RACE, SEXUALITY, AND GENDER AND THE MUSICAL SCREEN ADAPTATION

Race, Sexuality, and Gender and the Musical Screen Adaptation

*An Oxford Handbook of Musical
Theatre Screen Adaptations, Volume 2*

**EDITED BY
DOMINIC BROOMFIELD-MCHUGH**

OXFORD
UNIVERSITY PRESS

OXFORD
UNIVERSITY PRESS

Oxford University Press is a department of the University of Oxford. It furthers
the University's objective of excellence in research, scholarship, and education
by publishing worldwide. Oxford is a registered trade mark of Oxford University
Press in the UK and certain other countries.

Published in the United States of America by Oxford University Press
198 Madison Avenue, New York, NY 10016, United States of America.

Library of Congress Control Number: 2022042575

ISBN 978–0–19–766322–6

1 3 5 7 9 8 6 4 2

Printed by Marquis, Canada

In loving memory of my aunt,
Linda Riley (1951–2015),
who shared my passion for film musicals

CONTENTS

ACKNOWLEDGEMENTS

The initial inspiration for this volume came from a conference I convened at the University of Sheffield in May 2014. Titled *Restaging the Song: Adapting Broadway for the Silver Screen*, it brought together scholars from a range of disciplines to discuss stage-to-screen adaptations across the decades and ran alongside an exhibition and film festival at the Workstation and Showroom at Sheffield. I am grateful to all the presenters at the conference for their support, to Hannah Robbins and Danielle Birkett (then PhD students of mine) for their help in organising the conference, to Amy Ryall for her support in organising funding for the festival and exhibition through the University's Arts Enterprise scheme, and in particular to my fellow conference committee members, Stephen Banfield (who also acted as respondent to the conference), Geoffrey Block (keynote), and Jeffrey Magee, for their unswerving help and enthusiasm. The conference was especially important to me as it initiated a particularly close and important friendship between Geoffrey and me, and he has been incredibly helpful in reading and commenting on drafts of my material in this book.

I am also grateful to all the contributors to this volume, which was several years in the making. I am delighted that the original material is now available in paper form as three slimmer volumes. As always, I cannot begin to thank Norm Hirschy at Oxford University Press nearly enough for his incredible patience and support: it is difficult to imagine scholarship on musicals existing without his energy and enthusiasm in the background, and I am thrilled he was willing to make this new version of the *Handbook* available. Thanks also to Lauralee Yeary at Oxford, to the copyeditor, and to the team at SPi for seeing the volume through to completion. Special thanks are due to Cliff Eisen, who has been a wonderful mentor throughout my career and is now a very special friend.

As ever, my family and numerous friends are almost the only reason I managed to bring this volume to fruition, especially my partner Lawrence Broomfield, my mother Gilly and my late father Larry McHugh, and my friend Richard Tay. This volume is dedicated to the memory of my aunt Linda Riley, who died suddenly and unexpectedly in May 2015, leaving a gap in our family that will never be filled. She was a great fan of film musicals and I'm proud to leave behind this memorial to her.

Dominic Broomfield-McHugh
Sheffield, 2018

CONTRIBUTORS

Elizabeth Titrington Craft, Assistant Professor, University of Utah

Cliff Eisen, Emeritus Professor of Musicology, King's College London

William A. Everett, Curators' Distinguished Emeritus Professor of Musicology, University of Missouri-Kansas City

John Graziano, Emeritus Professor, City University of New York

Julianne Lindberg, Associate Professor of Musicology, University of Nevada, Reno

Hannah Robbins, Assistant Professor of Popular Music, University of Nottingham

Ian Sapiro, Associate Professor of Music, University of Leeds

Megan Woller, Associate Professor of Fine Arts, Gannon University

ABOUT THE COMPANION WEBSITE

www.oup.com/us/oxomtsa

Oxford has created a website to accompany *The Oxford Handbook of Musical Theatre Screen Adaptations*. Readers are encouraged to consult this resource in conjunction with each chapter of the book. Examples available online are indicated in the text with Oxford's symbol ▶.

Introduction

DOMINIC BROOMFIELD-MCHUGH

■ □ ■

FROM *SHOW BOAT* (1936) TO *The Sound of Music* (1965) and from *Grease* (1978) to *Chicago* (2002), many of the most beloved film musicals in Hollywood history originated as Broadway shows. And in the three years since the original publication of the chapters in this volume (as *The Oxford Handbook of Musical Theatre Screen Adaptations*, 2019) the phenomenon has persisted, with new adaptations such as *Cats, In the Heights, Tick, Tick . . . Boom!, Dear Evan Hansen,* and Spielberg's remake of *West Side Story*. Yet in general, the number of screen adaptations of Broadway musicals and operettas is far greater than the number that have met with success, especially both critical and commercial success (i.e., good reviews and a profit at the box office). This is all the more surprising since Hollywood tended almost (if not quite) exclusively to buy the rights to musicals that had been successful on the stage as a means of guaranteeing a profitable outcome. After all, musicals that had already enjoyed long runs and nationwide productions on the stage ought to have a readymade audience. One might also think that because the authors had puzzled over the individual challenges posed by such properties in their stage incarnations, it ought to be easier to turn them into strong film musicals. But for every *West Side Story* there were several *Finian's Rainbows*, *Man of La Mancha*s, and *Carousel*s: movies that simply did not do justice to the 'enchanted evenings'[1] these works provided in their stage incarnations.

This phenomenon is at the heart of this volume and explains why the book deals with as many unpopular films as it does popular ones. Rather than turning the wheel with a series of chapters on what makes the movies *My Fair Lady*, *West Side Story*, and *The Sound of Music* successful, I have invited a group of scholars on musicals to contribute articles on some of the deeper issues that are at the heart of Hollywood's troubled love affair with Broadway, as well as some of the more overlooked stage-to-screen adaptations that have appeared over the last ninety years or so. Thus, instead of a comparison of the screen adaptations of *Show Boat*, which have been discussed in print before, the volume contains explorations of the different film versions of *The Desert Song*, *Rio Rita*, and *Annie*, each of which pose different questions about the nature of changing media from stage to screen. Movies such as *Paint Your Wagon* and *Pal Joey*, which may not easily fit into some of the more obvious trends in the Hollywood musical, reveal new insights into the ways in which we might think about the nature of adaptation. Chapters on how Cole Porter's list songs and the George M. Cohan biopic *Yankee Doodle Dandy* might be thought of as types of adaptation expand our understanding of the concept, and the chapters as a whole examine how race, gender, and sexuality shape the process of adaptation. The book's aim, then, is not to provide an encyclopaedia of Broadway-to-Hollywood adaptations (such volumes already exist) but rather to sharpen the critical discourse on the subject and to share some of the latest scholarship on the topic from a range of disciplinary backgrounds.

Julianne Lindberg's opening chapter on the liberal movie adaptation of Rodgers and Hart's *Pal Joey* situates the musical in the context of postwar America, when traditional forms of gender and domesticity were being challenged and replaced by 'something more sexually "progressive."' In the film, Joey is now a singer rather than a dancer, vulnerable rather than a heel, and he gets the girl in the end. Lindberg explores how the film's promotion of 'a set of emerging gender archetypes that defy traditional, middle-class, suburban constructions of masculinity and femininity' is reflected in a new treatment of the score, which is 'reworked, repurposed, and in some cases eviscerated in order to promote the ethos of the film.' A good example is the film's presentation of the song 'The Lady Is a Tramp' (an interpolation from *Babes in Arms*), which, in Sinatra's version, 'emphasize[s] that he is offering his body to her.' 'Despite the lyrics,' Lindberg concludes, 'it is Joey who plays the part of the "tramp."'

Sexuality is also a topic of Hannah Robbins's chapter on the movie *Kiss Me Kate*, but it is also viewed through the lens of race. Although the film seems on the surface to be a comparatively faithful adaptation of the stage musical, Robbins highlights that it betrays the Broadway material by replacing the two African American characters, Paul and Hattie, with two white characters, Paul and Suzanne. The Broadway Paul's nondiegetic song 'Too Darn Hot,' which explicitly deals with male impotence during hot weather, is reassigned in the movie to Ann Miller, for whom it becomes a diegetic showcase of both her tap-dancing ability and her potent sexuality (she is heavily objectified in the number). Hattie's 'Another Op'nin', Another Show,' meanwhile, is cut apart from a brief piece of orchestral underscoring. In this, the film is a problematic reflection of its time, as is the manipulation of the direction for the briefly popular 3D technology that was used during the making of the film. Robbins concludes that 'the charisma of Sidney's adaptation lies in the conviction of our love for the score, the strength of the central performances, and the visual character of the film rather than in its deference to the original Broadway text.'

Megan Woller also focuses on sexuality in the much-maligned film adaptation of Lerner and Loewe's *Paint Your Wagon*, the least popular of the team's three 1960s film adaptations (*My Fair Lady* and *Camelot* are the others), but, in Woller's view, 'a fascinating adaptation study.' Situating the movie in the sexual revolution and second-wave feminism of the 1960s, Woller examines the characterization of Elizabeth and her only song, 'A Million Miles Away behind the Door,' as well as her polyandrous marriage to Ben and Pardner. Woller also reflects on 'not only how adaptations change the source but—due to changing social conventions and expectations—why they must.' In the case of *Paint Your Wagon*, the film matches Lerner's depiction of triangular relationships in *My Fair Lady* and *Camelot*; deletes Jennifer and Julio, the principal romantic couple of the stage version; omits the Mexican American perspective represented by Julio; adds the new character Pardner; and places Ben Rumson into a polyandrous relationship with Pardner and Elizabeth. Thanks to the shift from the Production Code to the Ratings System in 1968, *Paint Your Wagon* could portray a more liberal sexual situation than would have been the case over a decade earlier when the stage version appeared, and the screenplay exploits this possibility in a variety of ways, thereby reflecting its time.

Adaptation is considered with different meanings in Elizabeth Titrington Craft's chapter on the musical biopic *Yankee Doodle Dandy*. George M. Cohan was still alive when the movie about his life was made, and his influence is seen on how it depicts aspects of his life to suit his own account of it. But Craft also explores how the movie is 'a self-reflexive backstage musical and how its attention to theatrical authenticity served to deflect scrutiny from the lack of veracity in Cohan's biography.' Examples include the changing of details in scenes from the stage musicals *George Washington, Jr* and *I'd Rather Be Right* to serve the movie's hagiographic depiction of Cohan's life, as memorably played by James Cagney. But on the whole, Craft reveals, 'fidelity was the byword in the treatment of Cohan's musical oeuvre and the staging of musical numbers. James Cagney also took great care to capture Cohan's renowned, distinctive dancing style; his instructor Johnny Boyle had even performed in Cohan shows and staged dances for Cohan.'

Cliff Eisen also unmasks the mixture of the personal and the public in his chapter on Cole Porter's list songs on stage and screen. In his private life, Porter liked to make lists of things: Eisen uncovers a list made by Porter of things he required to be provided with during the out-of-town tryout of one of his musicals, as well as requests for lists of words and ideas for songs from *Can-Can*. The list song is a staple of most of Porter's shows, with key examples including 'You're the Top' and 'Let's Do It,' but their transposition to the screen is not always straightforward. For example, the film adaptation of *Kiss Me, Kate* moves 'Brush Up Your Shakespeare' from a song delivered in front of the curtain to the audience in the theatre ('literally' a show stopper) to a song performed in an alleyway 'to cheer up Fred.' Eisen proposes that this contextual dramatic change from the general to the specific 'hints at a fundamental aspect of filmed musicals that is inimical to list songs: their separateness and staticness, their drawing of attention to themselves and to words rather than, primarily, visuals or the narrative of the film, and their potential open-endedness may all work against the notion of what a film does.'

The final three chapters of the book offer comparisons of multiple adaptations of a single musical, demonstrating how a work can be fragmented into a web of interrelated cultural items, all of which remain related to the original in different ways. William Everett's chapter explores the fascinating screen journey of *The Desert Song* (1926), the Romberg-Hammerstein operetta. Warner Bros. released no less than three full-length screen adaptations of the piece, in 1929, 1943, and 1953, and a television version was broadcast in 1955. Everett's chapter addresses the work's 'shifting relationships, in terms of world politics, depictions of Otherness, and the interplay between reality and fantasy.' The 1929 version was the 'first full-length screen adaptation of a Broadway musical with all-synchronized sound' and it 'recreate[d] the theatrical original in a nascent medium.' However, the 1943 version (a story of 'Nazi machinations in North Africa') was a piece of 'home-front propaganda' and the hero (played by Dennis Morgan) was 'no longer a former French soldier but rather Paul Hudson, an American pianist who rides off to continue his fight for justice rather than remain with his beloved French chanteuse, Margot (Irene Manning).' Meanwhile, the 1953 Kathryn Grayson-Gordon MacRae version combined elements of the stage musical and the 1943 movie to create a 'Cold War' version of the story for a new political age.

Ian Sapiro also identifies intertextual relationships between different screen adaptations of a work in his chapter on *Annie*. The 1982, 1999, and 2014 films not only offer different takes on the material; they also contain connections to one another as part of the influence of *Annie* as a larger cultural text stemming back to the 1924 comic strip. This gives rise in Sapiro's chapter to an exploration of 'the re-inventions of *Annie* rather than . . . pass[ing] judgement on their respective levels of commercial, cultural or musical merit.' Sapiro observes how the 1999 Disney version is more influenced by the Broadway original than by the 1982 film, but the 2014 remake combines influences from Broadway and from the 1982 movie, including a chase through Manhattan that closely matches the climactic sequence from 1982; the 1999 version has not had an obvious influence on the 2014 movie, however. In this manner, each film's reinventions offer 'just enough of the original narrative and music for a new generation of viewers to recognize and accept it as "their *Annie*."'

There are similar contrasts in the movie versions of *Rio Rita* that form the focus of John Graziano's chapter. The first adaptation was released in 1929 and rereleased, due to its enormous popularity, in 1932; though largely faithful to the stage version, it contained numerous changes to the script and score, including the addition of a new number. In 1942, MGM bought the screen rights in order to readapt it into a vehicle for the celebrated comic team of Abbott and Costello. This was a much more liberal adaptation: only two of the original songs made it into the film, with a miscellany of other numbers being added, including a new song by Harburg and Arlen and a performance by Kathryn Grayson of the 'Shadow Song' from Meyerbeer's *Dinorah*. As with *The Desert Song*, Nazi characters were added to the film from this era: 'On its own patriotic terms, the 1942 version served its purpose; audiences would be entertained by the antics of its stars, but also be made aware of the secret foreign intruders who were threatening to overthrow the American way of life.'

NOTE

1. Here, I invoke the title of Geoffrey Block's seminal survey of the Broadway musical. Geoffrey Block, *Enchanted Evenings*, 2nd ed. (New York: Oxford University Press, 2009).

1

Adapting *Pal Joey*

Postwar Anxieties and the Playmate

JULIANNE LINDBERG

■ □ ■

*Now, in studying a case history of Joey, you must know his phi-
losophy—'you treat a dame like a lady, and a lady like a
dame.' . . . Didja get the message?*

–FRANK SINATRA[1]

THE 1957 SCREEN ADAPTATION OF Rodgers and Hart's *Pal
Joey* (1940)—starring Frank Sinatra as Joey, Rita Hayworth as
Vera, and Kim Novak as Linda—redeems Joey, the infamous
'heel' of John O'Hara's epistolary novel. Now a singer rather
than a dancer, Joey genuinely falls in love with the ingénue
Linda and makes seemingly selfless decisions that the stage
Joey would have scorned. The film praises Joey's vulnerability
and laughs conspiratorially at his self-seeking behaviour; in
the end Joey gets the girl. The 1957 screen version of *Pal Joey*
promotes a set of emerging gender archetypes that defy traditional, middle-class, suburban constructions of masculinity
and femininity. Joey's stage-to-screen evolution—from heel

to swinging bachelor—is mirrored by Linda's transformation from stenographer to sex kitten.

Both of these archetypes are responses to what cultural theorists have called the postwar 'crisis' in masculinity, and both reject traditional constructions of gender and domesticity in favour of something more sexually deviant, even potentially 'progressive.' Vera's character presents a foil to these seemingly uncomplicated archetypes. She more closely resembles the *femme fatale* of the 1940s: she is selfish, ruthless, and sexually experienced. Yet she is also played by Rita Hayworth, and in the end Joey tames her. The anxiety over contested gender roles is reflected in the alteration of the original score, which is reworked, repurposed, and in some cases eviscerated in order to promote the ethos of the film.

ADAPTING *JOEY*

Pal Joey centres on the antihero Joey Evans, who begins a self-serving affair with the hard, worldwise, sophisticated, and significantly older Vera Simpson, who in turn bankrolls Joey's dream club. Joey is, for the most part, happy to be Vera's object, and in return, Vera enjoys his physical charms: in the 1940 stage version of the show (which featured Gene Kelly and Vivienne Segal in the lead roles), this is a fairly straightforward, almost contractual agreement.[2] A side plot of the stage version involves the innocent Linda English (played by Leila Ernst), a stenographer who plays the part of the ingénue. In the absence of a true leading man, however, Linda's storyline fails to progress. Joey's two-timing, selfish ways are acknowledged, and both women eventually reject Joey, dramatized through the song 'Take Him.' Although many early audiences were won over by Joey's (or perhaps Kelly's) charm, there was no denying that he was a scoundrel: the sympathies of the narrative lie with the women.[3]

The film adaptation of *Pal Joey* was released by Columbia, headed by the irascible Harry Cohn. The film was directed by George Sidney; Dorothy Kingsley wrote the heavily revised screenplay. Both Sidney and Kingsley were veterans of Broadway-to-Hollywood adaptations.[4] Columbia had secured the rights to *Pal Joey* in the early 1940s, but they had a notoriously difficult time with casting. Early on they had considered casting Gene Kelly, again in the title role, with Rita Hayworth as Linda (their partnership had already proven successful in *Cover Girl*, from 1944).[5] MGM, however, refused to lend out Kelly. Other considerations for the title role included Marlon Brando, Kirk Douglas, and Jack Lemmon. At other points Marlene Dietrich, Ethel Merman, and Mary Martin were considered for the role of Vera.[6]

Although the basic outline of the original story remains, except for the Hollywood ending, much of the book was adjusted to satisfy a more conventional love triangle and the trio of stars who made it up. In the film, our story is set in San Francisco rather than Chicago, Vera is now a widow (rather than an adulterer), Linda is a chorus girl (rather than a secretary), the character Gladys (a conniving nightclub dancer) is reduced to almost nothing, and many subplots and characters are cut altogether, including Ludlow Lowell (an opportunistic 'agent') and Melba, a journalist who is immune to Joey's charms. Another major revision is the medium through which Joey's charms are communicated: instead of a third-rate nightclub dancer, Joey is now a third-rate nightclub singer.[7] The irony, of course, is that both Kelly and Sinatra were masters of their respective crafts, and part of Joey's charm is that, at least from the nondiegetic perspective of the audience, he is *not* in fact a hack.[8]

The score was also radically altered. Although some of Rodgers and Hart's songs from *Pal Joey* remain—including

'I Could Write a Book,' 'Bewitched, Bothered, and Bewildered,' and 'Zip'—many are cut or reduced to orchestral underscore, the latter skillfully arranged by Nelson Riddle. A handful of songs from earlier Rodgers and Hart shows are also strategically incorporated into the film, including 'There's a Small Hotel' (from *On Your Toes*, 1936), 'The Lady Is a Tramp' and 'My Funny Valentine' (from *Babes in Arms*, 1937), and 'I Didn't Know What Time It Was' (from *Too Many Girls*, 1939). As much as it was a vehicle for the lead stars, the show was also a Rodgers and Hart showcase, even though censors from the Production Code office ruthlessly purged much of Hart's lyrical wit. Joseph Breen's initial report on the script (from 14 February 1941) states that the lyrics to 'Happy Hunting Horn,' 'Bewitched, Bothered, and Bewildered,' and 'In Our Little Den' are 'entirely unacceptable,' and goes on to say that 'a number of the others contain unacceptable lines, which will have to be changed.'[9] Breen's report officially rejected the script for its inclusion of 'blackmail, sex perversion, adultery, [and] offensive dialogue.'[10] Between 1941 and the release of the film in 1957, Columbia engaged in a back-and-forth with the Production Code Administration (PCA) office regarding the 'unacceptable' elements of the film; the censored aspects were often the result of concessions made on the part of Columbia, while some of its racier elements were included due to a PCA policy that had relaxed, to a certain degree, by 1957. Still, Dorothy Kingsley recalls that it was Cohn who favoured the Hollywood ending, where Sinatra and Novak literally walked off into the sunset: 'Well, the story should have stopped with Pal Joey walking away, just alone, with the girl telling him, "That's all, brother," you know. But Harry Cohn insisted that we put on the traditional happy ending, that Kim and Frank must get together. And we fought and we fought but it didn't do any good.'[11]

For those critics who were expecting a true-to-the-original revival of *Pal Joey*, the film was a disappointment.

Lost were many of the book songs as well as some of the adult features that, in the words of Richard Rodgers, 'forced the entire musical comedy theater to wear long pants for the first time.'[12] Film critic Daniel O'Brien, in a book dedicated to the films of Frank Sinatra, said: 'If the 1950s revival had toned down some of the show's more controversial elements, Columbia's ultra-safe adaptation went for total emasculation.'[13]

PAL JOEY AND THE CRISIS IN MASCULINITY

O'Brien's critique is ironically relevant, as the film reacts in various ways to anxieties surrounding masculinity. As countless studies have outlined, attitudes towards gender and sexuality were shifting in the 1950s. Numerous publications in the popular press addressed what many saw as a 'crisis' in masculinity.[14] Not only were women in the workforce in unprecedented numbers, but many social critics saw the rise of corporate America (and office culture specifically) as emasculating, as well. Contemporary novels like *The Man in the Gray Flannel Suit* (1955) addressed these issues, questioning whether one could be personally fulfilled (or optimally masculine) in such an environment. For many, corporate environments went hand in hand with the 'feminization' of mass culture. The civil rights struggle offered yet another critique of white, patriarchal culture. Historian James Gilbert argues that there was a 'relentless and self-conscious preoccupation with masculinity,' and that this preoccupation led to new and varied masculine archetypes.[15] The official image of the cheerful 1950s housewife, standing behind her corporate, be-suited husband, was challenged by the reality of women in the workforce and new attitudes towards sex and sexuality.

Karen McNally, in a consideration of Frank Sinatra's film roles, traces new attitudes towards sex in the postwar era to ambivalent feelings regarding white, middle-class, suburban constructions of gender roles and to the infamous Kinsey reports (released in 1948 and 1953), which revealed that the sex lives of average Americans were far more varied than most publicly admitted to.[16] In 1953 (the same year the Kinsey report on female sexuality was released), the first issue of *Playboy* was launched, providing an antidote to the seemingly emasculated environment of corporate, suburban culture.[17] Early issues of *Playboy* were sophomorically misogynistic, blaming women for denying men their full masculine potential by trapping them in restrictive marriages.[18] Arguably the strongest proponent of the new 'swinging bachelor' archetype, *Playboy* carved a space out for a nonnormative form of virile heterosexuality, inextricably tied to material pop culture. By the mid-1950s, Frank Sinatra was their poster boy.[19]

Sinatra's hipness was signaled through pop culture references (especially urban slang), snappy dressing (with his hat tilted cockily to the side), and a disregard for traditional postwar views concerning marriage and domesticity. Joey's slang, which originated in O'Hara's libretto and was updated for the film adaptation, is rooted in the vernacular of urban African American culture, especially that associated with jazz and jazz musicians. The preface to Wentworth and Flexner's *Dictionary of American Slang* (1967) explains, in part, why Sinatra (or Joey, for that matter) might have adopted the vernacular of a minority social group: ' For self defense, and to create an aura (but not the fact) of modernity and individuality, much of our slang purposely expresses amorality, cynicism, and "toughness." '[20] The history of slang runs parallel to the history of American popular song: the so-called deviance of the material culture of marginalized groups is seen as both dangerous and desirable. When pulled into the mainstream, the dangerous qualities of a given cultural signifier are eventually neutralized, though they still retain the thrill of nonconformity.

One of the early trailers to *Pal Joey* plays up his use of slang, conflating Sinatra, the star, with Joey, the 'heel.' In the trailer, Sinatra/Joey gives us a crash course in Joey's 'slanguage,' and, incidentally, the film's attitude towards women. The trailer opens with Sinatra introducing himself to the audience as 'your pal Joey.'[21] He goes on to describe Joey's 'slanguage,' which is made up, according to Sinatra, of 'Joey-isms.' In particular, he outlines four terms: 'mouse' (a beautiful woman), 'gasser' (the 'very best,' typified by Rita Hayworth's form), 'loose' (Joey's unattached attitude towards life), and 'poppin' (demonstrated in a clip from the film, where Sinatra/Joey is peeping through a keyhole at a bathing Novak/Linda). He goes on to say that his philosophy in life is this: 'treat a dame like a lady, and a lady like a dame' (in *Pal Joey* the 'mouse' is the dame, and the 'gasser' is the lady). Some of the language Sinatra introduces was already a part of John O'Hara's Joey stories from the late 1930s (principally, the term 'mouse' to describe the various women that Joey encounters), and some of it shows up in jazz lexographies.[22] O'Hara actually invented some of the slang in the original stage production.[23] Joey/Sinatra's slang marks him as an outsider—he is socially deviant but also 'hip' and in line with the masculine archetype promoted by *Playboy*. His deviance was tied to signifiers that were in conflict with middle-class respectability.

Playboy also challenged dominant views of femininity, especially where sex was concerned. *Playboy*, whose playmates appeared each month as centrefolds, rejected the idea that women couldn't be both sexual and wholesome (the early centrefold features, for instance, were accompanied by other photos of the playmate, cooking, horseback riding, or even having dinner with her parents).[24] Although most studies of *Playboy* play up the misogynistic qualities of the magazine, which undoubtedly existed and persist today, the magazine also carved out a space (in an admittedly heteronormative, heavily conditioned universe) for the wholesome sex kitten, termed by *Playboy* as a 'playmate.' The sex kitten/playmate— naturally sexual, and perceived as somewhat innocent—helps complicate the virgin-whore dichotomy. To an extent, both Novak/Linda and Hayworth/Vera take on the role of the sex kitten in *Pal Joey*, though, undoubtedly, Hayworth's role is a bit more complex.

Clearly, the appearance of the sex kitten archetype is less illustrative of how women experienced their own sexuality and more indicative of how sexuality is embodied. The sex kitten/ playmate is the counterpart to the swingin' bachelor/playboy and perhaps says more about constructions of masculinity than about actual feminine desire. And yet, the 1950s discourse on sexuality was complex; in a discussion of the cultural discourse surrounding Marilyn Monroe, Richard Dyer states that 'the image of the desirable playmate, which Monroe so exactly incarnated, is an image of female sexuality for men. Yet so much does it insist on the equation women = sexuality, that it also raises the question, or spectre, of female sexuality for women.'[25] Dyer's insight might help us better understand the film versions of both Linda and Vera, who, to varying degrees, are cast as playmates.

THE PLAYMATE

Kim Novak's Linda is much more central to the narrative than the original stage role was. To ensure that the audience knows she is ingénue material, Ned, the bandleader, describes Linda as 'a nice kid' and goes on to say, 'She has ambition, too—she wants to be a singer.' Still, this observation occurs as Joey is sizing her up, appreciating her figure as she performs in the abbreviated

FIGURE 1.1 Still from Pal Joey (1957), Columbia pictures: 'That Terrific Rainbow' dance sequence.

costume of a nightclub dancer (see Figure 1.1). The visual portrayal of Linda is in direct contrast to the Linda of 1940, who is modest, reserved, primly dressed, and the antithesis of the nightclub dancer Gladys (see Figure 1.2).[26] Still, Novak's Linda is characterized as innocent, and even wholesome.

Novak's star image during this period—reflective of the sexual politics of the day—was dictated by her contract at Columbia, under the direction of Harry Cohn. As many accounts document, Cohn was cruelly controlling of his stars—especially his female stars—and both Hayworth's and Novak's relationship with Cohn were amongst the most publicly fraught. As Hayworth's career began to decline—and as she pushed against the strictures of her contract—Cohn

FIGURE 1.2 Jack Durant (as Ludlow Lowell), Leila Ernst (as Linda English), and June Havoc (as Gladys Bumps); photo by Vandamm Studio, 1940; NYPL Digital Collections.

sought out another star to replace her. Marilyn Monroe was contracted to 20th Century Fox, and in the early 1950s, Novak was regularly compared to her and to other famous blondes. It is likely that Cohn sought to reproduce the most marketable aspect of Monroe—her 'sexual readiness'—in Novak. He tried to do this by dictating what roles she played, how she behaved in public (and who she dated), and, crucially, how she looked. To differentiate her from other famous studio blondes, including Marilyn Monroe and later Jayne Mansfield, she was dubbed, and made into, 'the lavender blonde.' The studio also sought to create an air of relatability; as Sumiko Higashi observes, 'Since most *Photoplay* readers could not aspire to become a voluptuous blonde, stories continued to stress the star's awkward and gawky girlhood,' emphasized, for instance, in a story titled 'How to Be Good and Popular.'[27]

The song that introduces Linda/Novak—and, perhaps, best demonstrates her 'naturally sexy,' *Playboy* approved side—is 'That Terrific Rainbow,' a tune that was originally performed by Gladys and the nightclub dancers. In the stage musical, this tune is meant to reveal the depraved state of a cheap club in the South Side of Chicago. Although there is no audible record of the 1940 premiere, the Columbia studio recording from 1950, produced by Goddard Lieberson, includes the voice of the original Vera (Vivienne Segal). Conducted by Lehman Engel, the record also features Harold Lang, who would star as Joey in the 1952 revival (see Table 1.1 for a list of the principal roles and actors featured in the stage premiere, stage revival, and film adaptation). The Columbia recording includes a stellar orchestra, typified by the instrumental introduction in 'That Terrific Rainbow,' up to the task of improvising in the idiomatic way of jazz musicians in a club setting.[28]

On stage, the character Gladys sings the introductory stanza, and communicates the boredom of a nightclub chorine, a stark contrast to the virtuosic energy of the instrumental

Table 1.1

LIST OF ACTORS AND ROLES FROM THE FIRST TWO STAGE PRODUCTIONS OF *PAL JOEY*, AND THE FILM ADAPTATION

Year of Premiere	Role/Actor	
1940 (stage premiere)	Vera	Vivienne Segal
	Joey	Gene Kelly
	Linda	Leila Ernst
	Gladys	June Havoc
	Melba	Jean Casto
1952 (stage revival)	Vera	Vivienne Segal
	Joey	Harold Lang
	Linda	Pat Northrop
	Gladys	Helen Gallagher
	Melba	Elaine Stritch
1957 (film adaptation)	Vera	Rita Hayworth
	Joey	Frank Sinatra
	Linda	Kim Novak
	Gladys	Barbara Nichols[i]
	Melba	*role eliminated

[i] Nichols also played the part of Valerie, a nightclub dancer, in the premiere of the 1952 stage revival, and the part of Stella in the 1958 film adaptation of O'Hara's novel *Ten North Frederick* (1955).

introduction.[29] She is bored, jaded, and clearly cynical about the text she sings: 'my life had no color/before I met you./What could have been duller,/The time I went through?/You weakened my resistance/And colored my existence./I'm happy and unhappy too.' Hart's lyrics are brilliant, reflecting both the hackneyed nature of these sorts of club tunes and the manufactured tackiness that Rodgers and Hart enthusiastically embraced.[30] At the chorus, a raucous blues takes over, allowing Gladys, thus far portrayed as a bored chorine, to shift character from (in) sincere lover to unapologetically sexual nightclub dancer, complete with the requisite bumps and grinds. In addition to idiomatic gestures like blue notes and swung, syncopated rhythms, the harmonic progression clearly references the blues. Though not organized in a standard 12-bar or 16-bar format, the first 11 measures of the 32-bar chorus, excepting bar 12, follows a typical blues progression. Measure 12, the last measure of what would typically be the 'turnaround' (leading to a repetition of the form), instead sets up a harmonic extension (measures 13–16), completing the first half of the chorus. The second half of the chorus repeats the melodic figuration and harmonic progression of the first 6 measures of the chorus; the remaining 10 measures act as another harmonic extension, using standard techniques like strings of secondary dominants, in addition to some spicy altered chords, to bring Gladys home. In this way we can see that Rodgers adjusted a typical blues progression to satisfy the constraints of a standard 32-bar song.

The 1952, Capitol recording demonstrates well the aesthetic shift between the introductory verse and the chorus (see Table 1.2 for a list of significant recordings of *Pal Joey*). Helen Gallagher (Gladys in the revival and the Capitol recording) positively growls on the text 'I'm a red hot mama.' The lyrics to the chorus are delightfully clichéd: 'I'm a red hot mama/ but I'm blue for you/I get purple with anger/at the things you do/and I'm green with envy/when you meet a dame/but you burn my heart up/with an orange flame.' Each hue was originally matched by the appropriate shift in lighting (designed, in addition to all of the sets, by Jo Mielziner), a clever visual cue that made its way into the film. On stage, the tune creates not only an aura of tackiness but also brings into question the true attitudes of the nightclub chorines towards sex: perhaps they're bored with it. The playmate archetype is at odds with sexual boredom, for she is, seemingly, always 'ready.' In this way, the embodied sexuality of some of the nightclub dancers

Table 1.2

SIGNIFICANT RECORDINGS OF *PAL JOEY*

Recording	Featured Singers
1950 Columbia Records recording	Vivienne Segal (Vera), Harold Lang (Joey)
1952 Capitol Records recording[i]	Jane Froman (Vera), Dick Beavers (Joey), Helen Gallagher (Gladys), Elaine Stritch (Melba)
1980 London Cast Recording (Jay Records)	Sian Phillips (Vera), Denis Lawson (Joey)
1995 City Center Encores! Cast Recording[ii]	Patti Lupone (Vera), Peter Gallagher (Joey), Vicki Lewis (Gladys), Bebe Neuwirth (Melba)

[i] Billed as a cast album for the 1952 revival, nearly all of the original cast members are replaced. Froman and Beavers replaced Segal and Lang; only Helen Gallagher, who played Gladys in the stage revival, remains on the recording.

[ii] This is the most complete recording of Pal Joey (including oft-omitted songs like 'Chicago/Great Big Town' and 'Flower Garden of My Heart' and the music accompanying the Dream Ballet "Joey Looks into the Future"). There is also evidence to suggest that the orchestrations on this recording are, of all commercial recordings, closest to the original production. See Paul Christman, 'Pal Joey: reconstructing a Classic Rodgers and Hart Score,' Studies in Musical Theatre 3, No. 2 (2009): 174–176.

(and their calculated attitude towards it) sets them apart from the *Playboy* ideal.

The scene plays out a bit differently in the film: the introduction is thrown out—flattening out the characterization of the women—and each line of the chorus is given to a new dancer. All of the girls, except Linda, are either characterized as world-weary dancers, or empty-headed bimbos. None of them can sing, and many of them overact, to comic effect. When Linda eventually enters, appropriately on the lyric 'Doncha know your mama/has a heart of gold,' the aim is to set her apart from the other nightclub dancers. Her voice, dubbed by Trudy Erwin—a crooner known for her collaborations with Bing Crosby, and for dubbing vocals for other Hollywood starlets, including Lucille Ball and Lana Turner—is much more polished than that of her colleagues, and she moves naturally, without overacting. So, while the audience is encouraged to gaze upon the 'mouse with the built' (the words Joey uses when he sees her for the first time), they are also encouraged to view her as somewhat innocent of her sexuality. Although she does appear in full dress in the film, Linda/Kim Novak is often seen in short, strapless club numbers, or form-fitting gowns with severe slits up the skirt. A conspicuous bathtub scene is also included, which was played up in early promotional material (see Figure 1.3). But, in the words of Ned, the bandleader, we are assured that 'she's a nice kid.' The notion that women should be 'naturally' sexual (implying an innocence and a continual 'readiness'), while also exuding a niceness, or a wholesomeness, is in line with the fraught sexual politics of the 1950s, as well as the popular discourse surrounding Kim Novak herself.

Linda's wholesome side is exemplified by her performance of 'My Funny Valentine,' originally from Rodgers and Hart's *Babes in Arms* and here performed in the aspirational Chez Joey (this club, bankrolled by Vera, debuts in act 2 of the stage version of *Pal Joey*). 'My Funny Valentine' is both a gift to Linda (Joey allows her to sing the feature) and a love song to Joey who, as even the film concedes, is terribly flawed. Through the combination of soft-focus close-ups, string accompaniment, and the sultry, dark tones of Erwin's voice, this song is the true love ballad of the film (see Figure 1.4). The tune begins with a solo guitar—played by Bobby Sherwood—outlining a broken F minor chord, which sets the stage for the string orchestra's sotto voce entrance. Dominated by lushly orchestrated strings, 'My Funny Valentine' creates a romantic sensibility not yet heard in the film. While relatively short (Novak/Erwin sings through the form only one and a half times [the bridge and final chorus

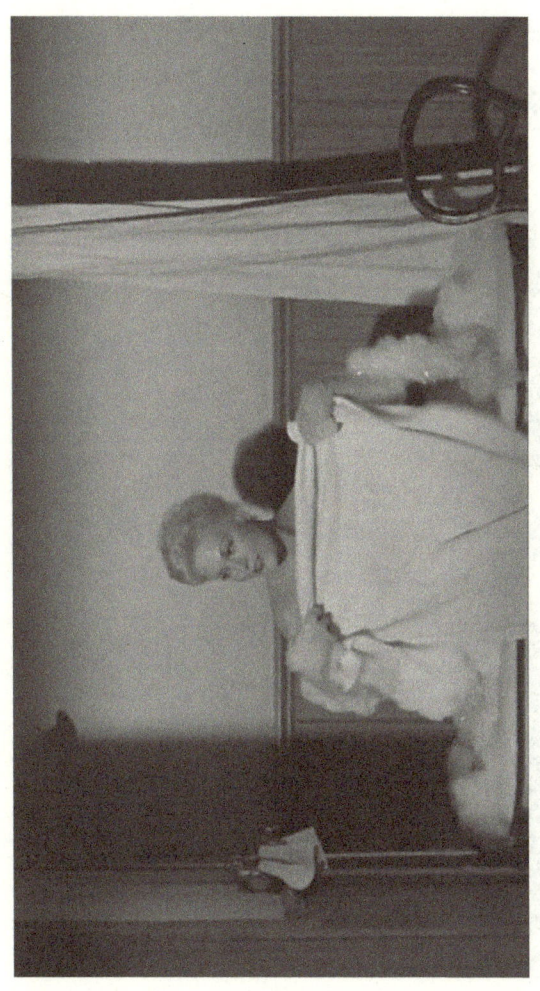

FIGURE 1.3 Still from Pal Joey (1957), Columbia pictures: Linda bathing at the Hotel.

FIGURE 1.4 Still from Pal Joey (1957), Columbia pictures: 'My Funny Valentine.'

are repeated]), the song carries narrative weight. It brings out Vera's jealous side, and she subsequently makes Joey fire Linda. It also convinces Joey, as well as the audience, that he is capable of a kind of selfless love not consistent with his stage persona.

Significantly, the original stage production of *Pal Joey* did not include a sincere love song: 'I Could Write a Book' is the closest version of one, and while it's true that it satisfies the requirements of a love song sonically, it is merely a pickup line within the narrative. 'My Funny Valentine,' however, transforms Linda from a cheap dancer into a romantic lead. By playing up the 'natural,' innocent sexiness of Kim Novak, the film reinforces the idea that a more calculated relationship to one's sexuality (as typified by the other dancers in the nightclub shows and Vera) is undesirable. The distinction between these two versions of sexualized femininity is demonstrated throughout the film.

Linda's performance of 'My Funny Valentine' signals the softening and taming of a kind of sexuality that, a decade prior, would have been considered dangerous. Consider the words of historian Elaine Tyler May, who argues that during the postwar era, 'knockouts and bombshells could be tamed, after all, into harmless *chicks, kittens,* and the most famous sexual pet of them all, the Playboy bunny.'[31] Surely, we can add to this list Joey's term 'mouse,' his pet name for Linda.

FEMME FATALE?

Novak's image in the film is deliberately set against Hayworth's. Significantly, this tension was also being played out in real life: Cohn was both goading Hayworth and paving the way for her replacement as Columbia's 'love goddess' when he helped cast Novak as Linda against Hayworth's Vera, originally a character decades older than the young ingénue. The press, predictably, saw the potential for scandal and played up what they saw as a certain rivalry between the two actors. The contrast between Hayworth and Novak was, at Cohn's hands, at the expense of Hayworth. In a cruel bit of symmetry, a comparison between the two actors has also been played up in scholarly literature, but to the opposite effect: Hayworth is often 'rescued' from her cruel treatment at the hands of Columbia and Cohn, but usually at the expense of Novak, who is characterized as vacant, against Hayworth's complexity, and lacking, against Hayworth's talent. Film scholar Adrienne McLean, in her illuminating study of Hayworth, admits in her conclusion that she set out to rescue Hayworth, too, at the expense of Novak. Through research, however, she found that Novak was not, in reality, the 'blank' (or, in the words of a 1956 *Time* cover story, the 'pudding-faced, undistinguished girl') that the press made her out to be.[32] Novak, in fact, received good reviews for many of her films, *Pal Joey* included. As McLean puts it, 'Novak (like Hayworth) did have something more than a face and body, and it is probably not mere nostalgia that leads headline writers to refer now to Novak with epithets reminding us of her "enduring magnificence." '[33] Further, the two women were, in fact, friendly on the set of *Pal Joey*: Hayworth sympathized with Novak (who was just a few years into her contract at Columbia), and Novak admired the film veteran.

Pal Joey was Hayworth's last film with Columbia and marked the end of a bitter relationship with Cohn and with the studio. Her last performance with Columbia is indicative of the kind of image Cohn tried to project, even as Hayworth 'rejected the binding stereotype that the Love Goddess represented.'[34] Hayworth's Vera undergoes a similar sort of 'softening' as Novak's Linda, though, for plot purposes, she remains the foil to the relationship between Linda and Joey. Vera can't quite achieve 'playmate' status because she is a bit too smart and a bit too ruthless: she 'owns' Joey for a good part of the film (despite Joey's insistence that 'nobody owns Joey but Joey'). Her age is also a barrier to 'bunny' or 'mouse' status, although Rita Hayworth was in fact a few years younger than Sinatra. And yet any power she has—whether it is through status, money, or sex—is consistently neutralized. The song 'Zip' demonstrates this well.

'Zip' presents perhaps the biggest alteration to an existing song in the screen version of *Pal Joey*. It was originally sung by Melba, a smart, cynical journalist who interviews Joey about his newly opened nightclub. In the course of the interview, and in line with his morally defunct character, Joey begins making up stories about his fictional high-class upbringing. Like most of the characters in both the stage and screen versions, she sees right through Joey, but rather than call him out on it, or indulge him, she simply brushes him off. Melba intimidates Joey, something even Vera can't accomplish. Melba is witty (thanks to Hart's clever lyrics), portrayed as somewhat masculine, and knows what she wants in a drink ('Double St. James and water, no ice').[35] Sadly, Melba doesn't exist in the screen version, or even in the most recent Broadway revival.[36]

The song depicts Melba's interview with the famous burlesque dancer Gypsy Rose Lee, a pop culture reference that resonates with the adult nature of the show.[37] Sung from the perspective of Gypsy Rose, Melba paints her as an ironic intellectual, a quality Lee played up in her own acts.[38] Like the character she sings about, Melba is transgressive in the way that she embodies femininity. Rather than play up the 'naturalness' of sex, Melba's performance promotes the idea that sex, or sex acts, might in fact be quite staged.

Rodgers's music is clever, and it amplifies the disaffected, cynical personality of Melba/Gypsy Rose. The opening lines of the introduction, for instance, comprise a repetitive, singsongy, broken B-flat major chord. This gives the effect of someone 'going through the motions,' perhaps like a bored child at the

FIGURE 1.5 Melodic introduction, Measures 3-6 of 'Zip.'

piano, letting her thoughts stray to playtime (see Figure 1.5). This contrasts delightfully with the decidedly un-childlike character of our soon to be introduced stripper, and yet they are both bored, mechanically going about their work.

The true humour of 'Zip' comes from the deliberate juxtaposition between the act of stripping and the inner intellectual life of the fictionalized Gypsy Rose: 'Zip! Walter Lippmann wasn't brilliant today/Zip! Will Saroyan ever write a great play?/Zip! I was reading Schopenhauer last night/Zip! And I think that Schopenhauer was right.' The humour is amplified when Melba— our hard-boiled journalist—pantomimes a striptease. Jean Casto was the original Melba, and she reportedly prepped for the role by attending (at George Abbott's and Rodgers's prompting) 'every burlesque show on Broadway' (see Figure 1.6).[39]

When Melba shifts into the character of Gypsy Rose in the last two measures of the introduction, most singers shift their vocal timbre to signal a new character.[40] Jo Hurt, from the 1950 Columbia recording, sings the part of Melba and gives a fair representation of the disaffected journalist. Hurt excels at bringing out the humorous mind/body disconnect through a distinction between timbres on the word 'Zip!' (which are alternately flat and bored, or nasal and flirtatious) and the rest of the lyrics (which she performs in a broad belt). The orchestral accompaniment also emphasizes the distinction, including exaggerated, muted trumpet 'wha-whas,' a clear reference to striptease, at the ends of phrases. As a character, Melba is the polar opposite of a playmate. Her mock striptease draws attention to the artifice of the seemingly sexy-all-the-time stripper and in doing so questions the authenticity of sex

FIGURE 1.6 Gene Kelly (Joey) and Jean Casto (Melba) in a Publicity still from Pal Joey (1940); photo by Vandamm Studio, 1940; NYPL Digital Collections.

acts altogether. Hart's biting lyrics—including the line 'I don't want a deep contralto/or a man whose voice is alto/Zip! I'm a heterosexual'—put the fictionalized Lee in the position of the knowing pursuer rather than the sexually 'ready' vessel for male sexual gratification.

Melba doesn't exist in the film; instead, Vera sings 'Zip.' This change marks a clear distinction between the stage and screen Veras: in the film, it is revealed that our sophisticated society dame was actually once a stripper known as 'Vanessa the Undresser.' Joey outs Vera at a society party (where he's performing, and where he first meets her), and, somewhat against her will, convinces her to perform the song. This maneuver effectively takes Vera off her gilt pedestal—the audience is made aware that she was once part of the same working class that Joey now occupies, and the power dynamics between the two shift considerably. As in the original, the tune is performed as a mock striptease, but now Vera sings the song in the first person, about her own mind/body disconnect when stripping. The bulk of Hayworth's version is dubbed over by Jo Ann Greer (as are the rest of her songs in the film), but Hayworth herself recites the introduction as a monologue, in a posh, affected manner, which, given her origins, we now know is a ruse. Some of the humour of the original introduction is lost, but Hayworth's version brings out the sultry side—the sexually experienced side—of Vera's character, which is amplified by Greer's lush, teasing, warm voice, a stark contrast to the bright timbres of Jo Hurt (or anyone who has played Melba on stage since, including Elaine Stritch [1952]). Joey appreciates the performance, and we can see that her sexual charms are not lost on him.

The lyrics of the screen version are also significantly altered. Given the references to contemporary pop culture (some which were out of date by that point), this is partially understandable, and, certainly, the PCA office flagged some of the original lyrics.[41] But it seems that one of the primary purposes of changing the lyrics was to transform the irreverent, critical, somewhat 'masculine' Melba (and by extension, Gypsy Rose Lee) into our screen Vera, who has lost her claws in favour of a more *Playboy*-approved performance. What is lost is the bulk of Hart's lyrical brilliance.[42] Instead, the jokes are transparent and not nearly as funny. Take Hart's caustic, culminating line: 'Zip! It too intellect to master my art/Who the hell is Margie Hart?' With each iteration of the chorus, our fictionalized Gypsy Rose references her stripteaser rivals: Margie Hart, Sally Rand, and Lili St. Cyr. In the film, Hayworth sings 'Zip! It took intellect to master my art/Zip! Every movement from the heart.'

Hayworth's performance is also self-reflexive—this scene immediately brings to mind another famous mock-strip performed by Rita Hayworth: 'Put the Blame on Mame' from her iconic *Gilda*, from 1946 (see Figure 1.7). Although performed by one of the most famous femme fatales of the 1940s, the lyrics to

FIGURE 1.7 Stills from Rita Hayworth's mock stripteases: 'Put the Blame on Mame,' Gilda (1946); 'Zip,' Pal Joey (1957); Columbia Pictures.

'Put the Blame on Mame' also comment on the way that women function as scapegoats in film noir. Richard Dyer argues that this song—in addition to Hayworth's star status, the film's objectification of the character Johnny, and the fact that Hayworth is given a number of nonpartnered dance features (perhaps as a form of self-expression)—might allow for a reading in which *Gilda* allows Hayworth a degree of agency.[43] *Pal Joey*, I argue, undercuts Hayworth's agency. 'Zip' not only comments on the character Vera but also on the star playing her, whose own status as a femme fatale was established by Columbia, a studio she was now on rocky terms with.[44] Linking Vera to Gilda provides the subtext that characters who use sex as a tool/weapon are necessarily punished. It also places Vera in the position of being objectified by Joey, a relationship that was reversed in the original (indeed, Vera refers to Joey somewhat condescendingly as 'beauty' in both the stage and film versions). As Karen McNally has noted, Joey 'forces her to revisit her relinquished identity as an erotic object and puts in place the power plays that will define their relationship.'[45] In a direct way, this scene helps Joey regain power over Vera, while Vera makes herself vulnerable to both Joey and to the viewer. It's a little hard to reconcile this difference, given our knowledge of the original character.

The film Vera is made even more vulnerable through her performance of 'Bewitched, Bothered, and Bewildered,' originally sung near the end of act 1 by Vivienne Segal, the original Vera. In its stage life, this song humanizes a hard-to-like character. The original Vera is a married woman, an experienced adulterer, and, at heart, a cynic where men are concerned. She is tough and seems to appreciate Joey's crude honesty. In this song, Vera acknowledges Joey's flaws and seems to be faintly baffled by her affection towards him. She also expresses, in language largely censored in the film, her appreciation for his sexual prowess, summed up in the line 'horizontally speaking/ he's at his very best.'[46]

The song is also one of passionate infatuation. As Geoffrey Block has argued, the repetition in the opening four measures of the refrain, reaching compulsively towards the tonic five times before cadencing at measure 5, perfectly accommodates Hart's obsessive lyrics: 'wild again!/Beguiled again!/A simpering, whimpering child again.' The lyrics, in Block's words, communicate 'the society matron's idée fixe,' though, as he points out, Rodgers would have written the music first, and Hart would have followed with the lyrics.[47] Typical of tin pan alley song form (this song is organized into an AABA structure), the A sections of the tune are thematically in contrast to the B section: in this case, the refrain represents Vera's rapturous longing, while the bridge (B) seems to represent her self-awareness (the melodic contour of the bridge is the reverse of the upward-reaching A section: the tune repetitively turns downwards, perhaps indicating that Vera is, ultimately, grounded in reality). While humanizing, this tune also demonstrates that even in the midst of infatuation, Vera is self-aware—and perhaps a little disgusted with herself for falling prey to Joey.[48] Depending on the performer, Vera is depicted as self-possessed but infatuated (as in Vivienne Segal's performance on the 1950 Columbia record), tough and diva-like (as in Patti Lupone's performance on the 1995 City Center Encores! cast album), or worldly yet tragic (as in Stockard Channing's performance in the 2008 Broadway revival). In all cases, Vera is a multidimensional character who is somewhat ambivalent about her feelings towards Joey.

Rita Hayworth's performance of the tune, however, dispenses with Vera's characteristic self-awareness and instead relies on her own 'love goddess' star image, which was cultivated, and exploited, by Columbia. Numerous scholars and critics have noticed that her costume in this scene—a yellow silk and lace negligee—is reminiscent of the outfit featured in her famous 'pinup' photo from 1941, published in *Life* magazine. Other references to the star's glory days are also made.

Karen McNally makes the case that Hayworth's strategic hair-styling in *Pal Joey* was in contrast to her typical image: 'by tying up and taming the star's trademark long, flowing hair, the film suggests that Hayworth's days as a misunderstood femme fatale may be behind her.'[49] And yet in the beginning of this scene, her hair flows freely: here she is much more 'love goddess' than 'society matron,' and more easily fits the *Playboy* ideal.

What's particularly telling about the scene is that while many of the lyrics are censored, Hayworth's performance is overtly sexual: this is communicated through Hayworth and Greer's vocals, Hayworth's gestures, and strategic film cuts. The tune begins with a sultry, spoken introduction (spoken by Hayworth, as in 'Zip'), as Vera rolls atop her bed, stretching suggestively for the camera: 'He's a fool and don't I know it/But a fool can have his charms/I'm in love and don't I show it/Like a babe in arms.' This morning-after scene is full of innuendo, even without the original lyrics. Jo Ann Greer's voice enters on the lyric 'Men are not a new sensation,' and Vera begins her morning routine: putting on her dressing gown, brushing her hair, pinning it up, taking tea, and eventually disrobing (on the line 'the way to my heart is unzipped again') before entering the shower. Here the sexual thrill is played up by mirrors, and quick camera cuts that barely avoid any nudity.[50] Since the original scene from the stage show doesn't include any of the afore-mentioned visual cues (it was originally set in a tailor shop), this scene was not altered to satisfy the censors.

On the contrary, Hayworth's performance of 'Bewitched, Bothered, and Bewildered' is meant to satisfy the typical sorts of roles Columbia afforded her. Though Vera seemingly expresses her own sexual desire, a scene like this undercuts her agency. As Dyer has said of Marilyn Monroe, her image reinforces a *Playboy*-approved attitude that women's sexuality is for men: the discourse on Monroe's body 'is not referring to a body she experiences but rather to a body that is experienced by others. . . . [B]y embodying the desired sexual playmate she, a woman, becomes the vehicle for securing a male sexuality free of guilt.'[51] Ultimately, Vera's three-dimensional inner life—conveyed partly through a worldwise cynicism and her unexpected affection for Joey—is reduced to a clichéd, two-dimensional portrayal of feminine desire.

JOEY'S CHARM: THE SWINGING BACHELOR

The sexual power dynamics of Hayworth's scenes are fascinating when compared to Sinatra's performance of 'The Lady Is a Tramp,' where Joey willingly objectifies himself. Like 'My Funny Valentine,' 'The Lady Is a Tramp' is from *Babes in Arms* (1937). In *Babes in Arms* the song was sung by the character Billie (Mitzi Green), a young girl who proudly rejects typical constructions of middle- and upper-class femininity.

Sinatra's version of the song transforms the gender dynamic by exploiting the two meanings of the term 'tramp.' His performance reveals yet another way that Joey's working-class identity is linked to Vera's (a clever pairing to 'Zip'). Dorothy Kingsley, the screenwriter, claimed that this song was chosen to advance the plot: 'We wanted Rita to get together with Joey and have him tell her that he knew the type of dame she was, I happened to think of this Rodgers and Hart song, "That's Why the Lady Is a Tramp." And when he looked at Rita and said, "that's why the lady is a tramp," I think the audience got the whole picture.'[52]

Though central to Joey's philosophy—'treat a dame like a lady and a lady like a dame'—his performance of this tune is a risk. Having already been snubbed by Vera—and prior to this performance, Joey goes to her estate to let her know that the only reason he was originally interested in her was because of her money—he rightly assumes that this atypical disregard for her social position will intrigue her. (There is a parallel to this in the original stage production, though instead of coming to her house, he calls Vera on the telephone and tells her to 'go to hell.') When she arrives at the club after hours and requests a song, it's a way of both exerting her power over Joey and letting him know that his earlier behaviour intrigued her.

The two uses of the term 'tramp'—associated both with overt sexuality and/or prostitution and with the free-spirited hobo—reveal a great deal about Joey's relationship with Vera: he is clearly offering her his sexual favours in return for her funding of his club, but he is also aligning himself with her working-class roots, which the lyrics regard as virtues (both of them like the 'free, fresh wind in [their] hair'). The careful balance with which Joey expresses his own freedom, while simultaneously offering it to Vera, is indicative of the power relations of the film, which are much more straightforward in the stage version (Rita Hayworth, after all, was a major, if aging, sex idol). The performance of the song, despite the lyrics, emphasizes that he is offering himself— namely, his body—to Vera. This is underscored when, at the bridge, he leaves the piano bench, and displays himself at the front of the stage, eventually leaning over her table, circling her, and, as Karen McNally observes, approaching her 'in a style sim- ilar to a flirtatious striptease act.'[53] At one point he spreads his arms wide (as a gestural articulation of the lyrics, which he leaves out), offering himself. After the performance, she accepts his proposal, saying 'Come now, beauty,' and takes him to her yacht. Despite the lyrics, it is Joey who plays the part of the 'tramp.' The parallel scene on stage happens entirely through dialogue; after he insults her, she slaps him, but soon after says 'Come on.' He replies 'Where to?' and her answer is pure, self-aware Vera: 'Oh, you know where to. You knew it last night. Get your hat and coat. I'll be waiting in the car.'

* * *

Though not addressed in this chapter, it would be worth further considering, as Karen McNally has, the inconsistencies in Joey's 'swinging bachelor' character, an interesting counterpoint to characterizations of the female leads (there are many inconsistencies. For one, he is securely working class and conspicuously without the bachelor pad. For another, he is routinely objectified).[54] What is clear, however, is that by 1957, Joey is not nearly as subversive as he was in 1940. This is due in large part to shifting conceptions regarding masculinity, which tended to valourize, rather than demonize, Joey.

Richard Rodgers seems to have been aware of the shifting climate as early as 1951. In an interview in anticipation of the 1952 revival, he remarked: '[Since the 1940 premiere of *Pal Joey*] characters in musical plays have become more human, and the attitude of the public toward these characters has become more human, too. It's very possible that Joey will have more friends today than he did eleven years ago.'[55] He was right, though he might not have anticipated that Frank Sinatra would be the star to immortalize Joey, who in turn helped immortalize Sinatra. To underscore this point, consider a quote by John O'Hara. When asked if he had seen Frank Sinatra as Joey, he remarked, 'I didn't have to see Sinatra: I invented him.'[56]

NOTES

1. Frank Sinatra, in an early trailer for *Pal Joey* (1957). Columbia Pictures, '*Pal Joey* Trailer,' online video clip, YouTube, https://www.youtube.com/watch?v=-chWouJQflw, accessed on 14 September 2014.
2. Indeed, Vera muses on the charms and practical functions of men in the song 'What Is a Man?' ('What is a man?/Is he an ornament/useless by day/handy by night?'). This song was cut from the film.

3. It's true, however, that despite being the only virtuous character on stage, Linda is portrayed as naïve at best and empty-headed at worst. Rodgers said: 'There wasn't one decent character in the entire play except for the girl who briefly fell for Joey—her trouble was simply that she was stupid.' Richard Rodgers, *Musical Stages: An Autobiography* (New York: Da Capo Press, 1995), 200.

4. Before working on *Pal Joey*, Sidney's stage-to-screen musicals included *Annie Get Your Gun* (1950), *Show Boat* (1951), and *Kiss Me Kate* (1953); Kingsley's included *Girl Crazy* (1943), *Kiss Me Kate* (1953; with Sidney), and the screen-to-(eventually)stage *Seven Brides for Seven Brothers* (1954).

5. Daniel O'Brien, *The Frank Sinatra Film Guide* (London: Batsford, 1998), 102,

6. In a letter from Harry Cohn to George Cukor, who was slated to direct the film as early as 1954, Cohn notes that he met with Brando: 'He was forthright, friendly and simple. . . . I had a very friendly and helpful talk with Richard Rodgers this morning. He is enthusiastic about the notion of Brando playing the part. He did make the observation that he hoped Brando could be light enough.' This is an interesting comment, in view of the fact that Brando would play Sky Masterson in the MGM film version of *Guys and Dolls* the following year (1955). Cohn goes on to say that he also heard back from Mary Martin, who was considered for the role of Vera: 'She could not imagine herself playing it.' Harry Cohn, letter from Cohn to George Cuckor, 2 May 1954, Margaret Herrick Library, Academy of Motion Picture Arts and Sciences.

7. Though Hermes Pan choreographed the diegetic club numbers and the 'dream' sequence at the end of the film (loosely tied to the dream ballet that closed the first act of the stage show), none of Bob Alton's original choreography remains.

8. In an unpublished interview held at the New York Public Library for the Performing Arts, Kelly describes the paradox inherent to Joey: 'Joey had to be attractive, and I had to make him attractive, so I had to dance well. . . . That created a bit of a paradox. Just because I could only get a job in a fourth-rate nightclub, I couldn't then dance like a fourth-rate dancer. So I had to start thinking about that problem. . . . So we combined, Mr. Alton and myself,

some things like unusual and energetic steps that might be done in a kind of a cheap act, but would be exciting at the same time.' Gene Kelly, Oral History Project of the Dance Collection of the New York Public Library (NYPL), interview by Marilyn Hunt, 10–14 March 1975.

9. Joseph Breen, letter to Harry Cohn, 14 February 1941, Motion Picture Association of America, Production Code Administration (PCA) records, Margaret Herrick Library, Academy of Motion Picture Arts and Sciences, Beverly Hills, California.

10. Breen, letter to Harry Cohn, 14 February 1941.

11. Dorothy Kingsley, interview with Leonard Spiegelgass, in 'Fade in . . . Fade Out. A Writer's Retrospective' (1970). Transcript held at the Margaret Herrick Library, Academy of Motion Picture Arts and Sciences, Beverly Hills, California.

12. Richard Rodgers, ' "Pal Joey": History of a Heel,' in the *New York Times*, 30 December 1951.

13. O'Brien, *The Frank Sinatra Film Guide*, 104.

14. Three of the most visible, by the decade's end, were William Atwood, George B. Leonard, and J. Robert Moskin's *The Decline of the American Male* (Random House, 1958); Arthur Schlesinger Jr's 'The Crisis of American Masculinity,' in *Esquire*, November 1958; and Philip Wylie's 'The Womanization of America,' in *Playboy*, October 1958.

15. James Gilbert, *Men in the Middle: Searching for Masculinity in the 1950s* (Chicago: University of Chicago Press, 2005), 2.

16. Karen McNally, *When Frankie Went to Hollywood: Frank Sinatra and American Male Identity* (Urbana: University of Illinois Press, 2008), 133–169.

17. For a thorough, enlightening exploration of the gender roles promoted by *Playboy*, see Carrie Pitzulo, *Bachelors and Bunnies: The Sexual Politics of Playboy* (Chicago: University of Chicago Press, 2011).

18. An article from *Playboy*'s inaugural issue, titled 'Miss Gold-Digger of 1953,' criticized alimony laws; another, titled 'Open Season on Bachelors,' warns men off marriage. For more, see Pitzulo, *Bachelors and Bunnies*, 23–24.

19. McNally makes the important point that Sinatra's persona didn't always line up easily with *Playboy*'s 'swingin' bachelor' archetype;

her chapter on *The Tender Trap* and *Pal Joey* aims to reveal the contradictions in Sinatra's *Playboy* persona, principally his unstable class status (in contrast to the middle-class aspirations of *Playboy*) and his routine objectification in film. McNally, *When Frankie Went to Hollywood*, 133–169.

20. Harold Wentworth and Stuart Berg Flexner, eds., *Dictionary of American Slang* (New York: T.Y. Crowell, 1967), xi–xii. This passage is quoted in Rick McRae's informative ' "What Is Hip?" and Other Inquiries in Jazz Slang Lexicography,' in *Notes 57*, no. 3, 575.

21. Frank Sinatra, '*Pal Joey* Trailer.'

22. The term 'gasser,' for instance, is defined in Robert S. Gold's *A Jazz Lexicon*: 'by analogy with the immobilizing effects of being, literally, gassed,' and is cited as 'current since c. 1942.' References for the term include *The New Cab Calloway's Hepster's Dictionary* (1944), and *Down Beat* (28 July 1948). *A Jazz Lexicon* (New York: Knopf, 1964), 119–120.

23. In a letter to William Maxwell, who took over as fiction editor at the *New Yorker* in 1936, O'Hara complained that Harold Ross, *New Yorker* editor-in-chief who roundly criticized his use of slang, didn't in fact understand it. 'I was the first person ever to do a piece about double talk, and God knows a lot of people still don't know what it is, but that was several years ago that I did the piece . . . and several things in that piece have become established slang. It is a point of artistry with me.' John O'Hara in Matthew J. Bruccoli, *The O'Hara Concern: A Biography of John O'Hara* (New York: Random House, 1975), 152.

24. For more on the normalization of the 'girl next door,' see 'Inventing the Girl-Next-Door: The Pulchritudinous Playmates,' in Pitzulo's *Bachelors and Bunnies*, 35–70.

25. Richard Dyer, 'Monroe and Sexuality,' in *Heavenly Bodies*, 2nd ed. (London: Routledge, 2004), 50.

26. In O'Hara's original Joey story, which was translated fairly faithfully to the stage, Joey meets Linda while she's looking through the window at a pet shop. Like the film musical, he sizes her up, but unlike the film, he tells her an outrageous story about his fictionalized upper-crust childhood. A reference to this scene occurs in the film, but only after Joey sees her dancing

in the club. John O'Hara, *Pal Joey* (New York: Duell, Sloan and Pearce, 1940), 49–61.

27. Sumiko Higashi, *Stars, Fans, and Consumption in the 1950s: Reading* Photoplay (New York: Palgrave, 2014), 78.

28. Listen, for example, to the clarinetist in the introduction. The published piano vocal score by Chappell includes clarinet cues (original stand parts held by the Rodgers and Hammerstein Org. reveal these as being doubled at the third), but this solo performer improvises the call and response between the clarinet and the brass melody. Richard Rodgers and Lorenz Hart, *Pal Joey* (New York: Chappell, 1962), 44.

29. On the 1995 City Center *Encores!* cast recording, Vicki Lewis, playing the part of Gladys, actually stifles a yawn in the introduction.

30. Rodgers states, in his autobiography, that 'Larry and I were able to have fun writing numbers burlesquing typically tacky floor shows.' Richard Rodgers, *Musical Stages*, 201.

31. Elaine Tyler May, *Homeward Bound: American Families in the Cold War Era* (New York: Basic Books, 1990), 108.

32. Adrienne McLean, *Being Rita Hayworth: Labor, Identity, and Hollywood Stardom* (New Brunswick, NJ: Rutgers University Press, 2004), 202.

33. McLean, *Being Rita Hayworth*, 203.

34. McLean, *Being Rita Hayworth*, 203.

35. This scene comes directly from O'Hara's 'Joey' stories (this one titled 'A Bit of a Shock') and remains close to the original. In O'Hara's story, though, Joey is much harsher in his appraisal of Melba's looks: he refers to her as a 'something,' rather than a woman, and later says 'I tho't to myself Lesbo.' His description of her dress is typical Joey: 'She is wearing this suit that you or I wd turn down because of being too masculine. Her hair is cut crew cut like the college blood. She is got on a pair of shoes without any heels and a pr. of glasses that make her look like she lost something but gave up the hope that she will ever find it.' In the short story, however, the real joke is on Joey, who later finds out Melba is in fact a conventionally attractive woman ('for the 1st time in many wks I forgot about Lana Turner'). This last bit (the 'shock') didn't make it into the Broadway version of the story (though O'Hara toys with it in a draft script) or into the film.

Note: Joey's shorthand and misspellings appear in O'Hara's original stories. John O'Hara, 'A Bit of a Shock,' in *Pal Joey*, 175.

36. Martha Plimpton, who played Gladys in the 2008 stage revival, performed the number (admittedly to great effect).

37. In a coincidence that was not lost on journalists of the time, Lee's sister, the then unknown June Havoc, was featured as Gladys in the original production of *Pal Joey*. Havoc was a child star in vaudeville (immortalized as Baby June in the largely fictionalized *Gypsy*), and had a difficult time transitioning after vaudeville died; *Pal Joey* was her first big break. As Havoc tells it, Lee was supportive of Havoc's stage career, and cried tears of joy after seeing her perform in the Philadelphia tryout. The same could not be said for her mother (the infamous Mama Rose), who, according to Havoc, left after seeing the first act of *Pal Joey*. June Havoc, *More Havoc* (New York: Harper & Row, 1980), 213, 209.

38. A performance of Lee's intellectual (mock) striptease can be seen in the 1943 film *Stage Door Canteen*.

39. Jean Casto, '"Zip"—It's Strip Tease: But All She Takes Off Is a Heavy Tweed Coat,' *New York Post*, 29 March 1941.

40. Take, for instance, Jo Hurt's version on the 1950 Columbia studio release, or Elaine Stritch's version on the 1952 Capitol studio recording of the revival cast.

41. In a letter to Harry Cohn contained in the Production Code files, Joseph Breen reveals that an early script had Linda perform 'Zip': 'It will be absolutely essential that there be no objectionable movements where Linda is pantomiming a strip tease.' Joseph Breen, letter to Harry Cohn, 4 May 1954, Production Code Administration records, Margaret Herrick Library, Academy of Motion Picture Arts and Sciences, Beverly Hills, California.

42. According to the Production Code file, Stanley Styne, son of Jule Styne, wrote the revised lyrics. Styne, in a PCA note dated 12 February 1957, Production Code Administration records, Margaret Herrick Library, Academy of Motion Picture Arts and Sciences, Beverly Hills, California.

43. Richard Dyer, 'Resistance through Charisma: Rita Hayworth and *Gilda*,' in *Women in Film Noir*, ed. E. Ann Kaplan, 2nd ed. (London: British Film Institute, 1998), 115–122.

44. Hayworth's rocky relationship with Columbia studio head Harry Cohn is well documented. *Pal Joey* was her last film as a contracted actor with the studio.

45. McNally, *When Frankie Went to Hollywood*, 163.

46. This line was adapted to read 'Romantic'lly speaking/He's at his very best,' but didn't end up in the film. One of Hart's favourite lines, however, which made its way past the Production Code censors and into the film despite the double-entendre, was 'he's a laugh, but I love it/because the laugh's on me.'

47. Geoffrey Block, *Enchanted Evenings: The Broadway Musical from Show Boat to Sondheim and Lloyd Webber*, 2nd ed. (Oxford: Oxford University Press, 2009), 107.

48. Vivienne Segal's performance, on the 1950 Columbia record, brings out this mild self-disgust: on the lyric 'Seen a lot/I mean a lot!/But now I'm like sweet seventeen a lot,' she mockingly affects a girlish voice on the words 'sweet seventeen.'

49. McNally also notes that this was Hayworth's last film with Columbia under contract. Other scholars and critics have noted Hayworth's uneasy relationship with Columbia's head, Harry Cohn, which, in addition to life circumstances, likely resulted in Hayworth's exodus from Columbia. McNally, *When Frankie Went to Hollywood*, 165.

50. The Production Code note from February of 1957 warns that 'care will be needed in this scene where Vera takes a shower, to avoid any undue exposure.' In the end, the studio just barely heeded this recommendation.

51. Richard Dyer, 'Monroe and Sexuality,' in *Heavenly Bodies*, 2nd ed. (London: Routledge 2004), 39.

52. Dorothy Kingsley, interview with Leonard Spiegelgass.

53. McNally, *When Frankie Went to Hollywood*, 166.

54. See McNally, *When Frankie Went to Hollywood*, 133–169.

55. '"Pal Joey": History of a "Heel,"' *New York Times*, 30 December 1951, in *The Richard Rodgers Reader*, ed. Geoffrey Block (New York: Oxford University Press, 2002).

56. John O'Hara, in 'Interview with John O'Hara,' *Morning Herald* (Uniontown, PA), 15 August 1961. Also quoted in McNally, *When Frankie Went to Hollywood*, 158.

2

'Too Darn Hot'

Reimagining Kiss Me, Kate *for the Silver Screen*

HANNAH ROBBINS

■ □ ■

OF ALL MGM'S WELL-LOVED ADAPTATIONS of stage musicals, producer Jack Cummings and director George Sidney's interpretation of Cole Porter and Samuel and Bella Spewack's *Kiss Me, Kate* is regarded as one of the most faithful to its source material. Following the impressive reception of the original Broadway production, which was deemed a surprise hit for all involved, the film version was widely anticipated and drew in large audiences in the United States, Australia, and Europe. Billed as the first-ever musical to be filmed with 3D technology, it received almost exclusively positive notices, with eminent *New York Times* film critic Bosley Crowther proclaiming it 'a beautifully staged, adroitly acted and really superbly sung affair—better, indeed, if one may say so, than the same frolic was on stage.'[1] Reviewers particularly noted the impactful casting of MGM stars Howard Keel and Kathryn Grayson in the leading roles of Fred/Petruchio and Lilli/Katherine as well as the dance spectacles featuring Ann Miller and Tommy Rall. The review in the *Hollywood Reporter* was one of many to note that balance of song and text in *Kiss Me Kate* that finally allowed Keel an opportunity to demonstrate his full potential as a 'big selling star.'[2] Other accounts of the film noted that while the 3D technology added fun to the audience experience, the film was equally arresting when seen flat, and indeed *Kiss Me Kate* was widely distributed in its 2D format.

The process of realizing *Kiss Me, Kate* on screen was not a simple one. Lemuel Ayers, Arnold Saint Subber (both producers), Cole Porter, and Samuel and Bella Spewack received several different offers (with their own creative priorities) before the film rights were secured by MGM. For example, in 1951, Bella Spewack briefly championed a hypothetical project with Columbia Pictures to star Rita Hayworth as Lilli, which Porter then quashed as a false rumour.[3] Two other directors proposed undertaking a live recording of the stage production featuring the original Broadway cast. As such, it seems that there was no one artistic vision for a film realization of the musical. This could perhaps have allowed MGM potential licence to change *Kiss Me, Kate* in comparison to other screen translations of stage shows. However, the emphasis on recording the original Broadway production perhaps indicates that the rights holders were more interesting in preserving the stage text than updating it.

Once the film rights were secured, there was some concern about how to cast *Kiss Me Kate*, and especially the part of Fred, appropriately. As part of the discussions of the Hayworth film concept, it is clear that Porter and the Spewacks' attorney Edward Colton were not in favour of using dubbed voice recording in a film adaptation of *Kiss Me, Kate*; they anticipated that the film adaptation would feature performers who could deliver the songs with some verisimilitude. Alfred Drake, who originated Fred on Broadway, was screen-tested for the part and provisionally cast for the film. However, he claimed he was then discounted for holding liberal political views, which made him a liability during the rise of McCarthyism.[4] In a recorded interview (later aired on the BBC), Keel recalled that although he was tested for Fred early on in proceedings, the producer Jack Cummings attempted to avoid casting him in the hopes of securing Danny Kaye or Laurence Olivier.[5] In Keel's estimation, they were looking for a performer who did not exist: 'You are looking for an Olivier that can sing like Lanza or a Lanza who can act like Olivier and there isn't anybody.'[6] Cummings was ultimately forced to make use of Keel (who was also championed by Grayson) as the best available option. However, Keel recalled experiencing considerable stress and anxiety at the pressure to counteract the negativity associated with his casting.

The MGM adaptation closely maintained the narrative of the original Broadway musical. Sidney created a sense of spectacle, bringing together a range of exciting choreography by Hermes Pan, compelling performances, and striking set designs (referencing Lemuel Ayers's aesthetic vision on Broadway). As a result, *Kiss Me Kate* is seen to be a 'remarkably faithful' adaptation of its source text,[7] allowing audiences to experience on screen some of what they may not have been able to see if they had missed the show on Broadway. Yet in addition to addressing practical concerns including casting, there were obvious aspects of the original Broadway libretto and lyrics that could not be translated to film. Under the terms of the Hays or Motion Picture Production Code, references to and demonstrations of sexuality were considerably limited, impacting the lexicology of *Kiss Me, Kate* on screen. As such, some of Porter's more explicit lyrics and references (e.g., to 'the Kinsey report'—Alfred Kinsey's pioneering research into human sexuality—in 'Too Darn Hot') were altered to suit more conservative regulations. Geoffrey Block provides a succinct summary of the significant points of difference between the stage text and the film adaptation in his monograph *Enchanted Evenings*.[8] In his second chapter on screen adaptations of canonical musicals, Block particularly highlights the 'cinematic expurgation'[9] of Porter's lyrics, the reordering of the songs, and the addition of a prefacing opening scene—a prerehearsal audition held in Fred's luxurious apartment—as salient areas of change.

This chapter investigates the distinct identity of *Kiss Me Kate* as a film that transmits much of the joy of the stage musical while also revealing some less appealing aspects of film adaptations of the period. The capacity for comedy, sumptuous set and costume design, visual effects (such as flame-eating in the 3D cut and exaggerated dance moves using strings and trampolines) in *Kiss Me, Kate* allowed Sidney to create a distinct visual culture for the musical in film. However, the erasure of the African American cast members and the changes that removed the chorus from active participation in the life of the film, which intersect with the expansion of the character of Lois Lane, give this *Kiss Me Kate* significant areas of difference from the stage musical that have been largely ignored. Using the revisions to the cast—removing the chorus and the characters Paul and Hattie—as a framing context, this chapter reviews the two most widely discussed aspects of the film: Miller's performance of 'Too Darn Hot' and the misogynistic potential of *The Taming of the Shrew* in *Kiss Me, Kate*. In so doing, it suggests that the charisma of Sidney's adaptation lies in the conviction of our love for the score, the strength of the central performances, and the visual character of the film rather than in its deference to the original Broadway text.

REPLACING THE ENSEMBLE: COMMUNITY AND REFLEXIVITY IN *KISS ME KATE*

There is a clear unity in the script amendments by Dorothy Kingsley and the changes made to the running order of songs in *Kiss Me Kate* (see Table 2.1). Whereas the stage musical is structured around 'full ensemble' numbers at the beginning and end of each act, this (arguably, stagey) feature of the original Broadway production has been largely eradicated from the film adaptation. Most notably, this has led to the recasting and rearrangement of 'Too Darn Hot' as a pseudo-Latin vamp performed by Ann Miller in the opening scene of the film. However, this alternative vision also diminishes the opening number 'Another Op'nin', Another Show' to a gesture in the underscoring, cuts one of the least well-remembered songs 'I Sing of Love,' and substantially reduces 'Finale Act One,' replaced by a new segue reprise, 'I Came and Wived It Wealthily in Padua.' This final adjustment resulted in two important changes from the source text: (1) it removed Grayson's opportunity to perform Katherine's outraged virtuosic tantrum, repeated on the word 'never' (after the 'flute cadenza' incorporated into Donizetti's *Lucia di Lammermoor*) and (2) reiterates the focus on Fred's Petruchio as the narrator and orchestrator of *The Taming of the Shrew* in a manner that is not present in original Broadway script.

The concept of ensemble in the original Broadway version of *Kiss Me, Kate* is defined by the backstage aspect of the musical. As such, 'the chorus' in *Kiss Me, Kate* contributes to the theatrical environment in which the narrative takes place. In 'Another Op'nin',' Hattie and the chorus build the sense of anticipation, of place, and provide the first musical spectacle of the show. One might say that they establish the identity of *Kiss Me, Kate* to the audience before the domestic dramas interfere

Table 2.1

BREAKDOWN OF SONGS IN THE ORIGINAL BROADWAY PRODUCTION AND FILM ADAPTATION

Kiss Me, Kate (1948)	Kiss Me Kate (1953)
'Another Op'nin, Another Show'	'So In Love'
'Why Can't You Behave?'	**'Too Darn Hot'**
'Wunderbar'	'Why Can't You Behave?'
'So In Love'	'Wunderbar'
'We Open In Venice'	**'So In Love (Reprise)'**
'Tom, Dick Or Harry'	'We Open In Venice'
'I've Come To Wive It Wealthily in Padua'	'Tom, Dick Or Harry'
'I Hate Men'	'I've Come To Wive It Wealthily in Padua'
'Were Thine That Special Face?'	
'We Sing of Love'	'I Hate Men'
'Finale Act One'	'Were Thine That Special Face?'
	'Finale Act One' [abridged]
'Too Darn Hot'	*'I've Come To Wive It Wealthily in Padua' (reprise)*
'Where Is The Life That Late I Led?'	
'Always True To You In My Fashion'	'Where Is The Life That Late I Led?'
'Bianca'	'Always True To You In My Fashion'
'So In Love (Reprise)'	
'Brush Up Your Shakespeare'	'Brush Up Your Shakespeare'
'I Am Ashamed That Women Are So Simple'	*'From This Moment On'*
'So Kiss Me, Kate': Finale Act Two'	'So Kiss Me, Kate': Finale Act Two'

Note: Titles in italics either indicate songs from the original Broadway production that were omitted from the film or are supplementary to the original Broadway score. Titles in bold highlight the songs that were moved in the organisation of the film.

with the onstage performance of *The Taming of the Shrew*. The chorus and minor roles (Paul, Hattie, Baptista/Harry Trevor) establish the environment, which is then disrupted by the catalytic secondary characters (Bill, Lois, and the Gunmen) while the central lovers' quarrel punctuates each aspect of the show (the production, the relationship between Bill and Lois, the resolution of the Gunmen's plot line, the performance of *The Taming of the Shrew*, etc.). Therefore, the centrality of this song is further demonstrated by its new placement as the very opening section of *Kiss Me, Kate* in Michael Blakemore's revised text, which opened on Broadway in 1999. In lieu of the overture in the original Broadway score, the chorus builds the set, proffering the first metatheatrical gesture of the musical. (In the original Broadway script, 'Another Op'nin' closes act 1, scene 1 as the ensemble recovers the atmosphere of excitement after Lilli has stormed out and Fred has given his pep talk.)

This gesture—having an 'establishing' opening number—is not unfamiliar to musical theatre audiences (e.g., 'Oh, What a Beautiful Mornin' in *Oklahoma!* [1943] or 'I Hope I Get It' from *A Chorus Line* [1975]) and also in the opening sequences of many well-known film musicals, especially those produced by Walt Disney Studios (e.g., *Aladdin* [1992], *Hercules* [1997], or *The Princess and the Frog* [2009]). However, the reflexivity of 'Another Op'nin' is the first indication that the ensemble exists like a contemporary American 'Greek chorus' in *Kiss Me, Kate*. To some extent, its role provides a relatively early model in stage musicals for the Aristotelian notion that the chorus is a character and essential to the identity of the work.[10] It becomes a living audience for the details of the backstage storyline. For example, the assembled 'company'—the principal and secondary cast and attendant chorus—provide the first reaction when Lilli calls Fred a 'bastard' during rehearsals in act 1, scene 1. This is recapitulated in the act 1 Finale as

Lilli/Katherine prepares to rebel against Fred and the gunmen holding her captive.

In *Gestures of Musical Theater*, Bethany Hughes highlights the frequent misconception that perceives the chorus as 'something that cleans up a musical, dancing and singing a bit while the important characters change costumes.'[11] While Hughes's chapter particularly interrogates the function of the chorus in Rodgers and Hammerstein's *Allegro*, she introduces the idea of the chorus as a community—the chorus members frequently spectate or participate in solo numbers as dancers if not supporting vocalists. However, by taking the 'major structural liberty'[12] of creating a new opening scene in which Fred and Lilli review 'So in Love' while 'Cole Porter' (Ron Randell) plays at the piano, the film adaptation loses 'the need' for 'Another Op'nin'.' The details of the production, the love triangle between Fred, Lilli, and Lois, and the basic parallels between their *Taming of the Shrew* characters are each established, giving extra context to the tensions in final rehearsals. This also foregrounds Fred, Lilli, and Lois as the stars of *Kiss Me Kate*, meaning that the contrasting attitudes of leading actor, supporting actor, and chorus member are less necessary to the vocabulary of the film. Yet the film adaptation loses a detail of satire and reflexivity present in the stage musical by removing the chorus as a functional body in *Kiss Me Kate*. This absence damages the duality of the dramatic layers in which a stagehand who is a backstage witness to the backstage drama is also a Shakespearean player in *The Taming of the Shrew* performance. It also dissipates some of the reflexive humour in 'Another Op'nin', Another Show,' echoed in 'We Open in Venice,' as structural landing points that acknowledge their function as establishing songs in musical architecture in the show. More gravely, the lack of a present and active ensemble and their music removes a meaningful context for one of the most progressive elements of the stage musical: the integration of two African American members of the back-stage cast.

ERASING PAUL AND HATTIE FROM *KISS ME, KATE*

In addition to the restructuring of the score to suit the filmic context, the MGM adaptation of *Kiss Me, Kate* recasts two secondary characters from the original Broadway show: Paul, Fred's African American dresser, and Hattie, Lilli's African American maid. In the stage musical, both characters are peripherally involved in establishing the central quarrel between Fred and Lilli that capitulates with the actors ad libbing on stage: Paul delivers Fred's good luck flowers to the wrong love interest (to Lilli and not to Lois) and Hattie discovers and gives Lilli the accompanying card that reveals their intended recipient. Interestingly, Paul makes an assumption that Fred is still emotionally connected to his ex-wife, which parallels unused dialogue between Lilli and Hattie that makes clear she has joined the production in order to win Fred back.[13] This is one of many symmetrical details that can be traced to the draft versions of the original Broadway libretto. However, it is also one superficial indication of the extent to which these characters are familiar with the emotional details of their employers' lives. They are not isolated from the key details of the plot. More significantly, Paul and Hattie are fully integrated into the backstage crew and achieve considerable agency by carrying major song moments—'Another Op'nin', Another Show' and 'Too Darn Hot'—that have little to do with their race or social status. Both these songs come at significant structural points—the opening scenes of act 1 and act 2, respectively—and feature the chorus as supporting players.[14] They also position Paul and Hattie as the leads of two potentially spectacular and show-stopping moments in *Kiss Me, Kate.*

In the context of removing the chorus as a present community that frames and reacts to the interpersonal collisions in *Kiss Me, Kate* with diminished song moments, Paul and Hattie's identities are changed. The vocabulary and demonstration of their individual statuses are absent and therefore, this negatively impacts the details of their characters, removing the progressivity of the original Broadway musical. For example, without 'Another Op'nin', Another Show,' Hattie becomes another African American maid following the caprices of her wealthy white mistress. To contemporary spectatorship, it would be problematic and part of a negative cultural legacy to watch an African American servant mutely appear to collect Lilli's clothes and look disapprovingly at Fred. This would also have potentially connotative associations to the Sapphire and Mammie stereotypes of protectively aggressive, emasculating, and servile African American women, which in Porter and Spewack's Hattie are largely absent.

Hattie's movie incarnation, a prim, elderly French woman called Suzanne, seems superficially to prevent this regression from taking place. However, it is also indicative of the systemic racism that either negates the role of African American performers or removes their visibility altogether. This gesture undeniably highlights uncomfortable truths about the social context of film adaptations in early 1950s America (especially MGM's film musical adaptations) while also drawing attention to the lack of visibility of African American performers in nonservile roles. In general terms, this detail of change in *Kiss Me, Kate* is indicative of a more insidious social context that facilitated the troubled trajectory of Lena Horne's career at MGM. The framing details of Horne's performance of 'Love' in *Ziegfeld Follies* (1946)[15] is an obvious example of the problematic representation of 'exotic temperaments' that is partly echoed in the Havana scenes of *Guys and Dolls* as well as other film musicals.

A brief reading of the film *Kiss Me Kate* might situate the alterations to Paul, who emerges as an aging and slightly comedic pastiche of an English gentleman's gentleman, as similar to the treatment of Hattie. However, the reinterpretation of 'Too Darn Hot'—Paul's song number—is more complicated in the context of the Motion Picture Production code. Given the prohibition of any nonmarital sexuality for anyone on screen, the original context of 'Too Darn Hot,' in which Paul describes the unbearable heat by suggesting it is too hot for sex, could not have been directly translated to the film. Furthermore, there was also no precedent for casting an African American performer to carry a song about sex or love in an otherwise all-white cast. Similarly, laws prohibiting interracial marriage were still active in most states in America in 1953 when the film was released. While there is no implication of interracial sex in *Kiss Me, Kate*, the demographic of the cast would have loaded this performance because of a lack of alternative context. There is no question that Paul (even attended by his two black companions as on stage) would have been considered for the film in this way. The relative emancipation possible in the context of the original Broadway production allowed 'Too Darn Hot' to be a playful showstopper dominated by male dancers without causing offence.[16] However, Porter revised many of the lyrics performed on Broadway and heard on the original cast album for the national tour. For example, 'And blow my top [for my baby tonight]' was replaced with 'And play bebop.'[17] 'Too Darn Hot' was already subject to censorship before reaching the screen, and yet, the method of reinterpretation present in the Sidney film also highlights other concerning aspects of racial portraiture in film musicals of the time.

In the film adaptation, the recasting of this song from Paul to Lois, and therefore from male to female, immediately dissipated some of the nuance of Porter's lyrics in 'Too Darn Hot,' sanitizing the thinly veiled allusions to male sexual experience ('be a flop,' 'blow my top,' etc.) in the original lyrics. The sung section of the song was considerably shortened and many of the remaining lyrics underwent further sanitization although subtler expressions like 'I ain't up to my baby tonight' remained intact. Late in the dance sequence, we watch Miller tap frenetically, framed by mirrors so we see her body from multiple angles, accompanied by the bongos. As is shown in ⓘ video example 12.1, the hands of the musician 'playing' the rhythm frame her dance so that this is a feature of the shot. This adds to the voyeurism of the moment and to the exoticization of Miller's performance. Given that this number was originally interpreted by three African American performers, this becomes an uncomfortable gesture. However, when we situate this interpretation of 'Too Darn Hot' in the context of some of Miller's other iconic dance sequences, it becomes clear that there is a pattern of design, which pairs her outstanding agility with crude exoticization. For example, during her performance of 'Prehistoric Man' in the film adaptation of *On the Town* (1949), Miller's dancing is framed again by the spectatorship of other characters who follow her movements, provide a physical frame to her 'on the spot' choreography, and play drums from the museum exhibit to accompany her as can be seen in ⓘ video example 12.2. In this last example, the supporting choreography crudely evokes a kind of tribalism that makes a subtle but uncomfortable connection between spectatorship, appropriation, and exoticism, which is supported by the percussion-led orchestration of the underscore. The fetishization of non-Western melodies and rhythms is certainly less evident in 'Too Darn Hot.' However, the obvious focus on Miller's body, her physicality, and the Latin features of the orchestration clearly connect the sexual nuances of the lyrics (even after censorship), the exhibition of the female body, and exoticism.

In his article 'The Gang's All Here: Generic versus Racial Integration in the 1940s Musical,' Sean Griffin argues that MGM prioritized musicals in which the songs substitute conventional dialogue, meaning that the performers (of any race) needed to play character roles related to the plot.[18] This, therefore, excluded actors of colour who might disrupt MGM's wholesome American utopia as depicted in a film such as *Meet Me in St Louis* (1944). Griffin continues to demonstrate that in the early 1940s, Twentieth Century-Fox embraced a more vaudevillian structure of film musicals allowing performers of colour (including Lena Horne, Carmen Miranda, and the Nicholas brothers) opportunities to perform in static, staged, or 'speciality' numbers. While he acknowledges that the limitations of this structure allowed more conservative distributors to simply erase these performers from their screenings, Griffin also analyzes how artists like Miranda or the African American actor Bill Robinson (most famous for his work with Shirley Temple) exercised control over their performances off-camera as well as on screen.[19]

In this context, the erasure of Paul and Hattie highlights how Porter created a unique space for two characters of colour in the original Broadway version of *Kiss Me, Kate*. While 'Too Darn Hot' might be considered a speciality number for Paul and his supporting dancers in the stage musical, this song situates *Kiss Me, Kate* in present-day America in juxtaposition to the heightened Shakespearean performance onstage. Both 'Too Darn Hot' and 'Another Op'nin'' are integral to the framework of this musical (on stage) and to the crucial contemporaneous aspect of the Baltimore scenes throughout. *Kiss Me, Kate* would lack a rousing backstage ensemble number to open and frame act 2 before its next *Taming of the Shrew* scene if 'Too Darn Hot' were cut. The fact that both these numbers are carried by African American characters is of note and highlights this particularly limiting aspect of the film adaptation. It also intensifies the problematic exoticism of Miller's performance of 'Too Darn Hot.' African American performers were not invisible in film musicals in the decade before *Kiss Me Kate* came to cinemas. Indeed, the Nicholas brothers' performance with Gene Kelly in 'Be a Clown' in MGM's musical adaptation *The Pirate* (1947) was the first '*racially* integrated number' to be performed in this way.[20] As 'Be a Clown' is contained as performance in *The Pirate*, it does conform to some of the limitations highlighted with the guest performances in the Fox musicals. However, it draws attention to a framework set up by MGM with a Cole Porter score that was entirely unrealized in the film adaptation of *Kiss Me, Kate*.

LOIS LANE: REPRESENTING SEX UNDER THE PRODUCTION CODE

Beyond the issues of fetishization and exoticization raised in the context of removing people of colour from *Kiss Me Kate*, 'Too Darn Hot' also provides a case study of the way that MGM navigated the representation of sex and liberal sexuality in *Kiss Me, Kate*. The narrative context frames Lois as a chorus girl (if not a nightclub performer) 'at the Copa,' which associates her with a different social framework than that of the other performers and enabled the costume designers to dress Miller in a spangled pink leotard. As she bursts into Fred's apartment, she throws off a deliberately oversized raincoat to reveal the costume underneath. The film dampens the sexualization of this gesture, her subsequent striptease (she removes and throws her gloves and jewellery at her audience), and the obvious emphasis on her dancing body in the context of the song's lyric by creating comedic contrast between Lois and Lilli. There is an obvious aesthetic barrier created by their costumes and hair and makeup design as Grayson's Lilli is buttoned-up in a beautifully tailored but modest black suit. Similarly, the strip details are made amusing by Lilli's icy disapprobation of the performance taking place. This sequence is predicated on social norms in which demonstrations of sexualization and exhibitionism create class distinctions.

Taken in isolation, the gestures that shape Miller's portrayal of Lois seem exclusively tied to this film itself and as logically connected to the sexualized details of her character in the original Broadway show. However, as highlighted previously, Miller's performance builds on a consistent portfolio of roles, which have often included specific details that are also evident in her previous film work. For example, the standout 'Too Darn Hot' tap sequence is not unreminiscent of Miller's performance of 'Shakin' the Blues Away' in *Easter Parade* (1948) or the deliberately charged 'I'll Be Hard to Handle' in the fashion tableau at the end of *Lovely to Look At* (1953). In *Easter Parade*, we see Miller pull away the drapes of her neon yellow skirt in the preface to the coming tap sequence (see Figure 2.1). Similarly, 'I'll Be Hard to Handle' begins with a close-up tease of Miller's leg appearing suggestively from behind a curtain. Later in this number, the supporting dancers (all male) watch her wind and position her hips so that the emphasis is not simply on Miller's ability to dance but also on her legs as objects of interest. However, both these examples are framed as static performances where the audience is separate from the dance sequence. (Robert Lawson-Peebles also explains how Miller's 'Too Darn Hot' costume and posturing have come after Rita Hayworth's 'Put the Blame on Mame, Boys' in *Gilda* [1946] and Cyd Charisse's cameo in the speakeasy section of 'Broadway Melody' in *Singin' in the Rain* [1952].)[21]

Given the reemphasis of Porter's lyrics for 'Too Darn Hot' from the original Broadway text to the film adaptation throughout the score, this early number establishes Miller's Lois as the vehicle for the most sexualized details in *Kiss Me*

FIGURE 2.1 Ann Miller releases her wrap skirt before the chorus of 'Shakin' the Blues Away.'

Kate. Furthermore, the connotative association of her dance, the strip, and the allusions to sex in the song are made more palatable by establishing Lois's backstory, polarizing her from Lilli, and making the song a cut number from the show. The connection to the exotic in the arrangement further distances 'Too Darn Hot' from any contrived realism in the scene. It also disconnects this audition sequence further from other parts of the film (set in the theatre) whilst conforming to the song-and-dance expectations associated with Miller and with the film musical vehicle more generally. It is worth noting that some of the nuances established in this original opening scene are threaded through Miller's performance in the rest of the film. For example, Lois repeatedly lifts and parts her skirts to reveal her legs. Indeed, Hermes Pan's choreography for 'Tom, Dick or Harry' incorporates Bianca's skirt into lots of the movement so that Miller is not simply working with her costume but featuring it (see Figure 2.2). Again, the potential sexualization

FIGURE 2.2 Miller throws up her skirts during 'Tom, Dick or Harry.'

of this moment is displaced with literalism of Bianca pursuing her suitors with a net. This performance is less about sex and more about the chase of catching one of her interested admirers.

Miller's Lois has some 'smarts' but is characterized on several occasions as genuinely stupid, which troubles her agency. Also, the film reframes one of Lois's key solo songs 'Always True to You (In My Fashion)' so that she performs the number as a duet with Bill. In so doing, 'Always True to You' becomes about playful appeasement rather than as the capitulation of Lois's characterization through the stage musical. As Bill poses some of the anecdotes in the verses to Lois, there is a structural change to the song that renders some of Lois's encounters with wealthy suitors hypothetical. Furthermore, her consistent interaction with Bill, her deliberately false posturing (clasping her hands as though praying or reaching out penitently—mimicking the 'virginal' Bianca in *The Taming of the Shrew*), and Bill's subsequent parody of her behaviour draw attention away from the content of the lyrics more generally (see Figures 2.3 and 2.4). This is a subtle shift from the original Broadway script (and

FIGURE 2.3 Miller mimics the choreography Lois performs as Bianca during 'Always True To You (In My Fashion).'

FIGURE 2.4 Tommy Rall (Bill) imitates her performance in a later verse of 'Always True.'

numerous other interpretations of this number)[22] in which Bill leaves the stage before or during the first verse of the song. As a result of this stage direction, Lois regales the audience with playful and self-aware anecdotes about her various infidelities in direct parallel to Petruchio's 'Where Is the Life That Late I Led?' The textual connection between these songs also affirms Lois's agency, as she (unlike Petruchio) has no intention of modifying, or reason to modify, her behaviour. This is reinforced by Bill's subsequent admission in the number 'Bianca' (cut from the film) in which he explains to the amassed chorus girls: 'Off-stage I've found, / She's been around, / But I still love her more and more.'[23]

The shift in audience from stage to screen is significant because, once again, it interferes with the immediacy of the meaning of the lyrics. On stage, it is hard to misunderstand the playful insincerity of the repeated refrain 'But I'm always true to you, / Darlin', in my fashion' and that Lois both enjoys her way of life and has no inclination to change. Indeed, in the recording of Michael Blakemore's revised version of *Kiss Me, Kate* (first performed on Broadway in 1999 and recorded during the London transfer in 2001), Bill darts in and out of his dressing room during 'Always True to You' so that Lois directs the refrain to him and her stories about the men to the audience.[24] In this example, Lois is seen to be caveating the truth behind Bill's back, giving her reassurances a disingenuous character. However, in the reinterpretation on screen, we focus on Tommy Rall and Miller's interplay, mirroring an earlier scene including the original appearance of 'Why Can't You Behave?' (Porter modified the verse of 'Why Can't You Behave?' to serve as the introduction of 'Always True to You' and Sidney's adaptation capitalizes on this parallelism.) Indeed, on screen (and presumably to adhere to the code), Bill seemingly reproves Lois for her conduct. Her lack of fidelity is a point of concern, which is hardly the case in the original Broadway musical.

Miller's effervescence and undeniable skill adds a further glamour to Lois that is not inherently present in the libretto. The context of her previous performances established her as an effective and appealing secondary lead who could also facilitate the dance moments with ease and polish. The reworking of 'Too Darn Hot' can be interpreted as an opportunity to objectify Lois but it also serves as an incredible vehicle for Miller's physical prowess, which sets her apart from so many of her contemporaries. Furthermore, it creates a new dance spectacle comparable to that envisaged in the act 2 opening of the stage show. To some extent, it highlights the craft of this opening scene, which establishes the key characters, their skills, their foibles, and frames the inevitable fallout that will result from Fred's trying to satisfy both Lilli and Lois in the same environment. It incorporates a short but striking performance of Porter's emotive torch song 'So in Love' featuring Grayson and Keel (loosely reminiscent of their performance of 'Make Believe' in *Show Boat* [1951]).[25] Read without context, 'Too Darn Hot' seems like a perfect flourish, characteristic of the static song and dance moments of parts of the original Broadway musical. Sidney acknowledges the nature of display, which forms part of the theatrical metatext of the musical. However, there are similarly uncomfortable details about the representation of Lois as a woman, as an object of desire, and of objectification that are noticeably regressive in comparison to Spewack and Porter's original renderings of the role.

REFRAMING EMANCIPATION ON SCREEN

Initially, it seems logical to suggest that MGM's *Kiss Me Kate* reflects the period in which the film was made. The use of Ansco Color and 3D technology can be situated alongside the relentless technological competition between studios to compel audiences back to the cinema during the rise of television and after the devastating effects of the Paramount decision (1948).[26] (Porter's song 'Stereophonic Sound' from *Silk Stockings* [1955] provides a humorous insight into this commercial imperative.) Again, the largely subtle changes to the narrative of *Kiss Me, Kate* seem shaped by the increasing social conservatism as the role of women and the agency of men were the subject of renewed social scrutiny. Furthermore, Alfred Drake's alleged dismissal on the grounds of being too liberal forms part of a familiar picture of the contours of American society in the early 1950s. To some extent, this film reacts to each of these concerns— commercial, social, political—and puts it in a different context from that of the original Broadway production, which had opened less than four years earlier. In *American Cinderellas on the Broadway Musical Stage*, Maya Cantu situates the original Broadway version of *Kiss Me, Kate* alongside the gender politics of screwball comedies in a wave of positive and largely affirmative texts, which include empowered and active female characters.[27] However, as has been explored earlier, the changes to *Kiss Me, Kate* for the screen seem to belong more with the 'princess and prostitute' tropes that Cantu highlights as part of the cultural zeitgeist of the 1950s, stemming from Cold War anxieties about the threat of 'sexual chaos' from women.[28]

This is partly demonstrated in the displacement of power from Lilli to Fred achieved in the film adaptation of *Kiss Me, Kate*. In the original Broadway musical, Lilli has wealth and social status, which is referenced at several stages in the libretto. She is able to poke fun at Fred, who has had limited commercial success while pursuing his ambitions as an actor/ producer.[29] This gives her important agency in a narrative that involves Fred's successfully (if temporarily) manipulating Lilli through the threat of violence posed by the Gunmen. In the new opening scene of the film adaptation, Fred is clearly 'successful and sophisticated,'[30] another film and theatre star, which limits Lilli's potential social currency in comparison to him. Robert Lawson-Peebles highlights Keel's 'characteristic chest-swelling masculinity'[31] as a feature of his performance. Not only is Keel's Fred disconnected from any former poverty he and Lilli experienced as young actors, but he is also given considerable distance from the woes of a struggling theatre impresario who cannot afford to pay off the IOU. His production of *The Shrew* is lavish: it involves a live donkey, special effects, and a travellator. Furthermore, Kingsley's film script also references an understudy (Jeanie) who is expected to replace Lilli onstage. Therefore, the impact of her absence in this version is specifically personal rather than part of a rupture in the wider structure of Fred's world.

As a result of this, Lilli's 'power' in the stage musical, which includes seriously damaging the opening try-out performance of Fred's new venture, is significantly diminished in the film. Grayson's Lilli remains a credible force of personality in confrontation with Fred. However, the film reduces the significance of her impact on anything other than Fred himself. Furthermore, the script develops the familiar trope—setting women against one other—which is only fleetingly realized on stage by having Lilli and Lois fight over parts in the opening scene. Similarly, Lilli reacts to Lois's posturing and lifting of her skirts, competing with her at several moments early in the film. Whereas Lilli has no active interest in Lois other than as Fred's possible girlfriend in the stage musical,[32] she engages with details of Lois's behaviour, how she carries herself, talks to Fred, and so on. In one of the promotional photos circulated for the film (also used as one of a set of lobby cards), Lilli and Lois's faces are shown confronting each other as opponents as though in a still from the opening scene. As has been noted earlier, some of the sexual charge of 'Too Darn Hot' is negated by the contrast in costume and demeanour between Lilli and

Lois. This example of promotional materials—of the visual culture associated with the film—deliberately polarizes these characters, limiting some of the nuance achieved on stage.

While the details of female emancipation in *Kiss Me, Kate* sometimes consider the characterization of Lilli, most discussions centre on the potentially misogynistic overtones of the penultimate song in the score: 'I Am Ashamed that Women Are So Simple.'[33] For some, Porter's musical setting of Katherine's controversial closing speech in *The Taming of the Shrew*—'Fie, fie! unknit that threatening unkind brow'— provides a detrimental frame to Fred and Lilli's reconciliation at the end of the musical. As there is some debate as to whether it is possible to perform 'the taming' of Katherine in Shakespeare's play as ironic, the fundamental message of Shakespeare's original speech, which advocates a wife's unfailing submission to her husband, presents obvious challenges to a contemporary feminist approach to *The Shrew*, and to *Kiss Me, Kate*. Followed through, this reading argues that both Lilli *and* Katherine are potentially subjugated to the tyranny of oppressive and damaging relationships at the end of *Kiss Me, Kate*. However, the musical is structured so that it is both simple and essential that we differentiate between Lilli and Katherine. We can acknowledge the intricately crafted narrative and character parallels developed by Bella Spewack and Porter in the original Broadway production without concluding that Katherine and Lilli eventually become the same character.

To some extent, the film adaptation addresses some of the potential concerns raised when analyzing the libretto and score of the stage musical by de-musicalizing this part of the plot. Firstly, the problematic speech is framed by Fred delivering Katherine's cue line with clear uncertainty about what Lilli is going to do or, vitally, *to say*, next. This is in contrast with the abridged 1958 Hallmark Hall of Fame television adaptation, starring Alfred Drake and Patricia Morison, in which Drake proclaims these prefacing lines with considerable exuberance. In the MGM adaptation, Grayson then speaks the abbreviated speech instead of singing it. It is striking that Porter's simple but idiomatic melodic writing would have particularly suited her abilities but that this (like the operatic cadenza in the first act finale) was removed from the musical language of the film. Grayson's performance of the speech is perhaps the least convincing 'Shakespearean' moment in the film; she appears to break character in the final lines of the speech (from Katherine to Lilli), smiling and then mouthing Fred's name. This gesture is captured by a tight close-up on Grayson's face in contrast to the wide-framed shots earlier, which show her with the rest of the cast and in perspective with the audience behind Fred watching her. As such, the film removes the potential musical appeal of the song and the dramatic currency this might add to the moment but also displaces the emphasis on the text by having Lilli and Fred acknowledge each other in their offstage personas. Kingsley and Sidney perhaps recognized the challenges of creating an 'onstage' environment where the backstage narrative is ever present and included this break of character to make Fred and Lilli's reunion more blatant than it can perhaps be interpreted in the original Broadway text.

The details of Fred and Lilli's personal relationship, such as her recognition of his character and his manipulation of temper, inform *Kiss Me, Kate* and shape our interpretations of equality, power, and the viable romance between the leading characters. When Lilli/Katherine pulls out Petruchio's 'little black book' that he has previously consulted in 'Where Is the Life That Late I Led?' in the final moments of the film and tosses it away, there is a moment of mutual understanding that is crucial to the power play of this musical, which is far less comfortably demonstrated when addressing the gender politics of *The Taming of the Shrew*. In reality, the MGM adaptation of

Kiss Me, Kate is not defined by its limitations. Lilli still carries out acts of rebellion. Lois continues to pay attention to male suitors other than Bill. Fred is emotionally affected by his lack of harmony with Lilli. Similarly, 'Too Darn Hot' includes exciting, visually arresting dance that might 'stop a stage show cold.' However, this film helps to reveal more complex aspects of the adaptation process than whether the narrative is identical to the original book or not.

The role of the ensemble in *Kiss Me, Kate* is more complex than in some other metatheatrical musicals; it is both a collective that supports or carries larger musical numbers/sections of dialogue and is also made up of individuals who exist backstage and onstage, occasionally with small narrative functions (as with Paul and Hattie). The nature of film changes the layers of scale that are apparent in a stage production, contained by the scope of a single stage. Also, the presence of a 'live' audience during certain scenes in the film removes the necessity of the 'onstage' ensemble as participants of the drama. In order to demonstrate the metatheatricality present in *Kiss Me, Kate* cinematically, some of the stage mechanisms that create points of difference between 'backstage' and 'onstage' in the musical are less necessary in the film. Similarly, the artifice of the film is evident in the *Shrew* dance sequences ('Tom, Dick or Harry' and 'From This Moment On') when the edge of the stage and the structure of the proscenium arch vanish to allow for more expansive routines. While we lose some of the character of the score by losing the 'voice' of the ensemble in the songs, we gain some exceptional dancing, including Bob Fosse's choreographic debut in 'From This Moment On.' This chapter does not argue that we cannot enjoy the MGM adaptation of *Kiss Me, Kate* but suggests that 'fealty' to the original Broadway production was not a primary focus of its creation nor the best measure of what it does well.

Keel, Grayson, and Miller are presented as stars in the film, changing the nature of the relationships at the heart of *Kiss Me, Kate*. Unlike the original Broadway production, in which Alfred Drake and Patricia Morison were seen as commercial risks and relatively unexciting casting choices, MGM capitalized on the 'bankable' names at their disposal. However, this also created expectations about how these actors would be presented. (For example: there is notable contrast between Keel's performance in the MGM adaptation and his careworn interpretation of the role in the later television recording made for the launch of British television channel, BBC2, in 1964.) The new opening scene provides a playful, reflexive opportunity for Grayson and Keel to sing 'So in Love' together while framed by trophies of Keel's other film performances. This includes a still of Grayson and Keel as Magnolia and Gaylord in the MGM film remake of *Show Boat* (1951). Robert Lawson-Peebles describes this set dressing as 'sketchily suggestive of contemporary movies,' highlighting the painting of 'Fred' as *Hamlet* (directly referencing a familiar image of Laurence Olivier).[34] Although he notes the cyclical dimension of this environment as drawing attention to the layers of performance—we are potentially watching Fred play Petruchio as he thinks Olivier might—Lawson-Peebles does not clarify how this scene deliberately draws attention to the identities of Keel and Grayson themselves, particularly during the song moment. Here we watch a contrived 'rehearsal' of the only sincere love ballad in *Kiss Me, Kate* while the mise-en-scene of the scene reminds us of Keel and Grayson's previous performances (e.g., of the similarly reflexive 'Make Believe' in *Show Boat*). As such, the film presents the reflexive layers of performance that exist in *Kiss Me, Kate* in a new way, providing an alternative, more cinematic approach to the musical.

The star dimension of this gesture adds to Miller's tap performance for those familiar with her previous routines: we become aware of the performers' identities which inform their interpretations of numerous film musical roles. Porter's *Taming of the Shrew* songs are less suited to the extended tap spectacles associated with Miller whereas 'Too Darn Hot' is dominated by the dance music at the end of the vocal section. While there are limitations to MGM's reimagination of this number, this decision also complements the framing of Grayson and Keel and builds on the metatextuality of watching actors playing actors performing a show. Although the 3-D rendering of the film continues to divide opinion, the additional sequence filmed to preface 'We Open in Venice' reveals the potential of this technology, when used sympathetically and idiomatically, to heighten special effects. It provides an interesting template when paired with the technique of tracking the movements of the dancers instead of capturing a static space in which the choreography is contained. As such, this *Kiss Me Kate* provides underestimated visual richness alongside more superficial directorial and cinematographic choices. Film scholar Richard Dyer defines entertainment in his writing on television revues (not dissimilarly structured to *Kiss Me, Kate*) as asserting 'the fact of human *energy* in the vitality of the dance number, the pow of the singing, the snap of the humour, the sparkle of the sexuality—so many showbiz clichés.'[35] This quality is as present in MGM's *Kiss Me Kate* as was reported in the outstanding reception to the original Broadway production and of many stage revivals. The 'faithfulness' of the film is complex to determine. However, it is clear how Sidney, Kingsley, and the other creative team members involved attempted to construct *Kiss Me Kate* to follow the 'fine singing, plus captivating personalities and performances, entertaining dancing, and stunning settings and costumes' that had previously been praised on Broadway.[36]

NOTES

1. Bosley Crowther, 'The Screen in Review: *"Kiss Me Kate,"* an Inviting Film Adaptation of Stage Hit, Has Debut at the Music Hall,' *New York Times*, 6 November 1953. Note that the stage musical has a comma in the title while the movie omits it.

2. W. R. Wilkerson, 'Trade Views,' *Hollywood Reporter*, 27 October 1953. See also Gene., *'Kiss Me Kate'* (Musical-Color-2D and 3D), *Variety*, 22 October 1953; Brog., 'Film Review: *Kiss Me Kate*,' *Variety*, 27 October 1953 or 'M-G-M Musical Is Splashy, Fast,' *Los Angeles Herald-Express*, 26 December 1953.

3. Letter from Bella Spewack to 'Salem' (Lemuel Ayers and Arnold Saint Subber), 19 July 1951, Sam and Bella Spewack Papers, Columbia University, New York.

4. James Klosty, 'Alfred Drake on The Life That Late He Led,' *Show Music*, Winter 1998–99, 25–27.

5. Howard Keel in interview, broadcast in Sheridan Morley, 'Introduction to *Kiss Me, Kate,*' *Kiss Me Kate* [live broadcast] BBC Radio 2, London, 5 October 1996. [This is available to hear at the British Library, London.]

6. Keel in interview.

7. Geoffrey Block, *Enchanted Evenings: The Broadway Musical from Show Boat to Sondheim and Lloyd Webber*, 2nd ed. (New York: Oxford University Press, 2009), 315.

8. Block, *Enchanted Evenings*, 314–319.

9. Block, *Enchanted Evenings*, 317.

10. Other early examples include Rodgers and Hammerstein's *Allegro* (1947) and Kurt Weill and Alan Jay Lerner's *Love Life* (1948).

11. Bethany Hughes, 'Singing the Community: The Musical Theater Chorus as Character,' in *Gestures of Musical Theater: The Performativity of Song and Dance*, ed. Dominic Symonds and Millie Taylor (New York: Oxford University Press, 2014), 263.

12. Geoffrey Block, *Enchanted Evening*, 315.

13. *Kiss Me, Kate* draft script (labelled *'Kiss Me, Kate* Script C with Notes'), 11 October 1948, Sam and Bella Spewack Papers, Columbia University, New York, 1-3-7.

14. Although this has not remained the case in all productions, the original Broadway production and published stage directions indicate that the three African American performers who lead 'Too Darn Hot' are joined by secondary lead Bill.
15. This sequence was directed by Lemuel Ayers, producer and designer of costumes and sets for *Kiss Me, Kate*.
16. It is perhaps worth noting that 'Too Darn Hot' was one of several songs in *Kiss Me, Kate* to be banned from public broadcast in Australia because of the nature of its lyrics.
17. This change (and others) is evident on piano-vocal scores for 'Too Darn Hot' in Porter's papers at the Library of Congress. Porter amended the lyrics in pencil, replacing the Broadway versions with sanitized alternatives. 'Too Darn Hot' fair copy, labelled 'Road Co.,' Cole Porter Papers, Library of Congress, Washington, DC. These changes are also noted in Cole Porter, *Kiss Me, Kate: A Musical Play*, ed. David C. Abell and Seann Alderking (Van Nuys, CA: Alfred, 2014), 189–194.
18. Sean Griffin, 'The Gang's All Here: Generic versus Racial Integration in the 1940s Musical,' *Cinema Journal* 42 (Autumn 2002): 21–45.
19. Sean Griffin, 'The Gang's All Here: Generic versus Racial Integration in the 1940s Musical,' 35.
20. Griffin, 'The Gang's All Here,' 39.
21. Robert Lawson-Peebles, 'Brush Up Your Shakespeare: The Case of *Kiss Me, Kate*,' in *Approaches to the American Musical*, ed. Robert Lawson-Peebles (Exeter: University of Exeter Press, 1996), 99.
22. There are examples available online and on DVD from the BBC Proms performance, the Opera North.
23. Cole Porter, Sam Spewack, and Bella Spewack, *Kiss Me, Kate*, in *Ten Great Musicals of the American Theatre*, ed. Stanley Richards (Radnor, PA: Chilton, 1973), 338.
24. *Kiss Me, Kate*, directed by Chris Hunt (n.p.: Arthaus Musik: 2010) [DVD].
25. There is conscious reference to this section of *Showboat* as the set is dressed with 'real-life' and fake memorabilia from 'Fred's' career. As such, there is a photo on the piano of Keel and Grayson as Ravenal and Magnolia, which is in the centre of the shot for a

considerable section of the song. It is also featured later as they reach the final phrases and Keel comes to stand close to Lilli. *Kiss Me Kate*, directed by George Sidney (Burbank, CA: Warner Home Video, 2003) [DVD].

26. As a result of the capitulation of several legal cases, the US Supreme Court ruled in 1948 that film studios could no longer own cinemas to show their films and saturate the market with their own output. Where companies like Paramount and MGM had previously offered subsidized distribution fees to the venues that the studios owned, they either had to form a new company as Paramount did in 1953 or sell their interests, causing a rise in the costs of showing films and a loss in relatively secure revenue from cinemas guaranteed to book a studio's films.

27. Maya Cantu, *American Cinderellas on the Broadway Musical Stage: Imaging the Working Girl from Irene to Gypsy* (New York: Palgrave Macmillan, 2015), 128–130.

28. Cantu, *American Cinderellas*, 159.

29. Cole Porter, Sam Spewack, and Bella Spewack, *Kiss Me, Kate*, 208.

30. Robert Lawson-Peebles, 'Brush Up Your Shakespeare: The Case of *Kiss Me, Kate*,' 96.

31. Lawson-Peebles, 'Brush Up Your Shakespeare,' 104.

32. In one draft of the original Broadway script, Spewack created a rehearsal built around Lilli and Lois, which was cut before rehearsals.

33. See, for example, Barbara Hodgdon, *The Shakespeare Trade: Performances and Appropriations* (Philadelphia: University of Pennsylvania Press, 1998), 20–21.

34. This frame is also noted in Robert Lawson-Peebles, 'Brush Up Your Shakespeare: The Case of *Kiss Me, Kate*,' 96.

35. Richard Dyer, *Light Entertainment* (London: British Film Institute, 1973) 39. Some of this text has been reprinted as a chapter, 'The Idea of Entertainment,' in *Only Entertainment*, by Richard Dyer (London: Routledge, 2002).

36. 'Plays on Broadway: Kiss Me, Kate,' *Variety*, 5 January 1949.

3

'A Humane, Practical, and Beautiful Solution'

Adaptation and Triangulation in Paint Your Wagon

MEGAN WOLLER

■ □ ■

THE 1969 FILM VERSION OF Alan Jay Lerner and Frederick
Loewe's *Paint Your Wagon* offers an incredibly interesting case
study on the subject of adaptation. The film represents the third
in a line of Lerner and Loewe 1960s musical adaptations. As
arguably the least respected and certainly the least faithful to
the original stage production of the three 1960s adaptations,
Paint Your Wagon highlights a number of questions and topics
that occur in the study of Hollywood adaptations of Broadway
musicals. By 1969, the Rodgers and Hammerstein film
adaptations of the 1950s had set a standard of relative fidelity.
The final Lerner and Loewe adaptation, however, adheres to
an earlier model of Hollywood musicals, in which filmmakers
freely made changes when adapting a show. Furthermore,
Paint Your Wagon diverges from the approach to fidelity in
My Fair Lady (1964) and *Camelot* (1967), both of which maintain a strong link with their stage counterparts. Yet, as I argue,

Paint Your Wagon in its cinematic incarnation can be viewed as the culmination of themes and relationships explored in these earlier musicals. Therefore, the film is a fascinating adaptation study. This chapter explores several interrelated threads: *Paint Your Wagon* in relation to other Lerner and Loewe adaptations of the 1960s, the concept of fidelity through an examination of the changes made from stage to screen, and the effect of as well as reasons for many of these alterations.

In particular, this chapter focuses on the changes made for the film surrounding the lead female character Elizabeth and her relationship with the two male leads. These changes reveal key intersections with sociocultural trends in the late 1960s, namely the so-called sexual revolution and second-wave feminism. Since Elizabeth sings only one song in the entire film, it plays a significant role in her characterization yet represents only one piece of the puzzle. My investigation considers Elizabeth's characterization and her only song 'A Million Miles Away Behind the Door' as well as her polyandrous marriage with Ben and Pardner. Through this analysis, this article addresses several key issues that surround not only *Paint Your Wagon* but film musical adaptations more broadly.

In conjunction with the work represented in this volume, this chapter dovetails with research on film musical adaptations that explores how the filmmakers balance fidelity with creativity in moving a work from stage to the screen. Investigating how much an adaptation adheres to its source provides an important starting point but represents only one aspect of adaptation theory. I find it essential to look at not only how adaptations change the source but—due to changing social conventions and expectations—why they must. Adaptation theory, as I use it, offers a framework that breaks away from value judgements rooted in ideas of fidelity, and therefore 'authenticity.' Since film musical adaptations have switched media, they engage in what Julie Sanders identifies as 'a transpositional practice.'[1] As such, the process can involve pruning as well as augmenting and reorganizing so that the adapted stage work succeeds onscreen. As Linda Hutcheon puts it, adapting a work for a new medium requires 'recoding [the work] into a new set of conventions as well as signs.'[2] Application of these ideas allows for a consideration of Hollywood adaptations on their own terms and emphasizes the reasons filmmakers make revisions. Key modifications often reflect not only differing practices but social implications. Since Hollywood movie musicals draw from theatrical productions, they use Broadway conventions by extension. However, they simultaneously strive to transform the original productions into cinematic entities.

Historically, Hollywood filmmakers have handled the amount of fidelity to the original show in various ways. Geoffrey Block observes that before the Rodgers and Hammerstein era Hollywood musical adaptations were often 'footloose and fancy free and at times unrecognizable vis-à-vis their stage counterparts' while film adaptations since the famed duo 'tend to be relatively faithful.'[3] Yet throughout the 1960s, the myriad approaches to fidelity in Broadway film adaptations often seems tied to larger goals, which may reflect social concerns, more individualized agendas, or a mixture of both. The adaptation of *Paint Your Wagon* certainly displays intersections with interests shown by one of its original creators, Alan Jay Lerner, as well as sociocultural concepts from the late 1960s.

TRIANGULATION IN LERNER AND LOEWE MUSICALS

The polyandrous marriage between Ben, Pardner, and Elizabeth in *Paint Your Wagon* reflects a fascination with triangulated relationships, which earlier Lerner and Loewe musicals similarly explore. It bears mentioning, of course, that love triangles have been prevalent in stories long before Lerner's particular interest—to which the adaptations of George Bernard Shaw's *Pygmalion* and even more strikingly, Arthurian legend attest. In other words, there is certainly nothing new in Lerner's interest in love triangles. However, his specific treatment of triangulation and its implications mean much. In particular, *My Fair Lady* and *Camelot* both contain similar sorts of love triangles as the film version of *Paint Your Wagon*, albeit presented more obliquely. Each of the earlier musicals introduces two overlapping triangles, which overtly involve or can be read as romantic or intimate relationships. Eliza Doolittle, Henry Higgins, and Freddy Eynsford-Hill comprise the most obvious 'love' triangle in *My Fair Lady*. At the same time, Eliza, Professor Higgins, and Colonel Pickering can be considered another triangle of sorts. Similarly, *Camelot* focuses on the legendary tale of forbidden love and tragedy surrounding King Arthur, Queen Guenevere, and Sir Lancelot. Once again, another older friend enters the relationship tangle through the character of Pellinore. As Raymond Knapp discusses, Pickering's relationships with Higgins 'strongly suggests homosexuality or its second cousin, a variation of the buddy trope.'[4] Pellinore, played by Robert Coote in the stage production (who also originated Pickering), provides a similar type of male-centred relationship with Arthur.

In terms of the main love triangles, *My Fair Lady* and *Camelot* offer important references for the film version of *Paint Your Wagon*. Dominic Broomfield-McHugh's study of character development in the genesis of *My Fair Lady* provides key insight to how Lerner altered both the character of Freddy and the relationship between Eliza and Higgins from George Bernard Shaw's *Pygmalion*. Importantly, McHugh notes that 'Lerner watered down Freddy's personality to render him an impossible choice of suitor for Eliza, thereby introducing the parting of ways with the published epilogue of *Pygmalion*, in which the two are united in marriage.'[5] Additionally, McHugh reveals that Lerner toyed with making the romantic connection between Eliza and Henry Higgins more explicit but states that 'in the end, Lerner tantalizes us with the possibilities of an alliance between Eliza and Higgins, but never quite delivers it.'[6] Even so, the changes Lerner made to Shaw's *Pygmalion* highlight the possibilities of romantic triangulation to a greater degree. In *Camelot*, Lerner once again adapts an existing source—this time taking on T. H. White's version of Arthurian legend, *The Once and Future King* (1958). Lerner chose to focus on the doomed love triangle of Arthur, Guenevere, and Lancelot. In the stage version, Knapp identifies the unconsummated love between Guenevere and Lancelot as part of the musical's idealism and its impossibility reflects the doomed nature of Camelot itself.[7] Thus, Lerner's *Camelot* builds on the idea of a love triangle, making it more explicit as well as a source of tragedy.

Furthermore, the way in which the film adaptations specifically handle the love triangles in these musicals makes a strong case for *Paint Your Wagon* representing the symbolic (in addition to the literal) culmination of the 1960s Lerner and Loewe adaptations. *My Fair Lady* and *Camelot* are much more faithful to their stage counterparts than the film version of *Paint Your Wagon*. Yet how they handle romance, the concept of triangulation, and the implications offered by these relationships presents an almost linear progression from the earliest film adaptation to the latest.

As in the stage production, two triangles form in the film version of *My Fair Lady*: Eliza Doolittle, Henry Higgins, and Freddy Eynsford-Hill as well as Eliza, Higgins, and Colonel Pickering. As mentioned above, the musical does not present Freddy as a serious choice for Eliza. Jeremy Brett, largely known as a British theatre actor, was cast in this pseudo-romantic role. At the time of filming, Brett had appeared in relatively few film roles. Notably, however, he played Count Nikolai Rostov in the 1956 film *War and Peace,* also starring Audrey Hepburn (who played Nikolai's sister Natasha). At the beginning of the film, Freddy actually appears onscreen before Higgins; he accidentally bumps into Eliza, spilling her flowers. While he apologizes, Freddy almost immediately dismisses her. In fact, they make very little impression on each other in general. Eliza, too, only cares that her flowers have been ruined. In contrast, the audience soon learns that Higgins notices her and her atrocious accent, finding it fascinating. From the outset, Freddy overlooks a lower-class flower girl while Higgins is drawn to her. Freddy does not appear onscreen again until about an hour and twenty minutes after the first brief encounter when he becomes smitten with Eliza at the Ascot races. Eliza, now cleaned up and dressed well, attracts Freddy with her good looks and amuses him with her unconventional behaviour. This encounter, of course, leads to Freddy's only song, 'On the Street Where You Live.' One of the hits from the Broadway production, the lovely song has a catchy lyrical tune and is highly extractable. 'On the Street Where You Live' had already been popularly recorded by the premiere of the film adaptation. Vic Damone's version reached number 4 on the Billboard charts, making it the most popular version of the decade. And in 1964, Andy Williams had a version that reached number 3 on the adult contemporary chart and number 28 on the Hot 100. Thus, the song was quite well known at the time of the film's release.

'On the Street Where You Live' represents some of the best singing in the film without the more personal, narrative connection of several of the other songs. Although Jeremy Brett could sing, the studio chose to dub 'On the Street Where You Live' with tenor Bill Shirley.[8] Shirley had experience on radio as well as other film dubbing and provided the singing voice of Prince Phillip in Disney's *Sleeping Beauty* (1959). It seems that the studio was taking no chances with an already popular hit. Once the opening verse ends, this song could be sung by anyone about anyone. Thirty minutes after 'On the Street Where You Live,' we discover that Freddy spends his time loitering on the street of Higgins's house, and he reprises the song. Eliza finally appears (as he sings 'any second she may suddenly appear' while looking away from the house).

In an attempt to woo her, Freddy sings a romantic verse, which Eliza interrupts with 'Show Me.' The humour of this song comes from Freddy's attempts to act while Eliza constantly obstructs him. While her words ask him to show his love, her actions clearly demonstrate that she does not truly want it. Freddy has a remarkably unceremonious final appearance in the film. He comes to collect Eliza after she has tried to go home and discovered she no longer belongs. Practically speaking, a suitor who appears onscreen for less than half an hour in a nearly three-hour film makes less impression than characters with more screen time. The audience does not have the time to become emotionally invested in the Freddy/Eliza relationship, despite his charming song. On the surface, Freddy appears to be a lover on the order of Lancelot or Pardner. However, he never quite makes the grade. Higgins's obvious dismissal of the younger, attractive rival makes this abundantly clear. In their final argument, Eliza makes two threats to Higgins: to marry Freddy and to work for the Hungarian language expert. In the moment, Higgins responds more passionately to the second threat. In his rant during 'I've Grown Accustomed to Her Face,' Higgins assumes that any marriage between the young couple would be doomed to fail, even reveling in the possibility.

Furthermore, Higgins makes no objection to Eliza marrying another man—rather, he rejects a potential marriage with Freddy specifically because he feels that the young man is not good enough for her. In fact, Higgins twice mentions Eliza marrying. The first instance occurs after the ball when the uncertainty of her future upsets Eliza. Higgins points out that Eliza is attractive and now suited to marry an eligible man.

The second instance is even more telling: Higgins suggests that Eliza may marry Pickering. While Eliza dismisses Pickering as too old, the suggestion alludes to the already comfortably established triangle. Eliza has been living with not one—but two—'confirmed, old bachelors.'[9] Although Lerner gives hints as to the potential relationship between Eliza Doolittle and Henry Higgins, Pickering forms an important part of the picture. The threesome are nearly always together, and Pickering shares in many of their key moments. For examples, the 'Rain in Spain' number is not a private moment simply between Eliza and Higgins but all three of them. Additionally, Pickering, not Higgins, acts as Eliza's public escort at both Ascot and the Embassy Ball. Furthermore, Eliza freely admits to Mrs Higgins that Pickering's courtesy taught her how 'ladies and gentlemen behave towards one another.'[10] While meant as a barb to Higgins, the behavioural contrast between the two confirms the statement; Pickering coaxes Eliza with politeness and kindness while Higgins acts boorishly towards everyone. When Eliza leaves the house, *both* men storm around trying to find her. And while Higgins (selfishly and typically) assumes Pickering's concern is on his behalf, Pickering states in no uncertain terms to Mrs Pearce that *he* will miss Eliza's presence. Little romance—and even less sex—are apparent in this triangle and yet it is the more viable of the two. Eliza, Higgins, and Pickering live together comfortably. Shown all along with no ceremony whatsoever, they form the acceptable triangle, and we are given no reason to believe that this will change. When Eliza returns, the film ends with just her and the Professor at home, but the missing member of the household will certainly return and show his delight. In some ways, their living arrangement is a precursor to the three-way marriage in the film version of *Paint Your Wagon*. Two men live with a beautiful young woman, content to share her affections with the other in a pleasant home environment.

Although *Camelot* similarly remains quite faithful to the 1960 Broadway stage production, the film enhances the sexuality inherent in the love story between Guenevere and her two suitors. As I argue elsewhere, the film brings the feelings between Lancelot and Guenevere out of the ideal and into the earthly realm, from courtly love to consummated lust.[11] Through the use of bodies and other visual cues, the film strongly implies that Guenevere has had a sexual relationship with both Arthur and Lancelot over the course of the time period depicted. While the stage version certainly highlights the romance, albeit in an idealized manner, the 1967 film of *Camelot* takes the triangulation a step farther. Guenevere takes two lovers; Lancelot and Arthur share a knowledge of both her body and her mind. To some degree, each suitor acknowledges that the other knows about the illicit affair, thus tacitly agreeing to continue sharing Guenevere's affections until forced otherwise by outside forces. The shift in the portrayal of the love triangle from the Broadway to the Hollywood production suggests Lerner's strong interest in this type of triangulation. *My Fair Lady* and *Camelot* both indicate that Lerner was drawn to stories that had an element of triangulation built into the narrative. Furthermore, he chose to focus on this aspect of the source material and even enhance it to some degree.

Examining these earlier Lerner and Loewe film adaptations contextualizes *Paint Your Wagon* specifically in relation to Alan Jay Lerner's interest in this type of love theme. *My Fair Lady* and *Camelot* show Lerner's fascination with love triangles in which two men vie for—or perhaps more accurately share in—the affections of the same woman. Furthermore, Lerner worked on the screenplay for all three 1960s adaptations. As such, he made numerous changes to the plot, whether large or small, himself. Comparing the 1964 adaptation of *My Fair Lady* and the 1967 adaptation of *Camelot* already displays a propensity to highlight this notion of two men sharing the same woman as well as the sexual and emotional implications of such a relationship. *Paint Your Wagon* then offers the culmination of this particular interest. Notably, the original stage version does not contain this same type of triangulation to such a prominent degree.[12] The film, however, makes the newly conceived marriage between Elizabeth, Ben, and Pardner the central romantic relationship. As such, *Paint Your Wagon* more explicitly deals with elements only hinted at in *Camelot* and to a lesser extent, *My Fair Lady*. The Hollywood industry changes and the sociocultural context of the late 1960s allowed Lerner to explore this triangulation more fully.

ADAPTATION IN *PAINT YOUR WAGON*

Unlike the two other Lerner and Loewe musicals from the 1960s, the film version of *Paint Your Wagon* plays fast and loose with the original story and music of the original western musical. The stage production opened 12 November 1951 at the Schubert Theatre and received decent critical notices from reviewers. Brooks Atkinson called the score 'superb' and the musical as a whole 'heartily enjoyable' while identifying problems with the second act.[13] The show garnered no Tony nominations, however, and ran for only 289 performances. Both versions can be described as a musical comedy about gold miners in 1850s California. The two productions include the characters of Ben Rumson, an alcoholic miner, and Elizabeth Woodling, the Mormon wife whom he bought at auction. The general plot outline also remains, which involves Rumson discovering gold and the development of a mining town in the area. However, the similarities nearly end there. Although Lerner produced the film and ultimately wrote the screenplay, Paddy Chayefsky adapted the original script. Chayefsky produced a preliminary script which Lerner used as an outline for the final screenplay.

The film makes significant plot changes, including the removal of the Mexican romantic leading male and the addition of a polyandrous marriage.

The original stage production follows miner Ben Rumson, played by James Barton, and his daughter Jennifer, played by Olga San Juan. Rumson, a widower with a restless spirit, discovers gold in California. Subsequently, a gold mining town named after him springs up. For a time, Jennifer is the only woman in the newly populated town of 'Rumson.' The musical's primary romance occurs when Jennifer falls in love with a Mexican prospector named Julio Valveras, played by Tony Bavaar. The other miners constantly discriminate against Julio due to his ethnicity, forcing him to travel farther out of town in order to make a living in hopes of supporting Jennifer. Meanwhile, Ben buys the second wife of a Mormon traveler at auction. The marriage between Ben and his wife Elizabeth is not a happy one, and she runs away with another miner. While originally planning to leave Rumson for 'golder' pastures, Ben realizes his attachment to the town and chooses to settle.[14] Jennifer also remains, waiting for Julio's return. Julio eventually does come back despite not striking gold, and Jennifer and he begin their life together. The Broadway stage version tackles social issues surrounding ethnicity and prejudice in American history. The romantic lead is a Mexican character whom others constantly discriminate against and treat as an outsider despite his prior claim to the land. Through Julio's character as well as his romance with Jennifer, Lerner explores tolerance and multi-ethnic relationships. The narrative highlights the consequences of western expansion and questions the historic American dream. The removal of Julio Valeras and his plot omits these socially significant elements of the plot, missing an opportunity in light of the Chicano movement of the 1960s.

The film version of *Paint Your Wagon* keeps the Gold Rush Californian setting, the characters of Ben Rumson and Elizabeth

Woodling, and a very general outline of some of the original plot points. Chayefsky and Lerner change much, however. They completely omit the stage musical's principal couple, Julio and Jennifer. Consequently, the younger generation, and more importantly, the Mexican American perspective have also been removed. Instead, the film follows the partnership of Ben Rumson and the unimaginatively named Pardner. Rumson now appears as a bachelor with no children rather than a widower and father. An entirely male-populated town called No Name City develops around the gold veins where Ben and Pardner work and become friends. When a Mormon traveller passes through town with his two wives, he resolves to sell one, Elizabeth. A drunk Ben buys Elizabeth at auction and marries her. Unlike in the stage version, Elizabeth falls in love with the blustering drunkard Ben, who builds her a cabin of her own. For a time, Elizabeth remains the only female in No Name City, and this situation sparks consternation in her jealous husband. He thus concocts a plan to steal several prostitutes en route to a larger town. After some confusion, the two partners discover that Elizabeth loves both of them. They eventually agree to both be married to her.

The second portion of the film shows No Name City growing and becoming increasingly debauched. During this heady time, the polyamorous marriage thrives. A preacher arrives in No Name City and immediately condemns the raucous behaviour and questionable establishments. Soon, a winter storm brings a stranded churchgoing family to stay at the Rumson home. During their stay, both Pardner and Elizabeth realize that they no longer want to continue in their unusual situation. This realization coupled with his wandering nature prompts Ben to leave. After an emotional farewell to Ben, Pardner returns to Elizabeth as her sole husband. This brief plot outline of the original Broadway production versus the Hollywood version of *Paint Your Wagon* already demonstrates how much changed between the two productions.

The film features notable western stars Clint Eastwood as the taciturn yet sensitive Pardner and Lee Marvin as the blustering drunk yet kind-hearted Ben Rumson, with Jean Seberg appearing as their wife. The star text here reveals volumes in terms of marketing, genre associations, and musical ability. Director Joshua Logan chose nonsinging actors for all three of the starring roles.[15] As the polygamous Elizabeth, Seberg brought a European film pedigree to *Paint Your Wagon*. Although her career began somewhat unsuccessfully in Hollywood, the actress had since made a name for herself in French films, most notably in Jean-Luc Godard's *Breathless* (1960). Unsurprisingly perhaps, Logan emphasized the *western* atmosphere of *Paint Your Wagon* by casting two actors largely known for working in that genre.

By 1969, Lee Marvin had a well-established career as an actor 'identified with roles of violence and sadism,' known especially for his roles in westerns.[16] For example, he played one of the title characters in *The Man Who Shot Liberty Valance* (1962) opposite John Wayne and Jimmy Stewart. In the 1965 comedy western film *Cat Ballou*, Marvin played dual roles as two sharpshooters on opposite sides of a conflict and won the Academy Award for Best Actor for his performance. Like his costar, Clint Eastwood conjured associations related to the western. Eastwood had risen to international stardom through Sergio Leone's spaghetti western trilogy *A Fistful of Dollars* (1964), *For a Few Dollars More* (1965), and *The Good, The Bad, and the Ugly* (1966). All three of these films had US premieres in 1967 and gave Eastwood a star persona as an antihero with a 'laconic and even animal aura.'[17] As someone so identified with the western in the late 1960s, Eastwood's very presence in the film contributed greatly to the genre mixing in *Paint Your Wagon*. He was also cast against type as a gentle farmer who ultimately desires the moral strictures of society. Of both Eastwood and Marvin, Kelly Kessler states that they 'reflect variations on a form of contemporary masculinity that rejects the fifties ideals of marriage, white collar work, and family.'[18] The two actors bring their star text, developed from westerns, to bear on the film.

Several conditions in Hollywood in the late 1960s allowed for certain aspects of *Paint Your Wagon* to flourish. The film production of *Paint Your Wagon* occurred during the so-called early New Hollywood era. Two years earlier, the highly regarded, much-touted New Hollywood films *Bonnie and Clyde* and *The Graduate* premiered. Hallmarks of this style include narrative and character ambiguity, genre blurring, and techniques most associated with European art film (e.g., jump cuts). The casting of Lee Marvin and Clint Eastwood brought specific associations regarding the western as a genre. Similarly, the presence of Jean Seberg would bring to mind the French New Wave for those in the know, alluding to a connection with European art film. *Paint Your Wagon*, however, otherwise does very little in the way of New Hollywood filmmaking. For example, the camerawork, editing, and narrative devices are not New Hollywood in style. Ultimately, the film does not live up to its genre blurring potential implied by the creative casting. At the same time, the film contains elements that superficially attempt to forge this connection.

This time period also marks the final shift from the Hollywood Production Code to the Ratings System in 1968, which films exploited through an increased focus on sexual situations. Since the mid-1930s, the Production Code had provided a form of self-censorship that dictated what could and could not be shown on film. Although the Code varied throughout its lifetime, it affected the portrayal of sex, nudity, homosexuality, and drug use as some of the most notorious taboos.[19] As early as the 1950s, however, the Code began to lose its hold, and film found ways to get around the strict censorship system. In 1968, the Motion Picture Association of

America put into place an early form of the current Ratings System. With the new Ratings System, formerly prohibited subjects and images could appear in films with the caveat that the films received a 'more adult' rating.

Paint Your Wagon, in some ways, revels in the newfound sense of freedom pervading Hollywood at the time. However, the filmmakers relegate the emphasis on sex to the dialogue instead of the visuals. The most nudity that the audience sees occurs in a scene where Ben drunkenly rips off the bodice of Elizabeth's dress on their wedding night. The population of No Name City has lots of sex in the second half of the film, and with prostitutes no less, but the activity happens off screen. On the other hand, sex talk and bawdy humour permeate the film. Crude jokes and obvious references to sex replace the subtlety and double-entendres that infuse the dialogue and lyrics of many musicals. The acquisition of a bunch of 'French tarts' represents a turning point in the plot and leads the mining town into its debauched behaviour. To the chagrin of Paramount, the constant reference to prostitutes, sex, and of course the three-way marriage earned *Paint Your Wagon* a Mature (M) rating.[20]

In addition to the major plot changes, the film version of *Paint Your Wagon* alters the original score greatly. Without reprises, the film cut twelve major song and dance numbers (see chapter appendix for full song list from Broadway and Hollywood versions). These include romantic or mournful tunes sung by Julio and/or Jennifer, including 'Carino Mio,' 'Another Autumn,' and 'All for Him.' Lerner and collaborators redistribute a few of the remaining songs. For example, 'I Still See Elisa' understandably acts as Ben's torch song for his dead wife in the stage version. Since Ben is not a widower in the film, Pardner appropriates this tune. Pardner's version nonsensically becomes a song about an imaginary woman. Pardner also sings Julio's 'I Talk to the Trees.' In the stage version, this wistfully romantic number reveals the isolation experienced by Julio due to racism among the miners. In the film, it loses its poignant implications, simply revealing that Pardner tends to be a bit of a loner as well as showing his guilt for falling in love with his best friend's wife. Harve Presnell, the only trained singer cast in the film, unsurprisingly sings a lovely version of 'They Call the Wind Maria.' The decision to give this song to the best singer in the film makes sense given its popularity. Although *Paint Your Wagon* has never been among the best known of Lerner and Loewe's musicals, 'They Call the Wind Maria' did constitute a hit—due in part because folk revival group, the Kingston Trio, recorded the song in 1959. As the most recognizable song from the musical, the filmmakers took care to provide a well-sung version for the film.

Furthermore, the studio hired André Previn to write five new songs for the film. Ben receives two additional songs, establishing and affirming his rough ways. Clint Eastwood sings the tune 'Gold Fever.' Previn wrote the pseudo-gospel style song 'Here It Is' for the preacher, a newly created character who attempts to spiritually rescue No Name City from its sinful ways. The final new song, 'A Million Miles Away Behind the Door,' represents the only song in the entire film sung by a female character. Discussed in more detail later in the chapter, this is sung by Elizabeth as a tribute to her new home.

Additionally, the visual choices made by the filmmakers play a significant role in adapting a stage work for the screen. In *Paint Your Wagon*, the location shooting in Oregon represents the most notable aspect of the film's overall look. The cinematography tends to focus on the wide open spaces through an abundance of long shots and tracking shots that display the scenery. For the film's action, the editing and cinematographic choices are generally quite conventional. Mid-shots and longer shots that encompass several characters, coupled with the more seamless shot-countershot style of classic Hollywood, predom-inate. Given director Joshua Logan's reputation for somewhat unusual—and sometimes controversial—filmic choices in his musical adaptations, the sheer visual conventionality of *Paint Your Wagon* seems notable. Logan infamously added filters to the musical scenes in the film adaptation of *South Pacific*, giving the film an artificial appearance.[21] And in his other Lerner and Loewe adaptation, *Camelot*, he juxtaposed the grandeur of the legendary setting with myriad close-ups, sev-eral quite extreme, in order to depict the emotional anguish of the characters. For *Paint Your Wagon*, however, the choices of Logan and his collaborators reflect the connection to the genre of the western more than anything through the visual focus on the location shooting.

Film and musical theatre scholars alike tend to dismiss the film adaptation. Musical theatre scholars, for example, most often focus on *My Fair Lady* (1956; 1964 film) or even *Brigadoon* (1947; 1954 film) as representative of the duo's successful collaboration.[22] In film scholarship, authors lump the adaptation together with *Star!* (1968) or *Sweet Charity* (1969) as what Richard T. Jameson calls 'box office debacles (and lousy movies).'[23] Yet the figures reveal that *Paint Your Wagon* did much better than these other films. While *Star!* grossed $4 million and *Sweet Charity* grossed $8 million, *Paint Your Wagon* actually grossed over $30 million. In fact, it was one of the top ten highest grossing films of the year. While certainly nowhere near the more than $100 million mark of *Butch Cassidy and the Sundance Kid* of the same year, *Paint Your Wagon* would have done reasonably well if not for overspending.[24] We can speculate that perhaps the star power of Eastwood and Marvin contributed to this initial success and the sheer bizarre quality of the film itself to its later dismissal. Regardless, this disconnect makes an investigation of this ad-aptation an intriguing one.

RELATIONSHIPS AND SEXUALITY

A major change from stage to screen involves the alteration of the romances depicted. Initially, Lerner and Loewe clearly conceived of the relationship between Mexican prospector Julio Valveras and Ben Rumson's daughter Jennifer as the primary romance. Again, the film removes both of these characters. Without the young lovers, the film version compensates by building on the hasty marriage between Ben and Elizabeth. In the original stage production, Elizabeth does indeed come to the small mining town as the second wife of a Mormon traveller. She similarly agrees to be sold to another man, and Ben buys her. Elizabeth cares for the often-inebriated Ben, who still misses his dead wife, but she remains romantically dissatisfied. Ultimately, she falls in love with a minor character named Edgar Crocker and the two run away together—a decision which Ben respects. The film, however, adds Eastwood's character Pardner: a handsome, solitary, gentle young farmer who unwittingly becomes Ben's mining partner and just as unwittingly falls in love with his partner's wife. In the first half of the film, Pardner admits his love for Elizabeth and decides to leave town out of a sense of honour. Ben realizes that Elizabeth loves Pardner, prompting his decision to leave instead (which then begins a physical fight over which man will leave). Finally, Elizabeth, who loves both men, proposes what she calls a 'humane, practical, and beautiful solution.'[25] She cannot understand why she could be a second wife but not in turn have two husbands. The logic of her argument wins over unconventional Ben and the even more reticent Pardner.

The advent of this polygamous marriage seems to promote the type of alternative relationships advocated by the so-called sexual revolution. This social movement in the late 1960s notoriously challenged traditional modes of sexual behaviour, encouraging displays of sexuality and relationships outside monogamous heteronormativity. Trite ideas involving 'free love' associated with the predominant counterculture of the time as well as the increased visibility of second-wave feminism and the gay rights movement all contribute to the concept of the sexual revolution. Importantly, it seemed for a time in the film industry that sexual repression was a thing of the past. As discussed above, the move away from the Production Code to the Ratings System allowed many films to explore sexuality more fully. *Paint Your Wagon* portrays a harmonious marriage between a single female and two males, showing polyandry, which is the rarer form of polygamy. At the same time, however, the film implies that there is not a sexual relationship involving all three members. The two men trade off spending the night with their wife.

Interestingly, the film hints at the polyandrous love affair well before Pardner admits his feelings for Elizabeth. During the auction, Ben bids on Elizabeth while drunk and proceeds to pass out directly after winning her by doubling the previous bid. Pardner initially comes forward to withdraw Ben's alcohol-induced bid—an effort that proves unsuccessful. Thus, when Elizabeth enters the area, she sees the handsome Pardner and appears visibly pleased with her apparent new husband. Pardner quickly disavows her assumption and speaks on behalf of his incapacitated partner. Ben remains insensible throughout the entire preparation and wedding process. As such, Pardner walks him down the aisle and stands up with the couple. Furthermore, he actually answers 'he does' and 'she does' for Ben and Elizabeth, acting as the catalyst for their marriage. From the outset then, Pardner might be seen as an integral member of the marriage.

Although Elizabeth professes her love for both husbands and the two men similarly declare their love for her, the film contains only one real love song, 'I Talk to the Trees.' As mentioned before, Julio sings this song in the stage version, and it, in part, serves to highlight his marginality in the miner's community as a Mexican prospector. In the film, Pardner sings this song from the stage version as he struggles with his feelings for Elizabeth. The song comes on the heels of a brief montage of Elizabeth's and Pardner's interactions while Ben is away stealing prostitutes. Images of them spending time together fade into one another as an instrumental introduction to the forthcoming song plays.

The differences in sound as well as context for 'I Talk to the Trees' from the stage version emphasize specific elements about the film and the character of Pardner. Prior to this song, Pardner has sung only one other song, the wistful 'I Still See Elisa.' Both songs reveal Pardner's introspective nature as well as his romanticism. While Julio 'talks to the trees' out of necessity due to social ostracism, Pardner does so out of guilt and his own taciturn disposition. The orchestration further gives Pardner's song a particularly western type of romanticism, emphasizing the harmonica. In fact, the harmonica plays a counter-melody to Eastwood's vocal melody (⊙ video example 13.1). As the instrument has been used in numerous westerns as a symbol and a portable instrument used by cowboys, it holds strong associations with the genre.[26] Therefore, adding and even emphasizing the harmonica in Pardner's songs, and especially 'I Talk to the Trees' strengthens his association to the western. This song also becomes a turning point as it explicitly introduces the love triangle. However, the conflict displayed by Pardner during the song implies a more conventional love triangle than the one that will eventually occur.

Furthermore, Pardner's appropriation of the romantic ballad proves significant because he embodies conventionality throughout the film. Until Ben declares him his 'pardner,' Sylvester Newel intends to farm rather than search for gold in California. His wagon, which also contained his brother, turns over. While his brother died, Ben manages to save Pardner, whose gratitude to Ben for saving his life turns into loyalty and affection that gives the older man influence over the gentle Pardner. The contemplative 'I Talk to the Trees' permits Pardner to express his feelings and embody the romanticism that Ben lacks. While Ben's songs in the first half of the film tend to be boisterous, raucous numbers suited to a drunken miner, Pardner sings sweeter ballads. Once Elizabeth states that she wants to be married to both suitors, Ben and Elizabeth must convince the reluctant Pardner to agree. Although he eventually pronounces 'Hot damn, I think it's great. It's history-making!,' he soon passes out drunk.[27] The normally temperate Pardner turns to drinking in his discomfort with the situation.

In the second half of the film, a stranded churchgoing family come to stay in their home, and Pardner seems eager to readopt conventional behaviour. Since Elizabeth introduced Pardner as her husband first, she kicks Ben out of her home for the duration of the family's stay. Pardner quickly becomes a model 'only' husband. He begins to chide Ben for his wild ways and lead prayers before dinner. This taste of traditional marriage sours Pardner's conception of their original arrangement. He tells Elizabeth that he cannot return to the way things were; he needs a 'real' marriage with her. And finally, he achieves his desires. Ben gives in to his wanderlust and moves on from the soon-to-be respectable No Name City. Pardner dissolves their partnership and returns to Elizabeth. Despite the film's attempt to shock with its three-way marriage, *Paint Your Wagon* ultimately returns to traditional relationships and modes of behaviour.

FEMINISM VERSUS CHAUVINISM

Paint Your Wagon also contains a somewhat disconcerting tension between feminist and chauvinist perspectives. By the end of the 1960s, second-wave feminism was in full swing as a movement concerned with issues such as women's rights in the workplace and over their bodies. In film theory, second-wave feminism seeks to problematize and challenge traditional depictions of women onscreen.[28] As amongst the most seminal (yet not infallible) essays in feminist film theory, Laura Mulvey's discussion of the male gaze often informs Hollywood's onscreen women as well as those representations that subvert conventions.[29] Changing ideas of traditional gender roles also allowed for the possibility of more assertive and powerful female characters. And of course, this possibility sparks varied reactions and ways of looking at 'nontraditional' women who are no longer necessarily relegated to the domestic sphere. Nevertheless, mainstream films often depicted women who displayed behaviours such as intense sexuality in a more negative light (e.g., *The Graduate*'s Mrs Robinson). Indeed, the treatment of women and the characterization of Elizabeth in *Paint Your Wagon* reveal an ambivalence towards the feminist movement.

The film's basic plot elements display a highly chauvinistic treatment of women. Despite Ben and Pardner's love and even respect for Elizabeth, they view her as property on some level. Elizabeth comes to No Name City as the second wife of a travelling Mormon man. Having suffered the loss of her baby and being dissatisfied with her secondary status, she willingly agrees to be auctioned off to the highest bidder. The film adds a line not present in the stage version that briefly objects to this clearly odd practice. A member of the crowd shouts 'You can't buy a woman for money!'[30] However, this protestation is quickly overcome, and the auction commences. Thus, Ben buys Elizabeth, and their marriage ceremony resembles a claim-staking procedure. Similarly, the gentle, romantic Pardner uses rhetoric implying that he sees Elizabeth as a man's property. He tells Elizabeth that she 'belonged to Ben. He shared you with me.'[31] Only when Ben renounces her and leaves town does Pardner stay to build a life with Elizabeth. The idea of women as property that can be bought also comes through the centrality of the prostitutes in No Name City. The miners literally steal six women en route to a larger town in order to make use of their services. For the remainder of the film, these women are seen as objects for the male population's pleasure.

The score emphasizes the marginality of Elizabeth and other women in the town. The prostitutes who make up the female population of No Name City never sing. They simply exist as objects of visual (and implied physical) pleasure for the more active and audible men. While a prominent nondiegetic male chorus sings often, the only time offscreen female voices are heard singing is in Previn's newly composed 'Gold Fever.' Largely a solo for Pardner, which deals with the change that gold mining has wrought in his life, this song includes a background chorus of mixed voices. Additionally, Elizabeth sings only one solo number while both Ben and Pardner sing many. As such, the film marginalizes the female singing voice to the point that it is almost nonexistent.

Furthermore, the film privileges male homosocial bonds. Although the plot revolves around the three-way marriage, Ben and Pardner form the central relationship of *Paint Your Wagon*. Significantly, Ben gives Eastwood's character the name that he goes by for the majority of the film. Pardner's entire identity in No Name City is defined by his relationship to Ben—he is his partner. At the end of the film, Sylvester Newel (alias Pardner) finally reveals his true name to Ben as a parting gift. The first half hour of the film establishes the partnership and growing friendship between the two. The advertising for the film prepares this expectation from the outset. One tagline stated that 'Ben and Pardner shared everything—the gold, the laughs, the songs . . . even their wife!' This advertisement highlights their friendship as the film's primary relationship.

Throughout the beginning of the film, the pair open up to one another, and Pardner takes care of Ben when he lies drunk in the road. Only after their relationship is well established does Elizabeth enter the picture.

Thus, *Paint Your Wagon* begins as a 'buddy' film—a popular film type in the late 1960s and 1970s. In fact, the two most popular films of 1969, *Butch Cassidy and the Sundance Kid* and *Easy Rider*, privileged male relationships. Robin Wood posits that the buddy format exemplifies the 'repressed bisexuality that lurked (always ambiguously) in '70s Hollywood cinema.'[32] These undertones certainly materialize in this western musical. Ben and Pardner share a strong emotional connection, arguably deeper than their relationship with Elizabeth. When Ben abandons No Name City, he does not bother to say goodbye to Elizabeth but takes an emotional leave of Pardner. In fact, Ben willingly leaves Elizabeth alone in her house but had hoped that Pardner would travel with him. Pardner admits to Ben, 'Never liked a man as much as I liked you.'[33] Throughout their final conversation, relative close-ups on Ben's and Pardner's faces show their emotions throughout the exchange.[34] Furthermore, the plot relies on the near absence of women in a gold mining town. The men work and carouse together before and after women arrive in No Name City.

Once she arrives, Elizabeth is the only woman in No Name City. As such, she is both marginalized and objectified. She says very little at first and sings less, but the sex-starved miners track her movements. Elizabeth begins her time in No Name City as an object for male visual pleasure as described by Mulvey. At the same time, however, the film also subverts this viewpoint. The very first image of Elizabeth is presented in a long, full-body shot that shows her carrying supplies and struggling through the river on foot. As such, the audience's first view of Elizabeth shows a hard-working, travel-weary woman rather than a sexual object. She quickly becomes the object of No

Name City's male gaze as the shot-countershot technique illustrates, showing close or mid-shots of Elizabeth followed by men staring. In this way, the camera becomes conflated with the male characters' gaze, perhaps implying a male spectator as well. Yet the subsequent dialogue makes it apparent that the men are just as enamoured by the presence of a baby—even asking to hold her—as by the sudden appearance of a woman. This interest subverts the visual message to some extent, becoming part of the humour of the scene. Furthermore, her presence disrupts the camaraderie among the miners as Ben becomes prone to jealous rages, which prompts the town members to steal prostitutes in the first place. More importantly, she comes between Ben and Pardner until she announces that she wishes to take both as her husband.

This development leads to an additional element of homoeroticism since the two men share one woman. The situation in the second half of the film contains strong similarities to the *Camelot* love triangle. As mentioned earlier, *Camelot* makes clear that Arthur notices the feelings that Lancelot and Guenevere have for one another and even tolerates their relationship. Likewise, Lancelot admits to Guenevere that he believes Arthur knows of their clandestine meetings. However, the two men do not admit this knowledge to each other until forced by Mordred. Bruce Kirle claims that love triangles of this sort represent a 'classic, closeted homosexual fantasy; one man symbolically sleeping with his powerful friend by seducing the friend's wife.'[35] Kirle's analysis of the situation in *Camelot* can comfortably be applied to *Paint Your Wagon*, and he calls this film 'the most startling version of this gender-fluid fantasy.'[36] The fact that both men knowingly and willingly make love to the same woman renders the homoerotic subtext even more explicit. The social and industry context of the late 1960s gives further credence to a homoerotic reading. The film, however, stops short of implying a sexual relationship between Ben and

Pardner, or indeed, even both men engaging in sexual intercourse with their common wife on the same night. They switch off spending the night at home (in the cabin's one bed) while the other husband visits the gambling house. Although the film indicates that they do not have sexual relations, the living arrangements (especially when considering that they lived with one another prior to Elizabeth's arrival) and close emotional relationship expose marital intimacy between Ben and Pardner.

The music enhances the homosocial aspect of *Paint Your Wagon*. An integral part of the original production, which Ethan Mordden claims gives the works 'its *tinta*, its unique sound,' the male chorus becomes even more present in the film.[37] Both versions of the musical contain a male-heavy cast. The stage version, however, includes more than ten songs featuring a female singer (see chapter appendix). The miners do sing in several numbers throughout the show, but solos and duets without them is just as common. In the film version, a nondiegetic or onscreen men's chorus sings or accompanies a male soloist in the majority of the film's songs, including 'I'm On My Way' (and its many reprises), 'Hand Me Down That Can o' Beans,' 'They Call the Wind Maria,' 'Whoop-Ti-Ay,' 'There's a Coach Comin' In,' 'Wand'rin' Star,' and the reprise of 'Here It Is.' Therefore, the uniformity and tight harmonies of the studio-enhanced men's chorus become the film's primary aural marker, marginalizing the female voice. The dominant soundscape has significance in any film but especially in a musical. The cyclical way in which the film begins and ends further emphasizes the male population in the wilds of California. 'I'm On My Way,' sung by the ubiquitous male chorus, opens and closes the film, accompanied by various shots of people travelling in wagons (as can be heard and seen in ⏵ video example 13.2). These scenes show wagons moving through wild country in a series of location shots, and at the end, revisit individual characters. Indeed, the last image of the film shows Ben in his wagon, reinforcing the dominance of the male voice.

Despite her ostensible position, Elizabeth demands respect and asserts her control throughout the film. In the original stage production, Elizabeth steadfastly keeps house for Ben and nurses him in his drunken state. She rebels, but in secret, until finally leaving Ben for the miner with whom she secretly fell in love. And the stage version of Ben applauds her spirit and ability to make her desires come true. Elizabeth in the film version actively asserts her will on her men when she deems it important enough. From the outset, she uses the rather disconcerting proposition of being sold to the highest bidder as an opportunity to gain a better situation for herself. She clearly sees her current position as the second wife untenable. The visuals during this scene reinforce her stance. Elizabeth appears in mid-shot, sitting and eating at a table with a smirk on her face at the attention from No Name City's men. She listens to the debate about auctioning her off and actively argues for her present husband to sell her. When Ben comes to his senses enough to realize he has a wife, he unappealingly tries to force her into sexual submission on their wedding night. When Ben lunges at her and rips her bodice, however, Elizabeth pulls a gun on him and exclaims that she was 'bought as a *wife*, not as a *whore*.'[38] She insists that he respect her and build her a proper cabin.

Her only song 'A Million Miles Away Behind the Door' expresses her long-held desire for a home and subsequent joy when it has been built. André Previn and Lerner wrote this song for the film. It conforms closely to a conventional love song with moderately slow tempo, lyrical vocal melody, and a full, particularly lush orchestration that often accentuates the string section. In some ways, the song fits into a popular trope in musicals, which Jeffrey Magee has identified as the 'cozy cottage' trope: finding a home that represents domestic bliss.[39] For Elizabeth, however, the romantic notions behind the home are secondary. The lyrics emphasize her desire. She sings 'four cabin walls would be just right for me, I need a threshold I can cross where I can sit and gather moss,'[40] as can be heard in ⊙ video example 13.3. While she acknowledges the joy of having 'someone smiling from his chair across the floor,' this is clearly not the main purpose of the house.[41] The visuals further enhance this point. Ben does not appear onscreen until halfway through the song then largely has his back to the camera. Instead, the camera follows Elizabeth as she revels in her new home. Significantly, Ben remains mute rather than joining Elizabeth in her song as might be expected in a more traditional 'cozy cottage' type love duet. Taken together, the music, lyrics, and visuals, emphasize Elizabeth's love of her home and subvert focus on conventional romance. First and foremost, she wants a house that she can call her own. In fact, Elizabeth refuses to leave her home regardless of whether her husbands remain. She also makes it clear that the cabin is her property, not Ben's nor Pardner's—a fact that Ben freely concedes and allows her to kick one or both of them out of the house at will.

Furthermore, it is Elizabeth who initially proposes the idea that she take both Ben and Pardner as her husbands. While they are possessive of her, she wants something from each of them and actively works to get it. Her argument quickly persuades Ben, and even Pardner cannot form an adequate rebuttal for why she should not have both men, if she wants. Throughout the three-way marriage proposition scene, the cinematography includes shots that encompass all three members of the romantic triangle. As such, the visual construction echoes the polyandrous relationship being formed. Once married to both, she easily rules over their home life. Tellingly, she refuses to leave her house in No Name City even when the gold veins begin to run dry, and the men must bow to her wishes. And she throws Ben out of the house when the stranded family comes to stay. Elizabeth is a strong-willed woman who is not afraid to challenge either husband in spite of her subordinate status.

CONCLUSION

In a film such as *Paint Your Wagon*, the changes in plot loom large since the filmmakers altered it so drastically in meaningful, if somewhat bizarre, ways. One cannot help but comment on the polygamous marriage, particularly when it becomes apparent that this relationship was an addition not present in the original Broadway production. Yet the plot—significant as it is—only gives one piece of a complicated puzzle. And in a study of a musical, the score represents another key element. As this article explores, the music in *Paint Your Wagon* also changes quite a bit from the stage version and in ways that highlight the narrative approach taken in the film. Much of the film was shot on location in Oregon, in an attempt to give it the feel of a western with an emphasis on wide open landscape spaces. The location shooting, of course, differentiates the film from its stage counterpart. While the success and even meaningfulness of this might be seen as debatable, the treatment of Elizabeth and the other few women in the film through camerawork and editing do offer significant interpretations. Finally, the potential reasons behind these changes also become important.

Indeed, *Paint Your Wagon*, a seemingly strange adaptation of a lesser known Lerner and Loewe musical, proves to be very much a product of its time. Although it certainly explores a well-worn trope of triangulation, with which Lerner had long been fascinated, the means by which the film shows this relationship reflects the social and industry conditions of the late 1960s. Through its many alterations, the film exhibits a tension between traditional gender roles and marriage and the sense of freedom brought on by the sexual revolution, second-wave feminism, and the end of the Production Code. As the only lead female character in what essentially amounts to a buddy film, Elizabeth appears highly marginalized and certainly objectified by the male town. At the same time, she grasps at an opportunity to better her life. In agreeing to be sold, she no longer settles for being the second wife. Elizabeth demands respect, insists on a home, and even takes a second spouse herself. By the end of the film, however, it look as if she and Pardner will settle down to a quiet life of farming and domesticity. In this move and indeed throughout the film, *Paint Your Wagon* reflects a deep ambivalence towards significant social movements of the late 1960s.

As *Paint Your Wagon* makes abundantly clear, the process of adapting a work is a creative endeavour with many factors at play. The concept of fidelity—not only what changes are made in translation, but why they occur—remains an important part of musical adaptation studies. At the same time, I propose that forming value judgements based on ideas of fidelity can be shortsighted and even detrimental to the study of adapted works. It remains necessary to keep in mind the various other factors that impact adaptations. In the case of Hollywood film musical adaptations, the change in mediums makes alterations of some sort essential. The artistic success of a work does not depend solely on its faithfulness to the original source. While there is nothing inherently wrong with altering an original work, the types of changes made can certainly lead to questionable artistic choices, influencing the reputation of the musical. Adaptation—or in a broader sense the concept of combining familiarity and novelty—can provide a way for these works to remain relevant yet it can also have adverse effects. In the case of *Paint Your Wagon*, the original Broadway stage production never garnered the critical and popular success of *My Fair Lady, Brigadoon*, or even the film musical *Gigi*. As such, audience expectation—or lack thereof—allowed for myriad changes in the film version. At the same time, the film has acquired an extremely poor reputation. While neither version is as well known as other Lerner and Loewe musicals, the film remains widely available and potentially the more familiar version.

Therefore, looking at the changes and specific approaches that a single Hollywood adaptation makes can tell us much about adaptation in general. Perhaps the first question is why was the musical adapted in the first place? From an industry standpoint, adapting a successful stage musical can make studios a great deal of money. This was certainly the case during the studio era and the enormous popularity of *The Sound of Music* would give many studios cause to hope in the late 1960s. Another prominent line of inquiry deals with the involvement of any of the original creators and team members. Producers have used multiple approaches throughout the history of the film musical, and of course, Rodgers and Hammerstein maintained a significant amount of control in their film musical adaptations. While Frederick Loewe did not work on any of the 1960s film adaptations, Alan Jay Lerner involved himself in all of them to some extent, earning screenwriting credit for all three. This knowledge, coupled with the fact that Lerner tinkered with *Paint Your Wagon* throughout his long career, indicates that he may have viewed the film adaptation as an opportunity to try to 'get it right.' Lerner also potentially shaped the storyline to better fit his interests. All of this speaks to a wider issue: potential agendas of the various people involved in the making of an adaptation.

Furthermore, adaptations can tell us much regarding historical context and how changes over time might impact an artistic work. *Paint Your Wagon* represents a remarkably good example of this issue. To some extent, the film version misses a real opportunity, ignoring important movements such as civil rights and, relevantly, the burgeoning Chicano movement. Dovetailing with the momentum of these social movements could have bolstered the themes of bigotry versus love and acceptance and the repercussions of western expansion inherent in Lerner's original script. The whitewashing of the film version of *Paint Your Wagon* proves particularly problematic in light of these social movements, which pushed for equality for people of colour. Instead, the film intersects with the sexual revolution and reacts to second-wave feminism. As such, this film offers a look at how an adaptation can connect with the social mores of its time, whether explicitly or implicitly. The social movements the filmmakers choose to interact with and those they seemingly ignore provide a great deal of information.

In conclusion, I find that an in-depth exploration of a single Hollywood adaptation of a Broadway musical provides invaluable insight in myriad ways. While not all adaptations take the same approaches, studying these film musicals and their changes reveal ideas regarding fidelity to the original show, the aspects considered to earn success (typically financial), and the sociocultural context that may impact its creation. *Paint Your Wagon* might not be the most successful film musical of the late 1960s—though neither was it anywhere near the worst flop—and it might not have endured to be particularly well known or well respected in the twenty-first century. Yet a comparison of the film with its earlier stage counterpart reveals a great deal about the industry, individual filmmakers, and the times in which it was produced. This type of fruitful comparison makes a reconsideration of this film, and others like it, worthwhile.

APPENDIX

Stage:	Screen:
Act 1	Act 1
I'm On My Way	I'm On My Way (opening credits)
Rumson	I'm On My Way (choral reprise)
What's Goin' On Here?	I Still See Elisa
I Talk to the Trees	The First Thing You Know*
They Call the Wind Maria	Hand Me Down That Can o' Beans
I Still See Elisa	They Call the Wind Maria
How Can I Wait?	Whoop-Ti-Ay
Trio	A Million Miles Away Behind the Door*
Rumson (reprise)	I Talk to the Trees
In Between	There's a Coach Comin' In
Whoop-Ti-Ay	Act 2
How Can I Wait? (reprise)	Here It Is*
Carino Mio	The Best Things in Life Are Dirty*
There's a Coach Comin' In	Wand'rin' Star
Finaletto	Gold Fever*
Act 2	Here It Is (reprise)
Hand Me Down That Can o' Beans	I'm On My Way (reprise)
Rope Dance	
Can-Can	
Another Autumn	
Movin'	
I'm On My Way (reprise)	
All for Him	
Wand'rin' Star	
I Talk to the Trees (reprise)	

* New songs by Alan Jay Lerner and André Previn.

Source: Alan Jay Lerner and Frederick Loewe, *Paint Your Wagon: A Musical Play in Two Acts* (New York: Coward-McMann, 1952), and Alan Jay Lerner, *Paint Your Wagon* DVD. Directed by Joshua Logan (Hollywood, CA: Paramount Home Video, 1969).

NOTES

1. Julie Sanders, *Adaptation and Appropriation* (New York: Routledge, 2006), 18.
2. Linda Hutcheon, *A Theory of Adaptation* (New York: Routledge, 2006), 16.
3. Geoffrey Block, *Enchanted Evenings: The Broadway Musical from Showboat to Sondheim and Lloyd Webber*, 2nd ed. (New York: Oxford University Press, 2009), 153–154.
4. Raymond Knapp, *The American Musical and the Performance of Personal Identity* (Princeton, NJ: Princeton University Press, 2006), 286.
5. Dominic McHugh, *Loverly: The Life and Times of My Fair Lady* (New York: Oxford University Press, 2012), 83.
6. McHugh, *Loverly*, 87–88.
7. Knapp, *The American Musical*, 178–180.
8. Brett discusses the fact that Shirley provided the playback vocals in Suzie Galler, 'More Loverly than Ever: *My Fair Lady* Then and Now,' in *My Fair Lady*, Special Edition (Burbank, CA: Warner Bros., 1994).
9. Higgins refers to both himself and Pickering as such on several occasions. Alan Jay Lerner and George Bernard Shaw, *Signet Classics: Pygmalion and My Fair Lady* (New York: Penguin, 1980), 166.
10. Lerner and Shaw, *Signet Classics*, 183.
11. An expanded article that focuses on the following conclusion regarding sexuality in the film version of *Camelot* can be found in Megan Woller, 'The Lusty Court of *Camelot* (1967): Exploring Sexuality in the Hollywood Adaptation,' *Music and the Moving Image* 8, no. 1 (Spring 2015): 3–18.
12. It should be noted, however, that the stage version of Elizabeth does fall in love with another gold miner—a minor character—and actually runs away with him.
13. Brooks Atkinson, 'Swell Folks: *Top Banana* and *Paint Your Wagon* Are Acted by Some Vivid Performers,' *New York Times*, 18 November 1951.
14. Notably, Ben Rumson dies at the end of the stage version.

15. Logan did, however, cast classically trained singer Harve Presnell in the minor role Rotten Luck Willie to sing the already popular song 'They Call the Wind Maria.' Presnell made his film debut as Johnny Brown, a role he originated on Broadway, in Meredith Wilson's *The Unsinkable Molly Brown*. Ray Walston played another minor character, Mad Jack Duncan. Walston had previously appeared in musicals in roles such as Luther Billis in *South Pacific* (1958) and Mr Applegate in *Damn Yankees* (1958).

16. Norma Lee Browning, 'On the Wilderness Trail with Paint Your Wagon,' *Chicago Tribune*, 16 February 1969.

17. Paul Smith, *Clint Eastwood: A Cultural Production* (Minnesota: University of Minnesota Press, 1993), 12.

18. Kelly Kessler, *Destabilizing the Hollywood Musical: Music, Masculinity, and Mayhem* (New York: Palgrave Macmillan, 2010), 100.

19. Thomas Doherty, *Hollywood's Censor: Joseph I. Breen and the Production Code Administration* (New York: Columbia University Press, 2007).

20. *New York Times* articles reveal that the studio appealed the Motion Picture Association of America's (MPAA) decision twice. The rating controversy is discussed in Matthew Kennedy, *Roadshow! The Fall of Film Musicals in the 1960s* (New York: Oxford University Press, 2015), 183.

21. Logan called the use of the garish filters 'one of the major mistakes of my career.' Joshua Logan, *Movie Stars, Real People, and Me* (New York: Delacorte Press, 1978), 123.

22. Joseph Swain, *The Broadway Musical: A Critical and Musical Survey* (Lanham, MD: Scarecrow Press, 2002), 193–220, and Block, *Enchanted Evenings*, 260–278.

23. Richard T. Jameson, 'Dinosaurs in the Age of the Cinemobile,' in *The Last Great American Picture Show: New Hollywood Cinema in the 1970s*, ed. Thomas Elsaesser, Alexander Horwath, and Noel King (Amsterdam: Amsterdam University Press, 2004), 155.

24. Kennedy, *Roadshow!*, 184.

25. Alan Jay Lerner, *Paint Your Wagon* DVD. Directed by Joshua Logan (Hollywood, CA: Paramount Home Video, 1969).

26. The examples are too numerous to list. However, one famous and prominent western musical scene that features the harmonica can be found in *Rio Bravo* (1959), starring John Wayne, Dean Martin, and Ricky Nelson.
27. Lerner, *Paint Your Wagon* DVD.
28. Constance Penley, ed., *Feminism and Film Theory* (New York: Routledge, 1988).
29. Laura Mulvey, 'Visual Pleasure and Narrative Cinema,' in *Feminism and Film Theory*, ed. Constance Penley (New York: Routledge, 1988), 57–68.
30. Lerner, *Paint Your Wagon* DVD.
31. Lerner, *Paint Your Wagon* DVD.
32. Robin Wood, *Hollywood from Vietnam to Reagan . . . and Beyond* (New York: Columbia University Press, 2003), 199.
33. Lerner, *Paint Your Wagon* DVD.
34. I use the term 'relative' here as none of the closer shots in *Paint Your Wagon* can be considered extreme by any means.
35. Bruce Kirle, *Unfinished Show Business: Broadway Musicals as Works-in-Process* (Carbondale: Southern Illinois University Press, 2005), 164.
36. Kirle, *Unfinished Show Business*, 164.
37. Ethan Mordden, *Coming Up Roses: The Broadway Musical in the 1950s* (New York: Oxford University Press, 1998), 57.
38. Lerner, *Paint Your Wagon* DVD.
39. Jeffrey Magee, 'From Flatbush to Fun Home: Broadway's Cozy Cottage Trope,' keynote address, *Putting It Together: Investigating Sources for Musical Theatre Research*, 10–12 May 2016.
40. Alan Jay Lerner, Frederick Loewe, and André Previn, *Paint Your Wagon: Vocal Selections* (New York: Chappell, 1970), 13–17.
41. Lerner, Loewe, and Previn, *Paint Your Wagon: Vocal Selections*, 16.

4

'A Great American Service'

George M. Cohan, the Stage, and the Nation in Yankee Doodle Dandy

ELIZABETH TITRINGTON CRAFT

■ □ ■

AT THE INTERSECTION OF TWO popular film genres—the film musical and biographical motion picture, or 'biopic'—sits the hybrid subgenre of the musical biopic, films about the life and works of musical figures like composers, performers, or music industry professionals. Biopics, generally, are a sort of film adaptation, but the source material to be adapted is not an existing work but rather a personal history. In the 1930s and 1940s, they were a way of 'sober[ing] up' for a film industry tired of the 'extravagances' of 1920s romances, scholar Richard Gustafson has speculated.[1] But in merging musical and biography, musical biopics walked a middle path, promising the spectacle of entertainment as well as some semblance of authenticity. The success of *The Great Ziegfeld* in 1936 (about producer Florenz Ziegfeld Jr) set off a craze of 'epidemic proportions' for these films.[2] Among the subjects featured—with varying degrees of faithfulness to their actual lives—were the Austrian composer known as 'The Waltz King,' Johann Strauss II (*The Great Waltz*, 1938); American songwriters Stephen Foster (*Harmony Lane*,

1935 and *Swannee River*, 1939) and Paul Dresser (*My Gal Sal*, 1942); and a famous husband-and-wife ballroom dance pair (*The Story of Vernon and Irene Castle*, 1939). Many of these musical biopics spotlighted someone from American 'show business,' capitalizing on a ready-made story, natural 'backstage musical' set-up, and already popular songs and shows.

One of the most long-lived and critically acclaimed twentieth-century musical biopics is *Yankee Doodle Dandy* (1942) about George M. Cohan. A Warner Bros. film, *Yankee Doodle Dandy* was produced by Hal Wallis and associate producer William Cagney, was directed by Michael Curtiz, and starred James Cagney as Cohan, a career-defining role for which Cagney won Academy and New York Film Critics Circle Awards. Cohan's story offered Warner Bros. and audiences the advantages of a showbiz biopic with one of the most famous showmen in the United States, yet it was also unusual in several ways. For one thing, Cohan himself was an uncommon, even singular, Broadway theatrical figure in his manifold professional roles: he was a composer, lyricist, playwright, director, producer, and star actor to boot. His career, which started with his family's vaudeville troupe the Four Cohans, bridged historical and theatrical eras—from the nineteenth century into the twentieth, from vaudeville to musical comedy—and he was a key figure in the transition. Cohan was also a skilled self-promoter with a distinct interest in telling his own story; his many writings included an autobiography published when he was forty-six.[3] And unlike Stephen Foster or Florenz Ziegfeld Jr, long deceased when their biopics hit the screens, Cohan was still living at the time of *Yankee Doodle Dandy*'s writing and premiere. The film's contract stipulated that he would be an active participant in its development and have final approval of the product.[4]

Moreover, Cohan's shows and his self-constructed personal narrative had long emphasized his American identity and patriotism, themes that were particularly timely in the early 1940s as World War II loomed. Thus, the goals of biopic, backstage musical, and wartime propaganda intersect in *Yankee Doodle Dandy* in ways that would not have been possible with any other protagonist. This chapter explores how the film harnesses the particularities of Cohan's story as well as the communal, nostalgia-laden mythologies typical of the Hollywood musical to unify and glorify the United States in wartime, simultaneously solidifying the reputation of Cohan as a premier patriot and helping to position the musical as the nation's own, homespun art form.[5]

'THE STORY OF GEORGE M. COHAN BY HIMSELF'

Upon Cohan's death in 1942, only months after the release of *Yankee Doodle Dandy*, the *New York Times* declared 'he was patriotism on the stage' and that he 'almost represented the American flag.'[6] While Cohan was well known in the early twentieth century, especially for such patriotic shows and songs as 'Yankee Doodle Boy' and 'You're a Grand Old Flag,' the film solidified and made immortal—through the permanent fixity of recording technology—this image of him. It was only the culmination, however, of Cohan's extensive decades-long efforts to shape his patriotic persona through the press in an era when Gilded Age–wealth and mass circulation newspapers propelled the notion of celebrity in the United States.[7]

Born in 1878, Cohan was the grandson of Irish immigrants in an era when the Irish were considered racially distinct from—and inferior to—Anglo-Saxons. Both in spite of his heritage and because of it, however, he built his career on hyper-patriotic 'flag-waving' shows.[8] As his early, turn-of-the-century songs and musicals helped define a 'Yankee' national identity, he simultaneously linked himself to the patriotic heroes he portrayed onstage. He was so successful, in fact, that (long before the biopic chose the sobriquet as its title) he became known as the 'Yankee Doodle Dandy' celebrated in one of his hit songs. Programs, advertisements, and sheet music for Cohan's patriotic musicals abounded with national buzzwords and other signifiers. In *Little Johnny Jones* (1904), Cohan was billed front and centre as 'the Yankee Doodle Comedian,' a change of tack from his first two Broadway efforts in which The Four Cohans received joint billing.[9] *George Washington, Jr* (1906) was advertised as either the 'great National Song Show' or 'His Latest American Musical Play,' and its sheet music sported a flag design (see Figure 4.1). *The Yankee Prince* (1908) was said to open its first rehearsal with the singing of 'My Country, 'Tis of Thee,' and, building on the title of the show *The American Idea* (1908), Cohan sponsored a contest for the best statements of 'what the American idea is.'[10] Some critics disparaged his 'commercializing of the flag,' as one put it, but the tactics won ringing endorsement from the box office.[11] Cohan's output did include more than just 'flag-waving' shows, and the film adapts his anecdote on the point. As he tells it, when theatre magnate A. L. ('Abe') Erlanger asked him whether he could write a play without a flag, he countered, 'I could write a play without anything but a pencil.'[12] Nonetheless, his reputation for patriotism is what stuck in the public imagination.

Cohan's patriotic reputation was deliberately earned. A master of what today might be called personal branding, he took full advantage of the human-interest journalism that proliferated at the turn of the twentieth century. He bolstered his patriotic persona in countless interviews and articles, including, early on in his career, in *The Spot Light*, a bulletin 'devoted to the interests of Geo. M. Cohan and the Cohan and

FIGURE 4.1 Cover of the sheet music for 'You're a Grand Old Flag' (New York: F. A. Mills, 1906) from George Washington, Jr., University of Tennessee Library, Digital Collection, Sheet Music Collection, http://diglib. lib.utk.edu/utsmc/main.php?bid=320 (accessed July 26, 2018).

Harris attractions.' *The Spot Light* noted in 1905 that when Cohan 'makes himself sing' the line 'Born on the Fourth of July' in the song 'Yankee Doodle Boy,' 'he is singing the truth,' because he was indeed born on 4 July 1878.[13] Historians have disputed whether he was actually born on 3 July or 4 July, but Cohan certainly embraced sharing a birthdate with the national holiday, and it proved a convenient token of authenticity.[14] He attributed the shape of his career to being 'born under the Stars and Stripes' and even chose 4 July for his wedding date.[15]

By the time of *Yankee Doodle Dandy*, George M. Cohan's autobiography was well rehearsed and familiar, at least to fans. A series of articles in 1914 in *Green Book Magazine*, a theatrical periodical boasting 'timely articles by and about prominent stage folk' as well as coverage of motion pictures, fiction, and a 'play of the month,' was one of many places one could read about Cohan.[16] The magazine advertised its series as 'The Story of George M. Cohan by Himself' (though writer Verne Hardin Porter collaborated with Cohan and delivered the first installment about his parents), and its editor's note declared Cohan's life story 'the most American document we have ever read.'[17] The articles emphasize his strong family ties and theatrical upbringing, address character traits like his ego (or, as he preferred to put it, 'self-certain[ty]'), highlight his lack of formal education, and plainly acknowledge the simplicity of his methods and aims—in short, they cast Cohan as a self-made song-and-dance man.[18] Cohan's Irish background is not overlooked—the story talks about the years his father Jerry spent playing in the hibernicon, an Irish-themed moving panorama show—but his American pride is paramount.[19]

Cohan did his best to shape the storyline of *Yankee Doodle Dandy*, even offering his own screenplay at one point.[20] The film's first screenwriter Robert Buckner wrote in a memo to the executive producer, 'The picturization of his life story is an extremely serious matter with [Cohan]. He is independent as hell about it.'[21] Because of his assertive involvement in the film and because he had already so deliberately shaped his public image, it is unsurprising that the film echoes similar themes to those he had propagated.[22] The film presents his life story as an extended flashback during his visit to President Franklin D. Roosevelt's office, where he expects to be upbraided for his portrayal of the president in the musical *I'd Rather Be Right* (1937) but instead receives a Congressional Gold Medal.[23] As the flashback to the year of Cohan's birth begins, the scene shows a banner with the year 1878, and Cohan, in voiceover, describes the period as 'the beginning of the Horatio Alger age,' setting the scene for his own ascendance from immigrant to preeminent American, poor vaudevillian to famous actor and wealthy impresario.[24]

In keeping with Cohan's autobiographical writings, much of *Yankee Doodle Dandy* focuses on Cohan's childhood and relationships with his parents and sister. His father Jerry, mother Helen, and sister Josephine (called Josie) are central characters. As Patrick McGilligan notes in his introduction to the published screenplay, many of 'Cohan's anecdotes about his childhood and youth were adopted wholesale.'[25] In addition, the film ignored aspects of Cohan's life that were uncomplimentary to him or that he found objectionable for the big screen.[26] He famously insisted, for example, that there be no mention of his first wife Ethel Levey and no love scenes. Levey was, indeed, omitted, as were his children by both his first and second marriages, though Cohan eventually agreed to the film's portraying a fictionalized love interest named Mary.[27] The film also avoided any mention of Cohan's infamous hard-line stance against Actor's Equity Union, despite its major ramifications for his life and career. According to contemporaneous biographer Ward Morehouse, Cohan's daughter Georgette said of the film, 'That's the kind of a life daddy would have liked to have lived.'[28]

Two sequential scenes early in the film establish Cohan's 'Yankee Doodle Dandy' patriotic persona: his meeting with the president and his birth, related as a flashback. In both scenes, his Americanness is linked to his Irishness, helping to solidify cultural acceptance of a dual, patriotic Irish American identity at a time when the Irish had only relatively recently been accepted as bona fide Americans.[29] The scene with President Roosevelt introduces the theme of Cohan's Irish-tinged patriotism: remembering his youth, Cohan tells the president, 'I was a pretty cocky kid in those days—a regular Yankee Doodle Dandy. Always *in* a parade or following one.' The president comments, 'That's one thing I've always admired about you Irish-Americans. You carry your love of country like a flag, right out in the open. It's a great quality.' As historian Meaghan Dwyer-Ryan notes, this 'oft-repeated quote' from the film 'became an acknowledgement of Irish contributions to the country.'[30]

As in his own writings, Cohan's 4 July birthdate is critical to his historiography, and the birth scene in *Yankee Doodle Dandy* forcefully establishes both George's Irish heritage and his complementary fate as a patriotic American through closely intertwined aural and visual signifiers of Irish and US national identity. Initiating the extended flashback after the early scene with President Roosevelt, an image of Cohan in the president's study slowly dissolves to an American flag, then the camera pans downwards to Providence, Rhode Island, amidst Independence Day celebrations. We hear, then see, a marching band playing the nineteenth-century patriotic tune 'Columbia, the Gem of the Ocean,' then we see a sign for the Colony Opera House showing 'Week of July 1, 1878 / Mr and Mrs Jerry Cohan / "The Irish Darlings."' On the stage inside, Jerry sings and dances as Irish dancing master Larry O'Leary, costumed in breeches, a cape, and a 'jaunty Irish hat,' with shamrock appliqués on his hat and lapels, and carrying a shillelagh.[31] (His song, 'The Dancing Master,' was one performed by the real-life Jerry.)[32] He dashes off the stage as soon as his performance ends, and a Civil War veteran with an Irish brogue rushes him through the parade to his destination—the bedroom where his wife Nellie has just given birth to George. As they consider what to call the newborn, the doctor suggests George Washington Cohan, since he was born on the Fourth of July, but Nellie replies that 'Washington' is too long to fit on a billboard. They instead combine George with the 'nice short Irish [middle] name' Michael. When the veterans outside fire a cannon in George's honor and the baby breaks into a wail, Jerry exclaims, 'He's crying with a brogue!' and hands him an American flag (see Figure 4.2).[33] In continued voiceover, Cohan says, 'I guess the first thing I ever had my fist on was the American flag. I hitched my wagon to thirty-eight stars. And thirteen stripes.' Fulfilling the biopic's generic expectation of establishing its hero's 'sense of destiny,' the scene introduces the theme of patriotism as well as the literal symbol of the flag, one of many to be seen in *Yankee Doodle Dandy*.[34]

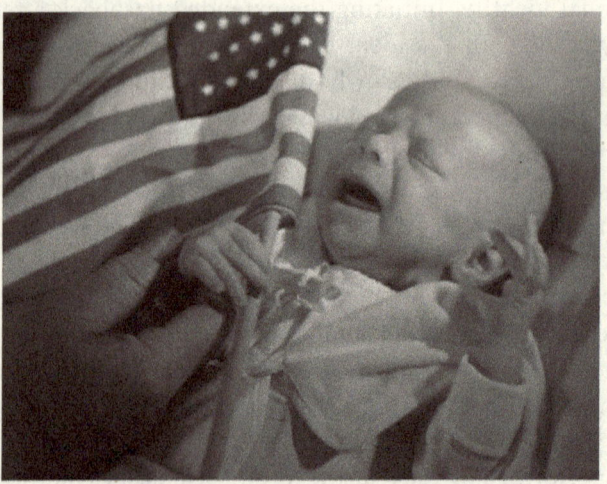

FIGURE 4.2 George M. Cohan at birth in Yankee Doodle Dandy (1942).

THE STAGE AND THE NATION

In its celebration of American theatre, *Yankee Doodle Dandy* exemplifies the stage and screen's 'intertwining of intimately shared histories,' as scholars Raymond Knapp and Mitchell Morris have put it.[35] The film is at once a chronicle of US theatrical history and a sort of backstage musical, with its attendant tropes.[36] While Cohan wrote plays as well as musicals, *Yankee Doodle Dandy* focusses almost exclusively on the latter. Occasionally musical and dramatic performances serve to advance the plot or develop a character, as when Mary plays and sings the song George has written for her ('Mary's a Grand Old Name') at the piano in her home. More often, however, songs—both snippets heard in montages and complete numbers—mark the passing of time or highlight key moments in Cohan's career. Dressing room scenes, backstage shots, and stage performances abound, and, with the notable exception of 'Over There' (discussed in this chapter's next section), the songs are part and parcel of show business, whether the characters are performing onstage, auditioning for a producer, or singing a newly written number at a living room piano.[37]

In tracing Cohan's journey through his theatrical experiences, from the touring circuits of vaudeville in small town America to the 'legit' stages in the heart of Broadway, *Yankee Doodle Dandy* strategically elides three simultaneous histories: those of Cohan, the musical, and the nation. Cohan's voiceover narration at the start of his flashback—with his quip, 'There weren't so many stars then, in the flag or on the stage, but folks knew that more were coming'—reveals the story's central metaphor while capturing the Gilded Age sense of optimism, confidence, and growth. After the scene of his birth, we see images of a family photo album, with Cohan's sister Josie (who was, in fact, the elder sibling) added to an empty frame (see Figure 4.3a), and a series of theatrical scenes. The imagery and narration continue to link the Cohans' experiences to the nation's. Cohan describes playing a Daniel Boone show on the 'kerosene circuit,' the term denoting low-budget companies performing a series of one-night engagements in very small towns.[38] We see a train traversing the countryside as Cohan, extending his use of flag symbolism, declares, 'They kept putting new stars in the flag, and the Cohans kept rushing out to meet them.' We see a young George playing the Irish 'Dancing Master' as his father had done, but with a novelty twist, playing (quite badly) the violin above his head. He also adds a patriotic flourish, shooting an American flag out of his shillelagh at the number's conclusion. In another scene, Josie sings and performs a dance to 'The Fountain in the Park,' a popular late nineteenth-century tune by Edward Haley, and in yet another, we see the four Cohans performing a black-face minstrel number with tambourines. Cohan's narration continues, 'We trouped through depression and inflation. Part of the country's growing pains.' Throughout, the Cohans' history touring the nation as performers is paralleled with the growth of the United States; their ups and downs are aligned with the nation's.

While *Yankee Doodle Dandy*, more than many Hollywood musicals, treats theatrical performance unabashedly as a commercial business, the film also partakes of similar generic mythologies, as described by scholar Jane Feuer. It valorizes entertainment, for instance, and presents a 'vision of musical performance originating in the folk.'[39] Show business is business, but it's also bound up with family ties (among the Four Cohans), romantic love (between George and Mary), and national sentiment. In one critical scene, the prominent producer Abe Erlanger tells the petulant star Fay Templeton,

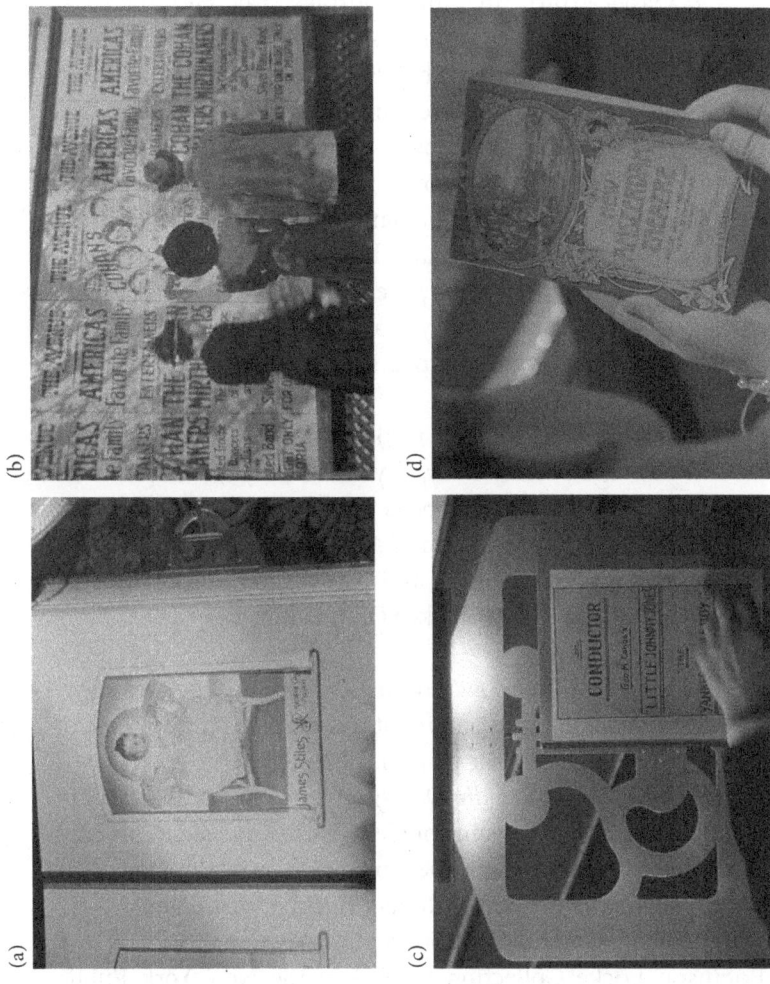

FIGURE 4.3A–D Images of Documents in Yankee Doodle Dandy (1942).

who has refused a role in a Cohan show, that she should reconsider.

> ERLANGER. You're making a mistake, Fay. He's the most original thing that's ever hit Broadway. And do you know why? Because he's the whole darn country, squeezed into one pair of pants! His writing—his songs—even the way he walks and talks—they all touch something way down *here* in people! (He lays a hand over his heart.) Don't ask me why it is—but it happens every time the curtain goes up. It's pure magic!
>
> TEMPLETON. I'm bored by magic. I know his formula—a fresh young sprout gets rich between 8:30 and 11:00 PM.
>
> ERLANGER. That's just it! George M. Cohan has invented the success story, Fay. And every American loves it because it happens to be his own private dream. He's found the mainspring in the Yankee clock— ambition, pride, and patriotism. That's why they call him the Yankee Doodle Boy.[40]

Cohan, *Yankee Doodle Dandy* insists, not only creates show business magic, but he embodies it. He becomes the epitome of Broadway because he's the epitome of America.

Within *Yankee Doodle Dandy*, even as great liberties are taken with the major events of George's life, considerable care is taken with the details of the Cohans' theatrical history. The film's original screenwriter Robert Buckner did extensive research using Cohan's autobiography, the scrapbooks of the Robinson Locke Collection housed in the New York Public Library, articles in newspapers and magazines, interviews with Cohan's acquaintances, and conversations with Cohan himself.[41] As one montage depicts, the family did indeed tour

together: with Jerry's hibernicon company, as 'The Cohan
Mirth Makers,' and later as the famous 'Four Cohans' act. The
film's iconography conveys a sense of authenticity; we see signs,
playbills, and other documents, frequently used to introduce
theatrical scenes (see Figure 4.3). The performance scenes are
fairly true to life as well. George M. Cohan did, indeed, play the
violin in his boyhood, Josie was known for her dancing, and
Cohan wrote in his autobiography about the family playing
'Daniel Boone on the Trail,' 'Peck's Bad Boy,' and other skits
and shows referenced in the film.[42] The plethora of seemingly
historical images, evocative of a visual archive, serves both to
commemorate theatrical history and to deflect from the film's
many biographical falsities.

Musical and choreographic decisions, too, were made with
the goal of authenticity as well as capitalizing on the popularity
of Cohan's songs. In the contract, Cohan agreed to provide
music and piano arrangements for the film.[43] (He was even to
provide three new songs, though that did not happen.) He was
quite concerned with the accuracy of the film's musical staging
of his numbers, and his assistance was appreciated more in this
realm than others.[44] While the final version of the film had a
few non-Cohan songs, the majority were his, including 'The
Warmest Baby in the Bunch' (1897), 'Mary's a Grand Old Name'
(1905), 'I Was Born in Virginia' (1906, originally published as
'Ethel Levey's Virginia Song'), 'Harrigan' (1907), and others.
The screenwriters took liberties with chronology as well as with
the arrangement of some numbers, like 'The Yankee Doodle
Boy' (1904) and 'You're a Grand Old Flag' (1906)—the first in
order to explain the song's role within the plot, and the second
(discussed in more detail later in the chapter) to evoke national
pride in wartime.[45] Overall, however, fidelity was the byword
in the treatment of Cohan's musical oeuvre and the staging of
musical numbers. James Cagney also took great care to capture
Cohan's renowned, distinctive dancing style; his instructor

Johnny Boyle had even performed in Cohan shows and staged dances for Cohan.[46]

The numerous special features on the 2003 DVD release, including a second disc of 'bonus material,' extend the film's approach to theatrical authenticity while also historicizing the film itself. These include feature-length commentary by film historian Rudy Behlmer; a short documentary chronicling *Yankee Doodle Dandy*'s making; *Warner Night at the Movies 1942*, a recreation of the various features (trailer, newsreel, and more) in a typical evening at the movie theatre during the period; listings of the film's cast, crew, and awards; *You, John Jones*, a wartime short starring Cagney; the Looney Tunes cartoons *Yankee Doodle Daffy* (1943) and *Yankee Doodle Bugs* (1954); an 'audio vault' including prerecording session outtakes and rehearsals; and the 'Waving the Flag Galleries' containing images of sheet music, set and scene stills, and publicity materials.[47] These supplementary features impart a similar veneer of authenticity to the film, as historical object, as the documents and performances do within the film's story, furthering *Yankee Doodle Dandy*'s almost archival aura and masking its notable departures from the facts.

'WITH THE AMERICAN SPIRIT AT A CRISIS'

The film's nostalgia for the late nineteenth and early twentieth century and its emphasis on the Americanness of the theatre were perfectly suited to the historical moment of its release during World War II. War was under way abroad when discussions about the film began, and Warner Bros. was already showing its keen interest in wartime intervention through anti-Nazi films like *Sergeant York* (1941).[48] For Cohan and Cagney, however, the initial attraction of the project lay elsewhere.

Cohan saw in the film a chance to preserve his legacy now that he was no longer so widely known.[49] Cagney, on the other hand, sought a chance to distance himself from recent charges of communism as well as the opportunity to escape his 'tough guy' typecasting and to do a musical.[50] William Cagney, associate producer of *Yankee Doodle Dandy* and James Cagney's brother, explained later that he told Warner Bros. studio head Jack L. Warner, 'We should make a movie with Jim playing the damndest patriotic man in the country,' George M. Cohan.[51]

The wartime climate and William Cagney's comment notwithstanding, patriotism was not necessarily to be *Yankee Doodle Dandy*'s primary theme. Rather, during the film's development, its writers struggled to choose their focus. In May 1941, Buckner and William Cagney despaired to executive producer Hal B. Wallis that 'we needed a romantic personal story,' but Cohan refused to let his 'private domestic life [be] a major element of [the] picture.' Buckner and Cagney explained a number of different approaches they had tried, like keeping the focus on the Four Cohans and developing a fictitious romance. Another tactic they tried, but found lacking, was 'develop[ing] the patriotic theme, George M. Cohan as the symbol of a dynamic and sincere American.' 'We gave this angle a tremendous workout,' they explained, 'But it spreads too thin.' Cohan, they acknowledged, was a good citizen, but they felt 'the evidence is neither complete enough or dramatic enough to ask any intelligent person to accept [it] as the key to his character.' Moreover, this theme failed as entertainment as well as biography; they thought it 'dangerous as a bore to a modern audience, for today Cohan's flashy type of patriotism sounds as cornily theatrical as it was in 1910'—a kiss of death for a motion picture that aimed first and foremost to entertain.[52] Finally, they were concerned about the implications of opportunism: 'Accidentally or not,' they wrote, 'the fact still blares at you that he made several million dollars with this act—<u>during the War</u>,' presumably referring to the way Cohan profited from his hit song 'Over There' and patriotism more generally during World War I.[53] The criticism of 'flag-waving' as a cheap trick pandering to the masses to make a buck that plagued Cohan during his career clearly troubled the makers of the film as well.[54]

By the end of *Yankee Doodle Dandy*'s production, however, the Japanese had attacked Pearl Harbor, the United States had formally entered World War II, and Warner Bros. had decided to sell Cohan and the world on the picture's patriotism. In part, when tensions between the recalcitrant Cohan and the studio came to a head in August 1941, stressing *Yankee Doodle Dandy*'s patriotism was a compelling way to persuade Cohan to allow the studio more liberties with the film's storytelling. In a lengthy letter to Cohan dated 29 August 1941, Hal Wallis, William Cagney, and Robert Buckner made a forceful, last-ditch effort to get approval for their script, including the plea: 'The dramatization of your life, Mr Cohan, has a great timely importance. It is the story of a typical American boy, who grew up with a strong love of his country, its ways and institutions. His life was spent in expressing and defending an American way of life.' By now, the team had settled on its through line; they stated, 'We believe that the deep-dyed Americanism of your life is a much greater theme than the success story.' The letter concluded, 'We have worked for six months because all of us here have an unshaken faith that this picture should be made—and today more than ever, with the American spirit at a crisis. It is our hope that perhaps you, too, will see this story of your life in its broader implications and give us your trust.'[55] A memo from a couple of days prior confirms the coercive intention of their pitch. William Cagney reported to Wallis that an outside party close to Cohan 'agrees with my point that Cohan should be made to realize that this is a great American message at the most crucial period in American history and he should patriotically bow to our efforts to dramatically present the story of this great American spirit.'[56] Had the filmmakers been swept up in patriotism as war loomed? Or was this a ploy to get Cohan onboard? It seems likely that both were true to some extent. Whatever the degree of their sincerity, Wallis, Cagney, and Buckner's appeal to Cohan's sense of patriotic duty was successful, and work on the film proceeded.[57]

Several elements of the film bear witness to its wartime roots and the ways in which the theme of patriotism came to dominate the story. The emphasis on wartime Americanism is legible from the opening credits, which use a stars-and-stripes pattern for the lettering of the names. (Warner Bros. had done the same for *Sergeant York* shortly earlier.)[58] Another indicator is the notable absence of Cohan's two real-life Japanese American valets. The first was Yoshin Sakurai, who Cohan also cast in his play *Get Rich Quick Wallingford* (1910); this is the earliest known appearance of an Asian American actor on Broadway.[59] The second was Michio 'Mike' Hirano, who had a small part in Cohan's 1936 play *Dear Old Darling*.[60] On 18 December 1941, only days after Pearl Harbor and during the filming of *Yankee Doodle Dandy*, Cohan telegraphed Attorney General Francis Biddle to request permission to travel with Hirano in the wake of the Presidential Proclamation making the Japanese in the United States who were not naturalized 'alien enemies.' Cohan wrote that he would 'personally vouch' for Hirano.[61] Recounting this story in an article for the magazine *Cabinet*, historian Scott A. Sandage points out that despite Hirano's importance to the Cohan family, 'the film did not portray Michio Hirano, not even for one line.'[62] We see instead an African American, whom Cohan calls Eddie, assisting Cohan in a mid-film dressing room scene. Japanese Americans were expelled from US society just as they were in the film: President Roosevelt signed Executive Order 9066 and the government began its forced 'relocation' of Japanese American citizens shortly before *Yankee Doodle Dandy* premiered.

The film's propagandistic tinge is most glaringly obvious, though, in the treatment of 'You're a Grand Old Flag.' In the original scene of the musical *George Washington, Jr* (1906), the song is prefaced by the hero encountering veterans who have come to Mount Vernon to decorate George Washington's tomb.[63] While the scene in the film likewise opens with a group of men in uniform (some with instruments, serving as the 'military band' mentioned in the song's verse), it is otherwise wholly divorced from the plot and setting of the original show, unlike the film's *Little Johnny Jones* number. The final screenplay contained little of the elaborate scene that ended up on the screen; its version was much shorter and emphasized the Cohans' love for one another and Mary's for George. According to that script, the Cohans would sing a verse and chorus, and then the company would have an ensemble dance number. 'The happiness on the Cohans' faces as they work together and smile at each other is something to see,' and Mary watches George from the chorus 'with much affection,' the directions note.[64] The number was also marked for spectacle early on—Buckner wrote in an earlier version of the screenplay that there should be 'flags all over the stage. This is an excellent opportunity for special trick effects.'[65] Still, the emphasis in earlier versions was the characters at least as much as it was the nation.

The final version of 'You're a Grand Old Flag' follows through with Buckner's ideas of spectacle, but it adds a sort of historical pageant of wartime scenes. In it, Cagney, as Cohan playing the hero of *George Washington, Jr*, sings a verse and chorus, backed by a group of Boy Scouts, then the Cohan song is intercut with various scenes representing key moments in US history with correspondent interpolated or newly composed tunes. Describing his plans for the number in a memo to William Cagney in January 1942, LeRoy Prinz, one of the directors of the musical numbers, cited as inspiration radio programs like 'Cavalcade of Am[erica],' which dramatized the nation's history in glowing terms.[66] In the final number as filmed, we see Betsy Ross sewing the flag. Visually referencing the iconic painting *The Spirit of '76*, as Holley Replogle-Wong has noted, revolutionary soldiers with fife and drums play 'Yankee Doodle.'[67] An African American soloist and chorus sing 'The Battle Hymn of the Republic,' and the Lincoln Memorial appears behind them; we hear Lincoln's voice deliver a line from the Gettysburg Address: 'And that government of the people, by the people, for the people, shall not perish from the earth.' Soldiers of the Spanish–American War led by Theodore Roosevelt march to 'When Johnny Comes Marching Home' (in fact, a Civil War–era song). We then seem to leave the musical's historical moment as we hear a group of citizens—the farmer, labourer, banker, as Prinz described them—sing a rallying cry for the then-current conflict: 'We're one for all and all for one, / . . . / And now that we're in it, / We're going to win it.' The closing musical phrase 'We'll fight as we did before' segues directly into "for 'my country, 'tis of thee . . .,' " quoting musically and lyrically from the well-known patriotic song by the same title. 'All the tableaux,' Prinz wrote to William Cagney, 'are to have a spiritual effect.'[68] The camera intersperses close-ups—for example, of the African American soloist's face and soldiers' bayonets—with long shots of the stage, moving between the 'real-world' framing of the stage, as the theatre audience would see it, and a more abstract, cinematic approach that invites film audiences to extrapolate to the present historical moment.

The finale of the number returns to the stage mode and the song 'You're a Grand Old Flag,' with Jerry Cohan costumed as Uncle Sam and Nellie Cohan as Lady Liberty, but replete with spectacular visual effects. We see, as Prinz described it, an 'ensemble of flags—entire group on treadmill across entire stage, walking towards audience' to create 'a finale of apparently hundreds of flags' (see Figure 4.4 and ⓥ video example 4.1). For this closing, he sought to evoke the theatrical rather than

FIGURE 4.4 'You're a Grand Old Flag' finale in Yankee Doodle Dandy (1942).

cinematic: 'This will not be a [Busby] Berkeley effect, but all legitimate stagecraft that could have been developed at this period.' The flag that appears on a scrim on the number's final bars, he notes, 'could have been done by Lantern projection.'[69] As the final chord rings out, the camera shows audience members jumping to their feet and applauding enthusiastically. The choice of staging marks the Cohans and the theatre itself as emblematic of wartime patriotism.

The scenes about Cohan's World War I hit 'Over There' are likewise written with pointed reference to current affairs. Upon learning about the sinking of the Lusitania, Cohan says, in voiceover narration, 'It seems it always happens. Whenever we get too high-hat and too sophisticated for flag-waving, some thug nation decides we're a pushover all ready to be blackjacked. And it isn't long before we're looking up, mighty anxiously, to be sure the flag's still waving over us.' The clear implication was that Cohan's brand of exuberant patriotism not only defined and celebrated the nation but also kept it safe, and the universal tone made its present-day applications patently obvious as well. In one scene, we see Cohan and a female singer, played by radio performer and film star Frances Langford, performing 'Over There' for the US troops. Langford's casting drew a connection to the contemporary conflict, since she also performed for military forces in real life: she later said that entertaining the troops was 'the greatest thing in [her] life.'[70] As they perform, the lights go out, and Cagney, as Cohan, runs out into the crowd to ask vehicles to turn on their headlights to light the stage—this borrowed from Cohan's own anecdotes.[71] Returning to the stage, Cagney conducts the audience for a few bars and calls out, 'Everybody sing!' (as can be heard in ⊙ video example 14.2). The troops join in heartily, a powerful scene of communal singing that engenders a sense of national pride and civic duty, inviting the film's audience, whether symbolically or literally, to join in.[72]

The scenes with Cohan and President Roosevelt that bookend the film bring the action to the present day; as Patrick McGilligan writes, 'History was manipulated so the president's summoning George directly from a performance of *I'd Rather Be Right* [which in reality opened in 1937] coincides with the outbreak of World War II.'[73] Lyrics referencing Hitler and the war were added for the performance of 'Off the Record' in the *I'd Rather Be Right* scene. When the president gives Cohan the Congressional Medal of Honor, Cohan protests that he's undeserving as he's 'just a song-and-dance man,' but the president insists, 'A man may give his life to his country in many different ways, Mr Cohan. . . . Your songs were a symbol of the American spirit. "Over There" was just as powerful a weapon as any cannon, as any battleship we had in the First World War. Today, we're all soldiers, we're all on the front. We need more songs to express America. I know you and your comrades will give them to us.' Cohan's response ties the Horatio Alger narrative of the film back to the nation's greatness and readiness for war: 'I wouldn't worry about this country if I were you,' he says. 'We've got this thing licked. Where else in the world could a plain guy like me come in and talk things over with the head man?' FDR concurs, 'Well, that's about as good a definition of America as any I've ever heard.' As Cohan leaves the White House, the soldiers and crowd outside are singing 'Over There.' He joins the troops, and a soldier asks him, 'What's the matter, old-timer, don't you remember this song?' Cagney, as Cohan, then joins in the singing, tears visible on his face. The real-life Cohan had indicated a scene of troops marching in his script, noting that 'this shot of the boys marching away might possibly be a delicate thing to do considering world conditions today, but if it is strongly planted that it is June 1917, and *not* 1941, you might get away with it.'[74] By the time of *Yankee Doodle Dandy's* filming and release, however, a marching scene set in the present was no longer risky but apropos.

The film's marketing and release established its reputation for wartime patriotism before audiences even stepped into the theatres. The premiere, which was moved from 4 July to 29 May in recognition of Cohan's failing health, was held in Times Square as a war bonds benefit, with tickets available for the price of bonds ranging from $25 to $25,000.[75] A second war bonds benefit labelled the 'Build Ships' premiere followed in Hollywood on 12 August. The reception at both was encouraging, and the day after the Hollywood premiere Jack Warner wrote to the heads of advertising and publicity at Warner Bros. that they should put forth 'a real campaign, telling not only the Exhibitors but America and the world that we are "first in the hearts of our countrymen," and "YANKEE DOODLE DANDY" is one picture every man, woman and child should see.'[76]

THE LEGACY OF *YANKEE DOODLE DANDY*

In the end, Warner Bros. and Cohan alike viewed the film as more than a commercial product or even a biopic: rather, it was their patriotic contribution to their nation. Jack Warner telegraphed Cohan on the day of the film's premiere, 'Dear George: I want to thank you from the bottom of my heart for permitting me to produce the story of your grand and glorious career. . . . It's more than a picture. It's the whole spirit of America rolled into one and by your permitting me to produce this picture you have done a great American service.'[77] Cohan's response echoed these hopes that the film 'may aid the theatre to contribute its share towards the realization of peace and civilization to follow the present tragic experiences. . . . With that thought I trust your statement in your telegram that *Yankee Doodle Dandy* is a great patriotic service will be true.'[78] While reportedly quite pleased with the film and likely proud of its contribution to the war effort, Cohan may have also recognized the potential downside of flag-waving patriotism at this late stage of his life. His son later shared with Scott Sandage that his father felt very bad about Mike Hirano, who disappeared during the war. Cohan 'finally made the connection,' as Sandage put it, 'between jingoism and prejudice.'[79]

Individual responses and reviews alike attest to *Yankee Doodle Dandy*'s impact at a pivotal time in US history. One enthusiastic viewer wrote to Jack Warner, 'This picture will undoubtedly receive all its praise from the Box Office, and what is more important to us all, from the uplift in the morale of the American public.' The letter closes, 'Viva J. L. Warner! A true (many words could be used here, but only one would do you justice) AMERICAN!!!'[80] Another wrote to Warner, '*Yankee Doodle Dandy* just makes you feel like being a better American.'[81] Critic Edwin Schallert described the film in the *Los Angeles Times* as 'patriotic, with plenty of flag waving, yet not too much for the present.' He further appreciated the film's interweaving of national and theatrical history, complimenting its 'delightful nostalgia attaching to the depiction of the old show days' and noting that the film 'brings to mind the passing pageant of American history through its chronicle of one man's huge success in the show business.'[82] The film also secured a permanent place in Hollywood film history. It won three Academy Awards, for Actor in a Leading Role, Music (Scoring of a Musical Picture), and Sound Recording. In 1993, it was inducted into the National Film Registry of the Library of Congress.

In adapting Cohan's life and works, the makers of *Yankee Doodle Dandy* depicted a rich theatrical history that corresponded with the nation's history. Drawing heavily on nostalgia for a mythologized past, they sought to show the nation's merit and resilience through its depth of historical experience—both cultural and military—and its national pride, exemplified by the rose-tinted character of one of its homegrown citizens. Demonstrating the Americanness of musico-theatrical entertainment, *Yankee Doodle Dandy* helped establish 'the American musical,' as a national art form, only a few months before *Oklahoma!* burst onto Broadway. It rejuvenated Cohan's legacy, which had begun to fade. And, furthering the project Cohan had already undertaken in his own public relations, it contributed mightily to his lasting image of patriot extraordinaire.

NOTES

1. This project was made possible by Warner Bros. Archives, School of Cinematic Arts, University of Southern California. I am deeply grateful to Brett Service, curator of the Warner Bros. Archives; Morgen Stevens-Garmon, associate curator of the Theater Collection at the Museum of the City of New York; and historian Scott Sandage for their assistance with the project. My thanks also to Louis Epstein, Frank Lehman, Hannah Lewis, Matthew Mugmon, and other colleagues who have generously shared ideas and feedback. Richard Gustafson, 'The Vogue of the Screen Biography,' *Film and History* 7, no. 3 (September 1977): 32.

2. Rick Altman, *The American Film Musical* (Bloomington: Indiana University Press, 1987), 235. On the musical biopic, see also John C. Tibbetts, *Composers in the Movies* (New Haven, CT: Yale University Press, 2005), 102–154.

3. George M. Cohan, *Twenty Years on Broadway and the Years It Took to Get There: The True Story of a Trouper's Life from the Cradle to the 'Closed Shop'* (New York: Harper and Brothers, 1925).

4. For an excellent account of the film's creation, see Patrick McGilligan's introduction to the published screenplay: 'The Life Daddy Would Have Liked to Live,' in *Yankee Doodle Dandy*, Wisconsin/Warner Bros. Screenplay Series (Madison: University of Wisconsin Press, 1981), 11–64. The contract with Cohan is discussed on pp. 16–17.

5. On the musical's mythologies, see Jane Feuer, 'The Self-reflective Musical and the Myth of Entertainment,' in *Genre: The Musical*, ed. Rick Altman (London: Routledge and Kegan Paul, 1981), and *The Hollywood Musical*, 2nd ed. (Bloomington: Indiana University Press, 1993), esp. 15–22 and 90–97.

6. Russell Owen, 'Yankee Doodle Dandy,' *New York Times*, 1 March 1942.

7. Charles L. Ponce de Leon, *Self-Exposure: Human-Interest Journalism and the Emergence of Celebrity in America, 1890–1940* (Chapel Hill: University of North Carolina Press, 2002); Fred Inglis, *A Short History of Celebrity* (Princeton, NJ: Princeton University Press, 2010).

8. For further discussion of Cohan's early, hyper-patriotic musicals, his construction of his public identity, and how he negotiated his Irish American identity (including in a series of Irish American–themed musicals from 1918 to 1927), see Elizabeth Titrington Craft, 'Becoming American Onstage: Broadway Narratives of Immigrant Experiences in the United States' (PhD diss., Harvard University, 2014), 30–158.

9. See, for examples, *Little Johnny Jones* Liberty Theatre playbill clipping, 'Week Beginning . . . Nov. 14, 1904,' box 819, Edward B. Marks Co. Collection on George M. Cohan, 1901–1968 (hereafter 'Cohan Collection') at the Museum of the City of New York (MCNY); *Little Johnny Jones* advertisement, *New York Times*, 6 November 1904; Cohan, 'They're All My Friends' (New York: F. A. Mills, 1904).

10. 'Rehearsing "A Yankee Prince,"' *New York Tribune*, 28 February 1908; 'The American Idea,' *Boston Daily Globe*, 10 September 1908.

11. Untitled article, *Life*, 12 October 1911, 618.

12. Cohan, *Twenty Years on Broadway*, 201.

13. *The Spot Light* 1, no. 28 (9 December 1905), Cohan Collection, MCNY.

14. Biographer Ward Morehouse uncovered a baptismal certificate naming 3 July as Cohan's birth date, but other official documents name 4 July and Cohan scholar John McCabe argues that 'the baptismal certificate hardly settles the matter.' McCabe suggests that the date on the certificate is a 'clerical error,' citing a diary entry by George's father as well as the fact that George's parents

always celebrated his birthday on the fourth and noting their 'utter probity.' Morehouse, *George M. Cohan: Prince of the American Theater* (Philadelphia: J. B. Lippincott, 1943), 24–25; McCabe, *George M. Cohan: The Man Who Owned Broadway* (Garden City, NY: Doubleday, 1973), 1–2.

15. Cohan, 'What the American Flag Has Done for Me,' *Theatre Magazine*, June 1914, 286; 'Agnes Nolan of Brookline to Become Mrs George M. Cohan,' *Boston Daily Globe*, 15 April 1907.

16. Table of contents, *Green Book Magazine*, December 1914.

17. Verne Hardin Porter, 'The Story of George M. Cohan,' *Green Book Magazine*, December 1914, 964.

18. George M. Cohan and Verne Hardin Porter, 'The Stage as I Have Seen It,' *Green Book Magazine*, February 1915, 247.

19. On the hibernicon, Jerry Cohan's role in it, and its function for the Irish transnational community, see Michelle Granshaw, 'Performing Cultural Memory: The Travelling Hibernicon and the Transnational Irish Community in the United States and Australia,' *Nineteenth Century Theatre and Film* 41, no. 2 (Winter 2014): 76–101; and Michelle Granshaw, 'The Hibernicon and Visions of Returning Home: Popular Entertainment in Irish America from the Civil War to World War I' (PhD diss., University of Washington, 2012).

20. On Cohan's script, which the initial screenwriter Robert Buckner described as an 'egotistical epic,' see McGilligan, *Yankee Doodle Dandy*, 30–34; Buckner to Wallis, 27 September 1941, folder 2375, '"Yankee Doodle Dandy" Story—Memos and Correspondence, 9/8/41–10/30/41,' Warner Bros. Archives, School of Cinematic Arts, University of Southern California, Los Angeles.

21. Robert Buckner to Hal Wallis, 25 November 1941, folder 2375 '"Yankee Doodle Dandy" Story—Memos and Correspondence, 11/1/41–11/28/41,' Warner Bros. Archives, School of Cinematic Arts, University of Southern California, Los Angeles.

22. One theme—Cohan's lack of formal education—is stressed less in the film than in Cohan's writings. As Patrick McGilligan notes, earlier efforts with the script had included attempts to dramatize the Cohan children's education (and problems therewith) but they were 'ultimately abandoned.' McGilligan, *Yankee Doodle Dandy*, 98, 211n14.

23. Cohan was, in fact, awarded a Congressional Medal of Honor. Although it was authorized by Congress in 1936, Cohan did not receive it from President Roosevelt until 1940. Cohan may have delayed the meeting for political reasons: see McCabe, *George M. Cohan*, 234, and Garrett Eisler, 'Kidding on the Level: The Reactionary Project of *I'd Rather Be Right*,' *Studies in Musical Theatre* 1, no. 1 (2007): 19–20.

24. All film quotations are from *Yankee Doodle Dandy*, based on the story of George M. Cohan, directed by Michael Curtiz, starring James Cagney (1942; Burbank, CA: Warner Home Video 2003), DVD.

25. McGilligan, *Yankee Doodle Dandy*, 21.

26. On Robert Buckner's attempts to show Cohan in a favourable light, see McGilligan, *Yankee Doodle Dandy*, 25.

27. McGilligan, *Yankee Doodle Dandy*, 20.

28. Morehouse, *George M. Cohan*, 229.

29. On the process of the Irish 'Becoming Caucasian,' see Matthew Frye Jacobson, *Whiteness of a Different Color: European Immigrants and the Alchemy of Race* (Cambridge, MA: Harvard University Press, 1998), 91–135. On the film's portrayal of Irish Americanness, see Meaghan Dwyer-Ryan, ' "Yankee Doodle Paddy": Themes of Ethnic Acculturation in *Yankee Doodle Dandy*,' *Journal of American Ethnic History* 30, no. 4 (Summer 2011): 57–62, and Christopher Shannon, *Bowery to Broadway: The American Irish in Classic Hollywood Cinema* (Scranton, PA: University of Scranton Press, 2010), 153–169.

30. Dwyer-Ryan, ' "Yankee Doodle Paddy," ' 61. The ability for Irish American characters in film to easily maintain both identities stands in notable contrast to other ethnic groups as portrayed by Hollywood, for instance, the Jewish American protagonist Jackie Rabinowitz in *The Jazz Singer*: Shannon, *Bowery to Broadway*, xxxi–xxxii, 161–162.

31. McGilligan, *Yankee Doodle Dandy*, 92.

32. McGilligan, *Yankee Doodle Dandy*, 38; Michelle Granshaw, 'Hibernicon and Visions,' 90.

33. When they filmed this scene, the war had recently begun and tensions were high, so director Michael Curtiz had to get permission from both Warner Bros. and the city of Burbank, California,

to fire the cannon: Behlmer commentary on *Yankee Doodle Dandy*, DVD.

34. Richard Gustafson describes a 'sense of destiny' as one of the archetypes of the early to mid-century biopic in 'Vogue of the Screen Biography,' 36. On the use of flags in American cinema, including *Yankee Doodle Dandy*, and this scene, see Robert Eberwein, 'Following the Flag in American Film,' in *Eastwood's Iwo Jima: Critical Engagements with Flags of Our Fathers and Letters from Iwo Jima*, ed. Anne Gjelsvik and Rikke Schubart (New York: Columbia University Press, 2013), esp. 85–86; and William H. Epstein, 'Biopics and American National Identity— Invented Lives, Imagined Communities,' introduction to 'Biopics and American National Identity,' ed. Epstein, special issue, *a/b: Auto/Biography Studies* 26, no. 1 (Summer 2011): 12, 15–17.

35. Raymond Knapp and Mitchell Morris, 'The Filmed Musical,' in *The Oxford Handbook of the American Musical* (New York: Oxford University Press, 2011), 136.

36. Rick Altman writes, 'The greater the star, we might expect, the less it is possible for Hollywood to fit his or her biopic into the familiar syntactic mold of the backstage musical, for the public would certainly be aware of at least the basic outline of the star's career. Such, however, is far from being the case' due to the 'American popular mythology' in which these larger-than-life figures operate. Altman, *The American Film Musical*, 236.

37. On the use of the framing of the stage as part of LeRoy Prinz's style, see Allen L. Woll, *The Hollywood Musical Goes to War* (Chicago: Nelson-Hall, 1983), 55.

38. James Fisher, *Historical Dictionary of American Theater: Beginnings* (Lanham, MD: Rowman & Littlefield, 2015), 252.

39. Feuer, 'Self-Reflective Musical,' 159–174, esp. 168.

40. McGilligan, *Yankee Doodle Dandy*, 157.

41. James and William Cagney were not happy with the versions of the script that Buckner submitted in October 1941, and Edmund Joseph, then Julius J. and Philip G. Epstein, were brought in to 'doctor' the script. The final production credits state that the screenplay is by Robert Buckner and Edmund Joseph; despite their significant contributions, the Epsteins agreed not to be listed. Robert Buckner to Hal Wallis, 15 April 1941, folder 2375 ' "Yankee

Doodle Dandy" Story—Memos and Correspondence, 1/16/41–4/ 28/41,' and Robert Buckner to Joseph D. Karp (*TS*, unsigned), 27 April 1943, folder 2375 '"Yankee Doodle Dandy" Story—Memos and Correspondence, 7/1/42—1/31/44,' Warner Bros. Archives, School of Cinematic Arts, University of Southern California, Los Angeles; McGilligan, *Yankee Doodle Dandy*, 19, 39–45, 54.

42. Cohan, *Twenty Years on Broadway*, 10–13, 22–26.

43. Heinz Roemheld and Ray Heindorf, however, were credited with the film's musical scoring, for which they won an Academy Award.

44. McGilligan, *Yankee Doodle Dandy*, 16–17, 30, 38, 54.

45. Seymour Felix, who staged the production numbers along with Leroy Prinz, wrote to Hal Wallis about going outside the bounds of the contract to interpolate small bits of music for dramatic purposes; for example, he stated: 'If the "Yankee Doodle" number is to be done as a production number, it . . . might be a good idea to inject about eight or sixteen bars of music and lyrics, advising the audience that Little Johnny Jones, the jockey, is going to ride in the Derby race, this done to gallop music, which will help to create musical excitement.' The additions 'Good Luck Johnny' and 'All Aboard for Broadway' were written by Jack Scholl and M. K. Jerome. Felix to Wallis, 12 November 1941, folder 2375, '"Yankee Doodle Dandy" Story—Memos and Correspondence, 11/1/41–11/28/41,' Warner Bros. Archives, School of Cinematic Arts, University of Southern California, Los Angeles; George Feltenstein, liner notes to *Original Warner Bros. Motion Picture Soundtrack: Yankee Doodle Dandy*, R2 78210, 2002, cd.

46. McGilligan, *Yankee Doodle Dandy*, 47.

47. Other features were directly related to James Cagney: a 'gallery' of trailers of Cagney films; a profile of Cagney hosted by Michael J. Fox; and a tribute to Cagney by John Travolta: *Yankee Doodle Dandy*, DVD.

48. During a 1941 congressional hearing to investigate purported 'Moving Picture Screen and Radio Propaganda,' initiated by the isolationist North Dakotan Senator Gerald Nye, Harry M. Warner gave a speech declaring outright, 'I am opposed to nazi-ism. I abhor and detest every principle and practice of the Nazi movement.' On Warner Bros. politically oriented prewar films, see Michael E. Birdwell, *Celluloid Soldiers: The Warner Bros. Campaign against*

Nazism, 1934–1941 (New York: New York University Press, 1999); Thomas Doherty, *Projections of War: Hollywood, American Culture, and World War II* (New York: Columbia University Press, 1993), 39–42; Woll, *Hollywood Musical*, 3–11, 33–44.

49. 'Four-fifths of the people who remember me are dead,' Cohan commented to Buckner. The film's opening, with Cohan's name in lights on a marquee, was designed in part to 'establish the importance of George M. Cohan for today's generation' according to a letter from director Michael Curtiz to Hal Wallis. McGilligan, *Yankee Doodle Dandy*, 14–15; Curtiz to Wallis, 14 November 1941, folder 2375 ' "Yankee Doodle Dandy" Story— Memos and Correspondence, 11/1/41–11/28/41,' Warner Bros. Archives, School of Cinematic Arts, University of Southern California, Los Angeles.

50. McGilligan, *Yankee Doodle Dandy*, 15–16, 46.

51. Thomas F. Brady, 'Facts Behind "Yankee Doodle Dandy," ' *New York Times*, 10 January 1943. The anecdote is related similarly on the *James Cagney: Top of the World* feature hosted by Michael J. Fox on the *Yankee Doodle Dandy* special edition DVD set.

52. One advertisement for *Yankee Doodle Dandy* proclaimed, 'Warner Bros. are on an all-out basis on the entertainment front. . . . All of us who *are* Warner Bros. . . . have one purpose and one only; to give you the kind of entertainment that raises your spirits, lifts your chin, and helps brighten things for any day ahead.' *Yankee Doodle Dandy* advertisement, undated, folder 2883, 'Yankee Doodle Dandy—Picture File,' Warner Bros. Archives, School of Cinematic Arts, University of Southern California, Los Angeles.

53. William Cagney and Robert Buckner to Hal Wallis, 5 May 1941, folder 2375, ' "Yankee Doodle Dandy" Story—Memos and Correspondence, 5/2/41–6/30/41,' Warner Bros. Archives, School of Cinematic Arts, University of Southern California, Los Angeles.

54. On critics' responses to Cohan and his 'flag-waving' musicals, see Craft, 'Becoming American Onstage,' 74–87.

55. Hal B. Wallis, William Cagney, and Robert Buckner to George M. Cohan, copying [story editor] Jacob Wilk, 29 August

1941, folder 2375, '"Yankee Doodle Dandy" Story—Memos and Correspondence, 7/1/41–9/5/41,' Warner Bros. Archives, School of Cinematic Arts, University of Southern California, Los Angeles.

56. William Cagney to Hal Wallis, 27 August 1941, folder 2375, '"Yankee Doodle Dandy" Story—Memos and Correspondence, 7/1/41–9/5/41,' Warner Bros. Archives, School of Cinematic Arts, University of Southern California, Los Angeles.

57. In response to this letter Cohan agreed to compromise according to 8 September correspondence from Buckner to Wilk. A 6 October telegram from Buckner to Hal Wallis reported a 'very encouraging conference with Cohan today' in which he 'assure[d] general approval of new script' with minimal changes. Robert Buckner to Jake Wilk, 8 September 1941, and Robert Buckner to Hal B. Wallis, 6 October 1941, folder 2375, '"Yankee Doodle Dandy" Story—Memos and Correspondence, 9/8/41–10/30/41,' Warner Bros. Archives, School of Cinematic Arts, University of Southern California, Los Angeles.

58. Eberwein, 'Following the Flag,' 85.

59. Walter Anthony, 'A Japanese Invasion,' *San Francisco Call*, 28 January 1912; Esther Kim Lee, *A History of Asian American Theatre* (Cambridge: Cambridge University Press, 2006), 14.

60. Scott A. Sandage, 'Old Rags, Some Grand,' *Cabinet* 7 (Summer 2002), http://www.cabinetmagazine.org/issues/7/oldrags.php; Cohen, 'Dear Old Darling,' *Variety*, 8 January 1936.

61. George M. Cohan to Hon. Francis Biddle, 16 December 1941, Cohan Collection, MCNY.

62. Sandage, 'Old Rags, Some Grand.'

63. Cohan, 'George Washington, Jr' script (Act I, pp. 37–40), box 519, Cohan Collection, MCNY.

64. McGilligan, *Yankee Doodle Dandy*, 169.

65. McGilligan, *Yankee Doodle Dandy*, 219n42.

66. LeRoy Prinz to William Cagney, 7 January 1942, folder 2375, '"Yankee Doodle Dandy" Story—Memos and Correspondence, 7/1/42–1/31/44' [filed out of date?], Warner Bros. Archives, School of Cinematic Arts, University of Southern California, Los Angeles.

67. Replogle-Wong's excellent analysis of this scene demonstrates how it presents 'an idealistic version of the American model of national inclusiveness, in which past offenses are absorbed by the spirit of unification': 'Coming-of-Age in Wartime: American Propaganda and Patriotic Nationalism in *Yankee Doodle Dandy*,' *Echo: A Music-Centered Journal* 8, no. 1 (Fall 2006): paragraphs 9–16.

68. LeRoy Prinz to William Cagney, 7 January 1942, in Warner Bros. Archives. Seymour Felix had been taken off the project in December 1941: Seymour Felix to Hal Wallis, 26 December 1941, folder 2375, '"Yankee Doodle Dandy" Story—Memos and Correspondence, 12/1/41–1/30/42,' Warner Bros. Archives, School of Cinematic Arts, University of Southern California, Los Angeles; Rudy Behlmer commentary on *Yankee Doodle Dandy*, DVD.

69. LeRoy Prinz to William Cagney, 7 January 1942, folder 2375, '"Yankee Doodle Dandy" Story—Memos and Correspondence, 7/1/42–1/31/44' [filed out of date?], Warner Bros. Archives, School of Cinematic Arts, University of Southern California, Los Angeles.

70. Richard Severo, 'Frances Langford, Trouper on Bob Hope Tours, Dies at 92,' *New York Times*, 12 July 2005.

71. McGilligan, *Yankee Doodle Dandy*, 221n52.

72. I draw here upon Sheryl Kaskowitz's discussion of communal singing, of another patriotic song from the same era, in *God Bless America: The Surprising History of an Iconic Song* (New York: Oxford University Press, 2013).

73. McGilligan, *Yankee Doodle Dandy*, 24.

74. McGilligan, *Yankee Doodle Dandy*, 221n53.

75. 'Exploitation: Treasury Dept Cued WB's $25,000 "Tickets" for 'Yankee Doodle,' *Variety*, 6 May 1942. On the premiere and publicity, see also McGilligan, *Yankee Doodle Dandy*, 58.

76. Jack Warner [to 'Messrs. Einfeld and Blumenstock'], 13 August 1942, folder 2375, '"Yankee Doodle Dandy" Story—Memos and Correspondence, 7/1/41–9/5/41,' Warner Bros. Archives, School of Cinematic Arts, University of Southern California, Los Angeles. The document is filed with the July–September 1941 documents. However, the 1942 date is probably correct given that it was common during the period for a film to move gradually to

different theatres and that the press reported that the national merchandising campaign would be rolled out following the film's premiere: 'Exploitation: Nat'l Campaign on "Yankee" Rests on Preem Results,' *Variety*, 27 May 1942.

77. Jack Warner to George M. Cohan, 29 May 1942, folder 2375, '"Yankee Doodle Dandy" Story—Memos and Correspondence, 2/2/42–6/20/42,' Warner Bros. Archives, School of Cinematic Arts, University of Southern California, Los Angeles.

78. George M. Cohan to Jack Warner, 17 August 1942, folder 2375, '"Yankee Doodle Dandy" Story—Memos and Correspondence, 7/1/42–1/31/44,' Warner Bros. Archives, School of Cinematic Arts, University of Southern California, Los Angeles.

79. Sandage, 'Old Rags, Some Grand.'

80. Donald A. Sardinas to [Jack] Warner, 29 May 1942, folder 2375, '"Yankee Doodle Dandy" Story—Memos and Correspondence, 2/2/42–6/20/42,' Warner Bros. Archives, School of Cinematic Arts, University of Southern California, Los Angeles.

81. Lydia Wilbur to Jack L. Warner, 21 July 1942, folder 2375, '"Yankee Doodle Dandy" Story—Memos and Correspondence, 7/1/42–1/31/44,' Warner Bros. Archives, School of Cinematic Arts, University of Southern California, Los Angeles.

82. Edwin Schallert, '"Yankee Doodle Dandy" Registers Super Success,' *Los Angeles Times*, 13 August 1942.

5

Cole Porter's List Songs
on Stage and Screen

CLIFF EISEN

■□■

LIST SONGS HAVE A LONG history: Leporello's catalogue
aria from *Don Giovanni* and 'I Have a Little List' from *The
Mikado* are only two of the best-known examples. And songs
made up primarily, if not entirely, of lists, figure prominently
among Cole Porter's works, including 'You're the Top,' 'Brush
Up Your Shakespeare,' and 'Let's Do It.'[1] As enumerations—
of things, places, and people, sometimes as themselves and
sometimes as metaphors—these songs juxtapose a variety
of objects, images, and ideas. 'You're the Top,' 'Let's Do It,'
and 'Can-Can' include references to people, places, and
things; 'Thank You So Much Mrs Lowsborough-Goodby'
satirizes high society entertaining like racing, card playing,
backgammon, hot cocktails, cold baths, and eating tinned
salmon that causes ptomaine poisoning; 'The Law,' also from
Can–Can, is about metaphors: the final version, dropped
during the Philadelphia tryouts in 1953, includes only the
line 'The law is my life, the law is my wife,' but when Porter

first thought about composing the song he wrote his librettist, Abe Burrows:

> Your notes concerning the song which I have to write about the law helped me so much that the song is nearly finished. Do you know other phrases besides the body of the law, the letter of the law and the arm of the law, which would also apply to a beautiful woman? If you could send me these I could write several more lyrics. My secretary just suggested the clutches of the law and the shadow of the law, but I need more.[2]

Burrows suggested the limbs of the law, the eyes of the law, the majesty of the law, legal lights, lovely loop-holes in the law, the statuesque beauty of a statute, the fine points of the law, the essence of the law, and the law is a mistress.[3] If a lyric sheet for 'Can-Can' is typical, Porter may have initially sketched out these songs by creating lists of appropriate rhyming words (Figure 5.1). But he was also not opposed to getting help constructing his lists. In addition to Burrows's potential contributions to 'The Law,' P. G. Wodehouse was co-opted to write additional lyrics for 'Anything Goes' when it was produced in London in 1935.[4] And Porter was receptive to the idea of others writing additional lyrics to his songs; indeed, he apparently saw his list songs—and others' adaptations of them—as something of a national poetical pastime. While composing *Can-Can* he wrote to Burrows:

> I am enclosing the lyrics to a new song which could easily be the most important in the Show. As far as numbers go, this song could be sung by a solist [*sic*] alone on stage or to several other people on stage. It need not be danced to immediately after the vocal is finished, but could be used as a dance number later in the Show. This is a real Can-Can in its tempo and in its feeling. I shall send you the music to this shortly.

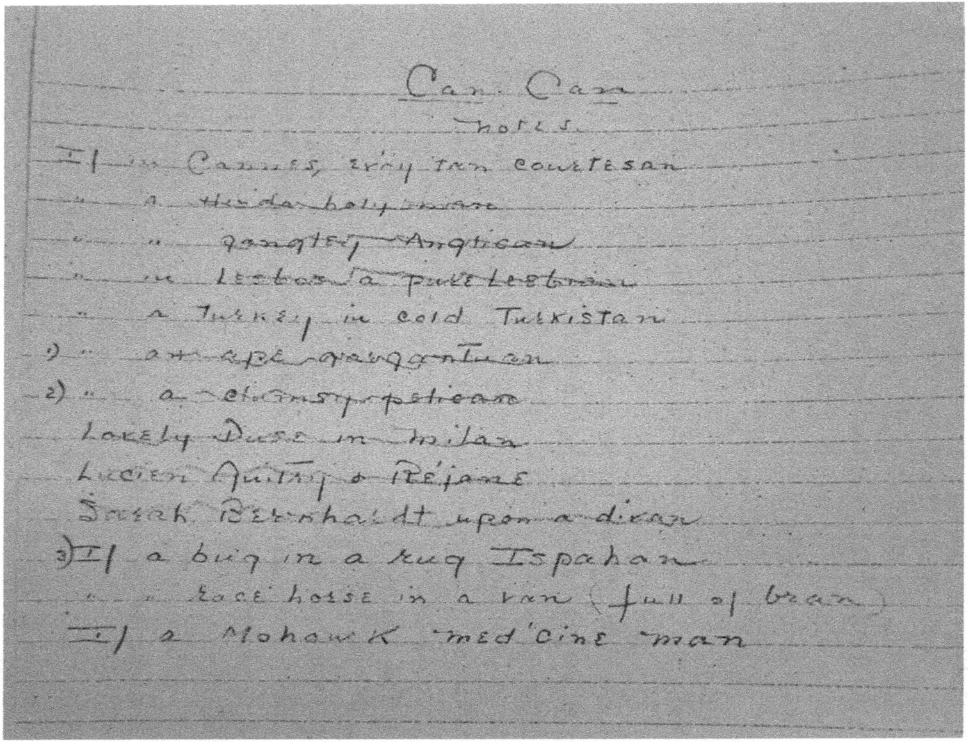

FIGURE 5.1 Notes for Can-Can. Reproduced with permission of the Cole Porter Literary and Musical Property Trusts.

I am already working on two other sets of lyrics which will become the fourth and fifth refrains. I hope to write even more lyrics, as this song can easily become a national game, such as was 'Your [*sic*] The Top' and 'Let's Do It.'[5]

According to David Savran, Porter's engagement with the public through list songs, and the public's willingness to embrace them, represent something fundamental about their nature, that they not only catalogue but also produce desires, whether desires for the objects, peoples, and places themselves, or more covert, sexualized desires that these objects, peoples, and places may stand in for.[6] (Parenthetically, Porter was himself attached to the idea of lists that catalogued his own needs, desires, and tastes: when he travelled to Philadelphia for the out-of-town tryout for *Out of This World* in 1950, he had his secretary write ahead detailing what he required in his hotel suite, even down to specific brands, including Ivanhoe shrimp, sturgeon, cocktail mushrooms, Persian melons, Saltine crackers, maraschino cherries, stuffed olives, Miracle Whip mayonnaise, Carnation condensed milk, Medaglio d'Oro coffee, Adams Chiclets (peppermint), Pabst Blue Ribbon beer, and Pard dog food (Figure 5.2)). At a more immediate but just as important level, list songs catalogue and encourage pleasure in ever more extravagant, creative, and extended verbal play, conceivably without end: list songs, like lists, are potentially infinite.

William Glass notes that many list songs juxtapose objects that seemingly do not 'belong' together—'You're a rose, / You're Inferno's Dante / You're the nose / Of the great Durante' from 'You're the Top'—and that in doing so, they create 'a site, something like [a] . . . universe of discourse, a place where everything on the list can co-exist, a common space.'[7] This is similar to Umberto Eco's notion of 'accumulations,' a common occurrence in biblical and medieval literature where linguistic terms 'belonging to the same conceptual sphere' appear in sequence and juxtaposition. Such accumulations need not be

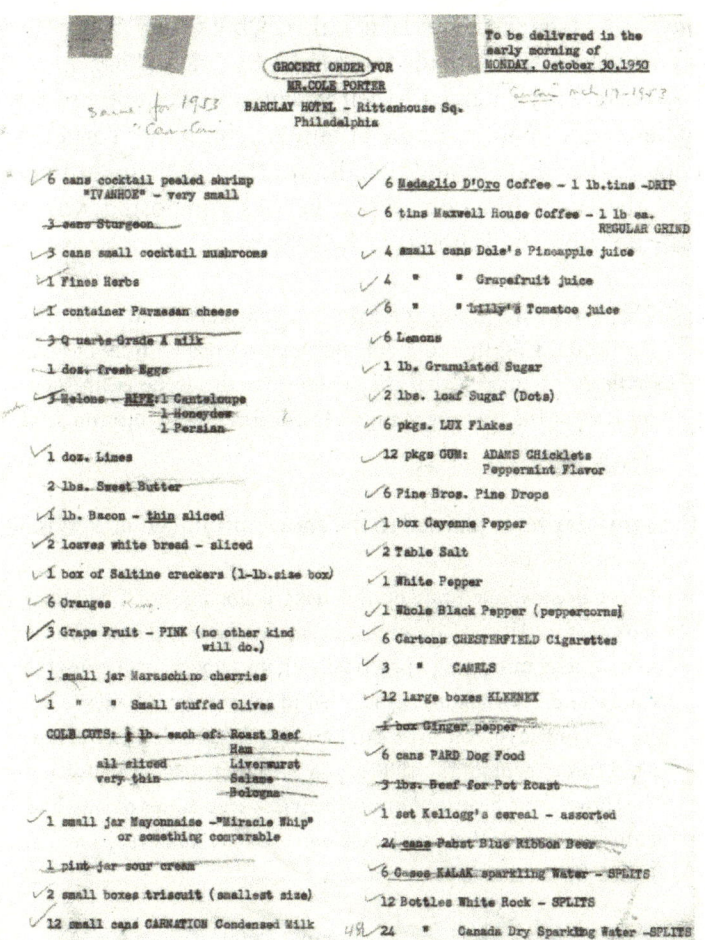

FIGURE 5.2 Cole Porter, list of requirements for his hotel room in Philadelphia, 1953. Reproduced with permission of the Cole Porter Literary and Musical Property Trusts.

coherent or may appear incoherent; their deeper coherence depends on just what the 'conceptual sphere' is.[8] Both Glass's and Eco's ideas derive from Leo Spitzer's notion of 'chaotic enumerations,' the 'lumping together [of] things spiritual and physical, as the raw material of our rich, but unordered modern civilization which is made to resemble an oriental bazaar.'⁹

Porter's list songs, with their potentially infinite expressions of desire and chaotic enumerations, are similarly a sort of 'oriental bazaar' and, in addition, he attached to them an important theatrical function. When he was composing *Kiss Me, Kate* he wrote to his librettist, Bella Spewack:

> I have written a . . . song for the two gangsters. I indicated that they could sing this song for their exit on page 2-6-29 of your book. . . . I suggest that they enter after the scene is finished, in front of the curtain & sing it just before we go into the final Shrew scene.¹⁰

The same day he explained to the show's producer, Jack Wilson:

> I have already taken care of [the] next to closing spot. I had been looking for that spot for weeks, as I always have had one of those low comedy numbers in practically all my shows, just before the final scene. . . . The number is titled Brush up your Shakespeare. It's [*sic*] music is reminiscent of East Side, West Side, i.e., the typical Bowery song of the 1900's, and I firmly believe it will tie up the show into a beautiful knot. The lyrics are a series of gags and I am almost sure that it will be a *show-stopper* and everyone that I have played it to is crazy about it.¹¹

For *Kiss Me, Kate*, the inclusion of 'Brush Up Your Shakespeare' necessitated a fundamental change in the script of the final scene: where originally Lilli/Kate had been given the whole of Kate's final speech from act 4, scene 2 of *The Taming of the Shrew*—'Fie, fie! unknit that threatening unkind brow'—now she was restricted to only a few lines. Perhaps to compensate Lilli/Kate, Porter wrote 'I am ashamed that women are so simple,'¹² which includes much of the text cut from her final Shakespearian speech. The result is an ending less Shakespearian but more in keeping with Porter's established musical theatre practice.

In the play, 'Brush Up Your Shakespeare' is delivered by the gangsters in front of the curtain (Figure 5.3). They—and the song—are set off from the rest of the show, creating a unique physical and psychological space, one different from the Shakespearian space of Petruchio and Katherine, the back-stage theatrical space of the protagonists Fred and Lilli, or the alley-behind-the-theatre space of 'Too Darn Hot.' This focuses attention solely on the gangsters and their list song: two singers alone on a stage illuminated by spotlights and in no identifiable physical location with respect to the rest of the show, enumerating at length, conceivably even infinitely if they do

FIGURE 5.3 'Brush Up Your Shakespeare,' New Century Theatre, 1948.

not run out of Shakespearian puns and wordplay. What is more, aside from the obvious Shakespearian textual connection, there is really no reason for this song—certainly no compelling dramatic reason—other than to enumerate and entertain, to be a 'low comedy number . . . just before the final scene.' To be—literally—a showstopper.

In the film version of *Kiss Me, Kate* from 1953, however, the gangsters deliver their list not to the audience (except for a brief moment at the end), but to a depressed Fred (Figure 5.4). The physical space, still the theatre, remains clearly attached to both Fred/Lilli and Petruchio/Kate while the text is considerably abbreviated (see Table 5.1) and the song remade in no small part into a soft shoe dance number. It also has a function: to cheer up Fred. Morose at the start of the song because he thinks he has lost Lilli, he is laughing by the end, the gangsters seemingly having told him there are other 'girls' out there and how to get them (Table 5.1). Possibly this restaging of

FIGURE 5.4 'Brush Up Your Shakespeare,' MGM, 1953.

Table 5.1

TEXTS: 'BRUSH UP YOUR SHAKESPEARE'
(*KISS ME, KATE*: STAGE SHOW 1948, FILM 1953).
LYRICS IN ITALICS ARE EITHER NEWLY WRITTEN
FOR THE FILM VERSION OR HAVE BEEN
MOVED FROM THEIR ORIGINALY POSITION IN
THE STAGE VERSION

Show:	Film:
VERSE	VERSE
The girls today in society	The girls today in society
Go for classical poetry,	Go for classical poetry,
So to win their hearts one must quote with ease	So to win their hearts one must quote with ease
Aeschylus and Euripides.	Aeschylus and Euripides.
One must know Homer and, b'lieve me, Bo, Sophocles, also Sappho-ho. Unless you know Shelley and Keats and Pope, Dainty debbies will call you a dope.	
But the poet of them all	But the poet of them all
Who will start 'em simply ravin'	Who will start 'em simply ravin'
Is the poet people call	Is the poet people call
The bard of Stratford-on-Avon.	The bard of Stratford-on-Avon.
REFRAIN 1	REFRAIN 1
Brush up your Shakespeare,	Brush up your Shakespeare,
Start quoting him now.	Start quoting him now.
Brush up your Shakespeare	Brush up your Shakespeare
And the women you will wow.	And the women you will wow.
Just declaim a few lines from 'Othella'	Just declaim a few lines from 'Othella'
And they'll think you're a helluva fella.	And they'll think you're a heckuva fella.

(continued)

Table 5.1

CONTINUED

Show:	Film:
If your blonde won't respond when you flatter 'er	If your blonde won't respond when you flatter 'er
Tell her what Tony told Cleopaterer,	Tell her what Tony told Cleopaterer,
If she fights when her clothes you are mussing,	*And if still she pretends to be shocked, well,*
What are clothes? 'Much Ado About Nussing.'	*Just remind her that 'All's Well That Ends Well.'*
Brush up your Shakespeare	Brush up your Shakespeare
And they'll all kowtow.	And they'll all kowtow.
REFRAIN 2	
Brush up your Shakespeare,	
Start quoting him now.	
Brush up your Shakespeare	
And the women you will wow.	
With the wife of the British embessida	
Try a crack out of 'Troilus and Cressida,'	
If she says she won't buy it or tike it	
Make her tike it, what's more, 'As You Like It.'	
If she says your behavior is heinous	
Kick her right in the 'Coriolanus.'	
Brush up your Shakespeare	
And they'll all kowtow.	

Table 5.1

CONTINUED

Show:	Film:

REFRAIN 3
Brush up your Shakespeare,
Start quoting him now.
Brush up your Shakespeare
And the women you will wow.
If you can't be a ham and do
   'Hamlet'
They will not give a damn or a
   damnlet.
Just recite an occasional sonnet
And your lap'll have 'Honey'
   upon it.
When your baby is pleading for
   pleasure
Let her sample your 'Measure
   for Measure.'
Brush up your Shakespeare
And they'll all kowtow.
REFRAIN 4
Brush up your Shakespeare,
Start quoting him now.
Brush up your Shakespeare
And the women you will wow.
Better mention 'The Merchant
   of Venice'
When her sweet pound o' flesh
   you would menace
If her virtue, at first, she
   defends—well,	

(*continued*)

Table 5.1

CONTINUED

Show:	Film:
Just remind her that 'All's Well That Ends Well.'	
And if still she won't give you a bonus	
You know what Venus got from Adonis!	
Brush up your Shakespeare	
And they'll all kowtow.	
REFRAIN 5	REFRAIN 2
Brush up your Shakespeare	Brush up your Shakespeare
Start quoting him now.	Start quoting him now.
Brush up your Shakespeare	Brush up your Shakespeare
And the women you will wow.	And the women you will wow.
If your goil is a Washington Heights dream	If your goil is a Washington Heights dream
Treat the kid to 'A Midsummer Night's Dream.'	Treat the kid to 'A Midsummer Night's Dream.'
If she then wants an all-by-herself night	If she fights when her clothes you are mussing,
Let her rest ev'ry 'leventh or 'Twelfth Night.'	*What are clothes? 'Much Ado About Nussing.'*
If because of your heat she gets huffy	*If she says your behavior is heinous*
Simply play on and 'Lay on, Macduffy!'	*Kick her right in the 'Coriolanus.'*
Brush up your Shakespeare	Brush up your Shakespeare
And they'll all kowtow,	And they'll all kowtow,
We trow, and they'll all kowtow.	We trow, and they'll all kowtow.

Table 5.1

CONTINUED

Show:	Film:
GRAND FINALE	
Brush up your Shakespeare,	
Start quoting him now.	
Brush up your Shakespeare	
And the women you will wow.	
So tonight just recite to your matey,	
'Kiss me, Kate, kiss me, Kate, kiss me, Katey.'	
Brush up your Shakespeare	
And they'll all kowtow.	

'Brush Up Your Shakespeare' was merely a directorial decision. Or possibly it hints at a fundamental aspect of filmed musicals that is inimical to list songs: their separateness and staticness; their drawing of attention to themselves and to words rather than, primarily, visuals or the narrative of the film; and their potential open-endedness may all work against the notion of what a film does.

The 1950s film version of *Anything Goes* (Paramount, 1956)—the 1934 show that featured 'You're the Top'—finds a similar solution to the filming of a list song. In the stage show, Reno Sweeney and Billy Crocker are alone on the deck of the S.S. *American* sailing to England; Billy has smuggled himself aboard so he can convince his true love, Hope Harcourt, not to marry Lord Evelyn Oakley. But he has a crisis of confidence and Hope tries to buck him up with 'You're the Top.' The 1954 film of *Anything Goes*, starring Bing Crosby, Donald O'Connor,

Zizi Jeanmaire, and Mitzi Gaynor, considerably rewrites the story, not atypically for film versions of stage musicals. Crosby and O'Connor are sailing for New York, each having promised a different actress the leading part in a new musical. But neither of them has the courage to break the news to them, the actresses, that they can't both star in the show. So they avoid each other, scheduling what should have been a joint rehearsal in two different places. The number they rehearse is 'You're the Top.' As with 'Brush Up Your Shakespeare,' the text is truncated and the song becomes a dance number, it is given a more fixed and identifiable physical location, and it serves to advance the plot, reinforcing the main characters' attempts to move forward with the show they are planning but not create havoc by owning up to their casting problem—or jeopardizing their love lives since each has fallen in love with the other's star actress (Figure 5.5).

Can-Can represents a more extreme example. The stage show, from 1953, included at least five list songs or songs made up mostly of lists: 'Maidens Typical of France,' 'Live and Let Live,' 'Never, Never Be an Artist,' 'Ev'ry Man Is a Stupid Man,' and 'Can-Can.' Neither 'Never, Never Be an Artist' nor 'Ev'ry Man Is a Stupid Man' made it into the 1960 film with Frank Sinatra, Shirley MacLaine, Maurice Chevalier, and Louis Jourdan (the list song 'Let's Do It,' from Porter's 1928 show *Paris* is smuggled into the film but in a much abbreviated version). The two that remain, 'Maidens Typical of France' and 'Can-Can' are so extensively reworked and altered as to eliminate them from consideration as list songs altogether.

In the stage show, the mini-list song 'Maidens Typical of France' is the first number and it is performed in a courtroom by Simone Pistache's dancing girls as a kind of legal defence against the charge that their show, and the can-can in particular, violates morality laws—it is, they are saying,

FIGURE 5.5 'You're The Top' from Anything Goes (Paramount, 1956).

entirely innocent. 'Maidens' not only represents an ensemble opening number but also sets the scene for the rest of the action: its short list not only juxtaposes high and low (in this case supposed moral rectitude though in fact meant to represent self-righteousness and social high-handedness as opposed to the club culture of Montmartre) but also, in keeping with literary enumerations, their legitimate and meaningful coexistence. This juxtaposition of high and low is also what fuels Judge Aristide Forestrier's falling in love with club owner and showgirl Simone Pistache, and his recognition, as well as the recognition by others who think like him, that he was wrong to be so strait-laced. The song is a microcosm of the whole.

'Maidens Typical of France' is *not* the opening number in the film. The opening number is 'Montmartre,' which in the stage show appears considerably later. 'Montmartre' not only sets a different kind of scene, identifying the place and culture that are central to the action, but it also serves more immediately to introduce the audience to two of the main characters, the younger, high-living lawyer Francois Durnais, and the older, high-living judge Paul Barriere. Or better, it serves to introduce Frank Sinatra and Maurice Chevalier who play parts that are less important in the stage version but central to the film. And when 'Maidens Typical of France' is introduced, not demurely in the courtroom but in a satirizing setting at Pistache's club Bal du Paradis, it is truncated: only one verse is given, a verse made up of bits and pieces from the original (Table 5.2). What is more, it is followed—even overshadowed—by a dance that reminds spectators they are watching a late 1950s film: whereas much of the dance is musically in keeping with the rest of the show, set in 1890s Paris, at the end it becomes modern and jazzy, with bump and grind gestures reminiscent of Adelaide's 'Take Back Your Mink'

Table 5.2

'MAIDENS TYPICAL OF FRANCE'
(*CAN-CAN*: STAGE SHOW 1953, FILM 1960)

Show:	Film:
REFRAIN 1	REFRAIN 1
We are maidens typical of France,	We are maidens typical of France,
In a convent educated.	In a convent educated.
From the wicked clutches of romance,	From the wicked clutches of romance,
We have all been segregated.	We have all been segregated.
We know how to sew, we know how to knit,	
We know how to read—at least a little bit,	
We know how to wash, we know how to clean.	
If also we know the difference between	
A pair o' panties and a pair o' pants,	
We are maidens typical of France.	
REFRAIN 2	
We are maidens typical of France,	
In a convent educated.	
From the wicked clutches of romance,	
We have all been segregated.	
We know how to sweep, we know how to dust,	

(*continued*)

Table 5.2

CONTINUED

Show:	Film:
We know how to stew—a rabbit if we must,	
We know how to bake, we know how to fry.	
If also we know a tart is not a pie	
It is because we had the lucky chance	
To be maidens typical of France.	
REFRAIN 3	
We are maidens typical of France,	
In a convent educated.	
We're all very pure, we're all very good,	We're all very pure, *we wash our dainties white*,
We all try to do exactly as we should,	We all try to do exactly *what is right*,
We all go to church, we all say our prayers,	We all go to church, we all say our prayers,
And if, when we dance, we show our derrieres	And if, when we dance, we show our derrieres
It is to show that, even when we dance,	It is to show that, even when we dance,
We are maidens	We are maidens typical of France.
POLICEMEN: They are maidens	
ALL: Typical of France.	

from *Guys and Dolls* or June's version of 'Let Me Entertain You' in *Gypsy*. As a scene-setting number, as an enumeration of high and low, as a microcosm of what follows—as a list song—the film version of 'Maidens Typical of France' is to a large extent eviscerated.

The handling of the song 'Can-Can' is more extreme. Coming at the end of the show, its chaotic enumeration and alliterations—'If the Louvre custodian can, / If the Guard Republican can, / If Van Gogh and Matisse and Cézanne can,/ Baby you can can-can too' is juxtaposed with 'If an ape gargantuan can, / . . . If a clumsy pelican can, / . . . If a dachshund in Berlin can, / If a tomcat in Pekin can, / If a crowded sardine in a tin can, / Baby, you can can-can too'—sum up the whole of the action, bring about a kind of general rapprochement, and represent a resolution to the supposed incompatibility among the characters, between high and low, between the moral and the licentious (Table 5.3). Yet in the film, 'Can-Can' is reduced to a dance only: there are no words, it is not sung, there is no list (Figure 5.6).

There are some common patterns here: in all of these examples much, sometimes all, of the text is omitted; in the cases of 'Brush Up Your Shakespeare' and 'You're the Top' the songs are given physical locations related to the action of the plot; they are meant to further the narrative rather than represent a static aside; and in every case, they become less songs and more like dance numbers.

A reason for this may be that in their original, full-length form, list songs represent an outlier among song genres that is potentially incompatible with film, especially musical films of the 1950s. A historical view might be that for the 1950s, list songs, showstoppers, were incompatible with the idea of the 'integrated' musical, a notion that first gained wide currency

Table 5.3

'CAN-CAN' (*CAN-CAN*: STAGE SHOW 1953, FILM 1960; NOT SUNG IN FILM)

REFRAIN 1
There is no trick to a can-can,
It is so simple to do,
When you once kick to a can-can,
'Twill be so easy for you. If a lady in Iran can,
If a shady African can,
If a Jap with a slap of her fan can,
Baby, you can can-can too.
If an English Dapper Dan can, If an Irish Callahan can,
If an Afghan in Afghanistan can,
Baby, you can can-can too.

REFRAIN 2
If in Deauville ev'ry swell can,
It is so simple to do,
If Debussy and Ravel can,
'Twill be so easy for you.
If the Louvre custodian can,
If the Guard Republican can,
If Van Gogh and Matisse and Cezanne can,
Baby, you can can-can too.
If a chief in the Sudan can,
If the hefty Aga Khan can,
If the camels in his caravan can,
Baby, you can can-can too.

REFRAIN 3
Takes no art to do a can-can,
It is so simple to do,
When you start to do a can-can,
'Twill be so easy for you.
If a slow Mohammedan can,
If a kilted Scottish clan can,

Table 5.3

CONTINUED

If in Wagner a Valkyrian can,
Baby, you can can-can too.
If a lass in Michigan can,
If an ass in Astrakhan can,
If a bass in the Saskatchewan can,
Baby, you can can-can too.
REFRAIN 4
If the waltz king Johann Strauss can,
It is so simple to do,
If his gals in Fledermaus can,
'Twill be so easy for you.
Lovely Duse in Milan can,
Lucien Guitry and Rejane can,
Sarah Bernhardt upon a divan can,
Baby, you can can-can too.
If a holy Hindu man can,
If a gangly Anglican can,
If in Lesbos, a pure Lesbian can,
Baby, you can can-can too.
REFRAIN 5
If an ape gargantuan can,
It is so simple to do,
If a clumsy pelican can,
'Twill be so easy for you.
If a dachshund in Berlin can,
If a tomcat in Pekin can,
If a crowded sardine in a tin can,
Baby, you can can-can too.
If a rhino with a crash can,
If a hippo with a splash can,
If an elm and an oak and an ash can,
Baby, you can can-can too.

FIGURE 5.6 'Can-Can' from Can-Can (Twentieth Century-Fox, 1960).

with *Oklahoma!*, in which narrative considerations trump performance. A list song, a potentially unending recitation devoid of action or even characterization specific to any show, as opposed to more universal notions of character and attributes, stops the narrative in its tracks. It is perhaps no coincidence that Porter's film musicals, as opposed to his stage musicals, do not include list songs at all (*Born to Dance*, 1936; *Rosalie*, 1937; *Broadway Melody of 1940*, 1940; and *The Pirate*, 1948). The one exception is 'Now You Has Jazz' from *High Society* (1956)—an exception explained by the fact that it is a 'live' performance number for Louis Armstrong.

Since the appeal of list songs is as much—if not more—the words as the music, they should perhaps be thought of as not just a musical genre but a literary genre as well (after all, Porter wrote that 'Can-Can' didn't *have* to be danced, hence the primacy of words over action), constructing meaning primarily through linguistic codes and conventions. This may also be why list songs are problematic in film: they represent a kind of open-ended literary structure that may be incompatible with the nature of the film musical itself and the demands of film narrative.[13] On a purely practical level, this appears to manifest itself in some well-understood rules about the length of a song, even in a film musical: in 1958, when Porter was working on *Aladdin* for CBS television, his producer, Richard Lewine, wrote to him that no song—for television or film—ought to exceed two and a half or three minutes, the maximum length for both the narrative and the audience.[14] Even then, the potential of an infinity of words, for an unending chaotic enumeration, seems to have been considered too much even for three minutes. In virtually all of the examples noted above, the songs mostly become action, become dances; as Rick Altman says, 'The beauty of dance is that it needs no words—indeed, it escapes words.'[15]

List songs, then, can also be thought of as representatives of a broader literary tradition, whether of rhetoric, as described by Eco, or chaotic enumerations, as described by Spitzer, and as theatrical traditions. They work on stage because they can 'become,' in a manner of speaking, literary works appropriate to live performance: the actors or singers can be physically isolated, even soliloquize, in front of the curtain; there is a recognized theatrical game to be played, whether encouraging applause at the false ending of a song like 'Brush Up Your Shakespeare' or the inclusion of, as Porter put it, a literal showstopper near the end; and because the immediacy of verbal performance in a theatre is different from the immediacy of visual performance on screen. List songs work in the theatre because they take centre stage all by themselves and invite listeners or watchers to be complicit in literary and theatrical conventions that go beyond a specific moment, scene, or show, conventions seemingly incompatible—to judge how Porter's list songs are presented on screen—with film.

NOTES

1. Considering that there is no fixed notion of what does or does not count as a list song, a rough account of the list songs in Porter's Broadway shows could conceivably include the following: 'The Physician' (*Nymph Errant*, 1933); 'You're the Top' (*Anything Goes*, 1934); 'Gather Ye Autographs While Ye May' and 'A Picture of Me without You' (*Jubilee*, 1935); 'From Alpha to Omega' (*You Never Know*, 1938); 'But in the Morning, No' and 'Well Did You Evah!' (*DuBarry Was a Lady*, 1939); 'Fresh as a Daisy,' 'I'm Throwing a Ball Tonight,' and 'Americans All Drink Coffee' (*Panama Hattie*, 1940); 'A Lady Needs a Rest,' 'Farming,' and 'You Irritate Me So' (*Let's Face It*, 1941); 'I Can Do without Tea in my Teapot' (*Something to Shout About*, 1943); 'The Good-Will Movement' and 'It's Just Like the Good Old Days' (*Mexican Hayride*, 1944); 'Drink'

and 'Hence It Don't Make Sense' (*Seven Lively Arts*, 1944); 'Brush Up Your Shakespeare' (*Kiss Me, Kate*, 1948); 'I Got Beauty' and 'Nobody's Chasing Me' (*Out of this World*, 1950); 'Never, Never Be an Artist' and 'Can-Can' (*Can-Can*, 1953); and 'Give Me the Land' (*Silk Stockings*, 1955).

2. Cole Porter Literary and Musical Property Trusts (hereafter CPT), Correspondence 1952.
3. Letter of 1 July 1952; New York Public Library (NYPL), Abe Burrows Papers, *T-Mss 2000–006, box 13, folder 19.
4. The London version of the lyrics for 'Anything Goes' survive at CPT.
5. CPT, Correspondence 1952.
6. See David Savran, ' "You've Got That Thing": Cole Porter, Stephen Sondheim, and the Erotics of the List Song,' *Theatre Journal* 64, no. 4 (December 2012): 533–548.
7. William H. Glass, 'I've Got a Little List,' *Salmagundi* 109–110 (1996): 22–23.
8. Umberto Eco, *The Infinity of Lists* (New York: Rizzoli, 2009), 133. Eco makes this argument in particular with respect to lists of God's attributes—since God is unknowable, the metaphor-attributes include the whole of existence. It is the larger 'conceptual sphere' of God's attributes that makes them cohere.
9. Leo Spitzer, 'Explication de Texte Applied to Walt Whitman's Poem "Out of the Cradle Endlessly Rocking," ' originally published in *Journal of English Literary History* 16 (1949): 229–249; reprinted in Leo Spitzer, *Essays on English and American Literature*, ed. Anna Hatcher (New York: Gordian Press, 1984), 23.
10. Letter of 16 June 1948 (Columbia University, Spewack collection). This reference, incidentally, dates a draft script for *Kiss Me, Kate* in the Hanya Holm collection (US-NYPL, (S) *MGZMD 135, folder 502) to 'before 16 June 1948' where the gangsters' exit is on page 2-6-29.
11. CPT, Correspondence 1948.
12. This is also described in Porter's letter to Spewack; see note 11.
13. This formulation is complementary to Jane Feuer's notion that film musicals are shaped by the loss of live performance: since list songs in stage shows are explicitly 'live performances,' their truncation or even elimination in film musicals, as well as their

recasting as part of the action and mis-en-scène, attenuates what would otherwise be a 'non-filmic' disruption. See Jane Feuer, *The Hollywood Musical*, 2nd ed. (Bloomington: Indiana University Press, 1993), especially chap. 2, 'Spectator and Spectacles,' 23–47.
14. US-NYPL, *T-Mss 2006–008, box 1, folder 31.
15. Rick Altman, *The American Film Musical* (Bloomington: Indiana University Press, 1987), 40.

6

The Shifting Sand
of Orientalism

The Desert Song on Stage and Screen

WILLIAM A. EVERETT

■ ◻ ■

SIGMUND ROMBERG AND OSCAR HAMMERSTEIN II's 1926 romantic operetta, *The Desert Song*, captured the hearts of countless fans in various stage productions. To capitalize on this popularity, Warner Brothers released three full-length adaptations of the adventurous romance, in 1929, 1943, and 1953, as well as a short version called *The Red Shadow* in 1932. In 1955, the classic operetta was broadcast live on network television. All versions of the tale, whether on stage or screen, explore the nebulous world of Orientalism, defined here as a Western construct of an imagined East. This chapter introduces each incarnation of *The Desert Song* and explores how the operetta's various manifestations over nearly thirty years, from the stage version in 1926 to the television version of 1955, address shifting relationships in terms of world politics, depictions of Otherness, and the interplay between reality and fantasy.

As an operetta, music takes centre stage, and no matter what the storyline, the performance of the musical score is what draws audiences. Romberg wrote some of his most beloved tunes for *The Desert Song*, including the evocative title song with its waltz refrain, the heroic 'Riff Song' featuring a thunderous male chorus, the perky 'Romance' with its coloratura obbligato, and the languid 'One Alone,' an ode to monogamy. What distinguishes this operetta from many of its counterparts, however, is its contemporary, though exotic, setting. While this element is not unique to the genre (Strauss's *Die Fledermaus* [1874] is set at the time of its creation), many operettas are set in a distant time and place with the express purpose of evoking a sense of fantasy, nostalgia, and nevermore. Against such backdrops, contemporary issues and attitudes are often reflected, refracted, and interrogated.

When it comes to the real-world setting of *The Desert Song*, France had established a protectorate in Morocco in 1916, in effect asserting colonial control while allowing Morocco to maintain its sovereignty. The first resident-general in Morocco, Hubert Lyautey (Louis Hubert Gonzalve Lyautey, 1854–1934) wanted to work with the Moroccan sultan Yusef ben Hassan (1882–1927, ruled 1912–27) to 'modernize' Moroccan society according to French principles. Lyautey held his post until 1925, though Morocco continued to be a French protectorate until 1956, when it gained its independence. Significantly, the original stage libretto for *The Desert Song* is set in 1925, the exact time that Lyautey was concluding his direct role in Morocco, and all versions of the tale discussed here were created while Morocco was a French protectorate and not a fully autonomous state.

Concerning Orientalism, John Maier remarks on the construct in *Desert Songs: Western Images of Morocco and Moroccan Images of the West*: 'Orientalism at its worst involves crude stereotyping of supposedly inferior peoples. Somewhat more frequently, the Orient is imaged [*sic*] as a backward place in need of modernizing and civilizing—in the direction, of course, of the West.'[1] In the 1926 stage play and the 1929 film, Morocco exists as an underdeveloped land of vast mystery and primal sexuality. This shifts in the version from the early 1940s, where the Moroccans are vilified and depicted as treacherous and devious Nazi collaborators. The next decade's version offers a blend of the two constructions (though without the Nazi element), while the television version returns to the spirit of the original. Music occupies a central role in each of these discourses. Romberg's musical stylings differentiate between European and non-European characters through the use of major and minor modes, and in the mid-century film adaptations, the indigenous-sounding musics add a sense of documentary realism, as do diegetic performances of several key musical numbers.

THE 1926 STAGE ORIGINAL: CHIC MEETS SHEIK

Among the central works in the American operetta repertory stands *The Desert Song*.[2] With a rhapsodic score by Sigmund Romberg (1887–1951), a contemporary book by Frank Mandel (1884–1958), and romantic lyrics by Otto Harbach (1873–1963) and Oscar Hammerstein II (1895–1960), the work opened at the Moorish-clad Casino Theatre on 30 November 1926 and played 471 performances in its original Broadway run. Mandel and Laurence Schwab (1893–1951) produced the work, which marked a change in Romberg's approach to operetta. Rather than having a bittersweet ending in which the principal lovers are not together at the final curtain (such as in *Maytime* [1917], *Blossom Time* [1921] or *The Student Prince in Heidelberg* [1924]), the lovers now embrace for a happy ending. Equally important is the show's setting in the immediate past. Whereas orthodox operetta recreated the past through rose-tinted glasses, *The Desert Song* looked to current events through an Orientalist gaze. Its creators sought to blend nostalgic sentiment with present-day situations, a difficult concoction and one that was not always convincing.

The show transferred to London, where it opened at Drury Lane on 7 April 1927 for 432 performances and subsequently appeared in translation throughout continental Europe. The stage show's popularity continued for decades, with scores of professional, amateur, and summer stock companies mounting productions throughout the English-speaking world.

The Story: Pierre Loves Margot, Who Thinks She Loves Paul, Who Is Lusted after by Azuri, Who Detests the General, Who . . .

The operetta's convoluted web of relationships is set in 1925 in Morocco. Pierre Birabeau (played by Robert Halliday), the nerdy son of the new commander of a military outpost, is in love with the beautiful Margot Bonvalet (played by Vivienne Segal), a woman he knew in France.[3] Margot, though, feigns disinterest in Pierre; she wants to be with a hero. Her wish to be with a champion actually motivated Pierre to come to Morocco, where he could earn medals for bravery, which in turn could help him win Margot's heart.

Margot, however, has come to Morocco to be with Paul Fontaine, a French officer with whom she thinks she is in love. Paul's father was the former commander of the French outpost and was known as 'the butcher' because of his desperate cruelty. Pierre, while under the elder Fontaine's command, was ordered to attack Riff villages, acts he found appalling. He resigned from the military and seems to enjoy a life of picking wildflowers. Since Pierre's resignation, the mysterious Red

Shadow keeps thwarting the French military's efforts. Hassi, a Riff, is the only one among his people who knows the truth: the Red Shadow is Pierre.

After the death of the senior Fontaine, the French appoint a new commander: Pierre's father. General Birabeau's primary goal in coming to Morocco is to dispose of the Red Shadow. The General is very disappointed with his son and even tells him at one point that he wishes he would just do one thing to make him proud.

Margot, meanwhile, has discovered that Paul isn't the man she thought he was and that he's only a 'military machine.'[4] She confesses to Pierre that even though he (Pierre) is far from heroic, he is the only person who truly understands her. But when Margot hears of the Red Shadow, she is captivated by his mystique and adventurous spirit. The General, hoping to embarrass Pierre for his lack of overt masculinity, tells his son that Margot wishes the Red Shadow would come and carry her over the sands. So, Pierre changes clothes, enters as the Red Shadow, and whisks Margot off to the desert as the first act ends.

Act 2 opens at Ali Ben Ali's desert palace, where a troupe of Spanish dancing girls entertains the guests. Ali Ben Ali simply cannot understand why Pierre is so smitten with Margot, one woman, and Moroccan and European cultural differences emerge in the musical-dramatic scene 'Eastern and Western Love.' General Birabeau arrives to rescue Margot and meets the Red Shadow, whom he challenges to a duel. Swords drawn, the Red Shadow drops his. By forfeiting the duel, the Red Shadow can no longer lead the Riffs and must be banished into the desert with only his broken sword. General Birabeau orders Fontaine to go into the desert and kill the Red Shadow.

Azuri, a native dancer who is obsessed with Fontaine and knows the Red Shadow's true identity, asks the General repeatedly and with increasing intensity, 'Where is Pierre?' The General finally realizes his son's dual identity. Fontaine returns and tells the assembled group that the Red Shadow is dead. When Fontaine confesses that it was Pierre who killed him, everyone is surprised, except for the General, who is relieved. Pierre enters, carrying the costume of the Red Shadow. In a short scene that follows, father and son pledge to work together to protect the Riffs. Margot enters, angry with Pierre that he killed an unarmed man. Pierre dons the Red Shadow's costume, joins her in a reprise of 'One Alone,' and kisses her as she realizes the truth.

Benjamin 'Bennie' Kidd, a newspaper reporter for the *Paris Daily Mail*, and Susan, his secretary, provide comic respite and serve as foils for the primary love story of Pierre and Margot. Bennie and Susan have a curious sort of platonic relationship, though Susan begs for something more intimate. Their duet, 'It,' is an ode to sex appeal. It is performed in a nearly speech-singing style reminiscent of music hall. The song's fast tempo, frequent rests, and references to Sigmund Freud and Elinor Glyn place it in a syncopated style closer to sexualized revue than to sentimental operetta. Glyn's novel *It*, from which the song takes its title, was first published serially in *Cosmopolitan* magazine in 1926, the same year in which *The Desert Song* appeared. Their characters further root the show in the present day. Benny resists the advances of not only Susan but also Clementina, the leader of the Spanish dancers, and explains his reticence as the result of women treating him badly when he was young in his quasi-pitiable song 'Bold Women.'

Orientalist Discourse in the 1920s

Edward W. Said's theory of Orientalism, as demonstrated in his landmark study, *Orientalism*,[5] permeates *The Desert Song*. Desert locales especially became symbols for underdevelopment—unchangeable terrains that were trapped in an uncivilized (by Western standards) stasis. These vast landscapes added to the

allure of Orientalist discourse. Furthermore, the Orientalist/
colonialist notion that the peoples living in the Orient needed
Western assistance is evident in *The Desert Song*, for near the
end General Birabeau and Pierre pledge to work together to
help the Riffs, who, ironically, might not need their help if the
French were not in Morocco in the first place!

When Howard Carter discovered King Tutankhamen's
tomb on 26 November 1922, a new wave of Orientalism erupted,
one that melded nineteenth-century perfumed exoticism
with contemporary media. New technologies of photography,
print media, and film brought news of ancient civilizations
to the world. Europeans (and Americans) subsequently became aware of current events in North Africa and the Eastern
Mediterranean. The character of Bennie, in a way, represents
homage to the foreign press corps of the time; he is in Morocco
to tell the world about the Red Shadow.

Following nineteenth-century models, the Orient was
being conceived as a land of overt sexuality, with rugged macho
men and alluring, barely clothed women vying for the attention
of Westerners. Rudolph Valentino (1895–1926), in the title role
of *The Sheik* (1921), embodied the image of a virile exotic male.
Valentino popularized sideburns as a symbol of male virility,
and his image of a kaffiyeh-covered man became the personifi-
cation of lust and violence.[6] This attitude appears in *The Desert
Song* in how the Riff men are imagined as physically (and sexually) superior to Europeans. For example, Margot tells Pierre
that the Red Shadow, who she thinks at this point is a Riff, is
'about a head taller than you.'[7] Later, Clementina, exasperated
with the strength of Arab men, tells Ali Ben Ali, 'Oh, I will
be so happy when I can meet a real man again—a nice, weak
Western man.'[8]

Regarding the female imagining of the Orient, a substantial
tradition existed whose musical incarnations included Camille
Saint-Saëns's *Samson et Dalila* (1877), with its sultry bacchanal,

and Richard Strauss's *Salome* (1905), most notably 'The Dance of the Seven Veils.' Significantly, both of these examples rely on the physicality of the female performer for their meaning. A reviewer of *The Desert Song* in Boston offered a contextually apt description of Pearl Regay, who played Azuri: 'Then, when tribal musicians drummed and piped, she wove Azuri's body into writhings, whirlings, bendings, archings wondrous to see.'[9] The nearly erotic element is also evident in the remarks of the Lord Chamberlain's Office when it reviewed the play for licensing in London. The examiner, George Street, noted that 'the scenes at Ali ben Ali's include a good deal of voluptuous dancing and so on, but we can be sure that kind of thing will be kept within bounds at Drury Lane.'[10] Orientalist fantasy held a potent allure for audiences.

Film emerged as a notable medium for Orientalist discourse, the exemplar being *The Sheik*.[11] The film's plot was an emblematic colonial rescue fantasy—a Western woman is kidnapped by an Arab and rescued by a European. In *The Sheik* (and in *The Desert Song*), the 'Arab' kidnapper is a disguised European, and the kidnapper and the rescuer are in fact the same person.

Valentino, star of *The Sheik*, died on 23 August 1926 at the young age of thirty-one.[12] At the time, Romberg and Hammerstein were working on *The Desert Song* at the Hotel Marie Antoinette, across the street from Campbell's Funeral Parlor, where Valentino's body lay in state. They saw and heard the tremendous outpouring of grief, and since their new work included tropes associated with the immortalized star, Romberg and Hammerstein were prepared to ride the wave of Valentino's legend. *The Sheik*, with its plot of disguise and dual identity, was an obvious influence on *The Desert Song*.

Real-life inspirations also existed for *The Desert Song*, including Lawrence of Arabia (Thomas Edward Lawrence, 1888–1935), an Englishman who donned dashing robes and whose exploits in the Near East were well known in the English-speaking world. He himself added to his celebrity status by privately publishing his autobiography, *The Seven Pillars of Wisdom*, in 1926, the same year that *The Desert Song* appeared. His personal account had the flavour of a heroic epic adventure, the spirit of which infuses much of *The Desert Song.*

Gertrude Bell (1868–1926) also figures into the story. Here was an Englishwoman who became famous for her travels in the Arab world through the books she wrote about her experiences.[13] Her contributions to Arab culture were greatly lauded after her death on 12 July 1926 in Baghdad, five and half months prior to the opening of *The Desert Song*. Bell could have been an inspiration for intrepid women like Margot and Susan, who travel to distant climes.

Finally, there was Abd El-Krim (1882–1963), a real-life Riff leader who detested foreign rule in Morocco. In 1904, Spain and France divided Morocco into spheres of influence, and in 1920, Abd El-Krim led a four-year revolt that eventually drove the Spaniards out of Morocco. In 1925, France and Spain formed an alliance to defeat Abd-El Krim and his Riff forces. They achieved victory the following year (the year of *The Desert Song*'s premiere), though it took 25,000 French and Spanish troops to do so. The Red Shadow's efforts paralleled those of Abd El-Krim, though the real Riff leader was not a disguised European.

Speaking of the Riffs, they are an actual Berber tribe that resides in northern Morocco and Algeria. Adult men wear a long blue veil (a tegelmoust) to cover their faces, with a slit for the eyes.[14] This level of costume accuracy would not be possible in *The Desert Song*, for the actors must have their mouths uncovered in order to project their singing voices.

In short, the Orientalist perspective reflected in *The Desert Song* conflates a sense of present-day realism, notable in the appearance of Riffs in French-controlled Morocco, with Orientalist images inherited from the nineteenth century, especially sexual allure. The appeal of Rudolph Valentino in *The Sheik* with the general attraction of Orientalist cinema as well as the autobiographical tales of Lawrence of Arabia and Gertrude Bell similarly played into *The Desert Song*'s tale of romance, disguise, and desert fantasy.

Musical Orientalism in The Desert Song

In 1928, Romberg offered his views on modes and their ethnic associations. 'Music is in two categories: major and minor. Hungarian, Russian, and Balkan States, Persia, and India take music in the minor key; Anglo-Saxon and Latin countries are written in major.'[15] To extend this axiom to *The Desert Song*, European characters sing resolutely in major, while Moroccan ones perform in minor, often with chromatic inflections. When ambiguity exists, as in the case of the dual identity of Pierre and the Red Shadow, Romberg employs musical means to accentuate this split personality.

This tonal trope is readily apparent in the 'The Desert Song,' the luscious waltz duet that is also the operetta's title song. Pierre begins the verse by singing in Margot's major-mode language, 'Why waste your time in vague romancing,' in D-flat major. As he dons the persona of the Red Shadow, though, he shifts to C-sharp minor (the enharmonic parallel minor) to intone the inviting 'My desert is waiting' in a largely pentatonic vocal line. When he reaches the refrain, he is again Pierre the Frenchman and expresses the wistful 'Blue heaven and you and I' in D-flat major. He is being truthful in all things—his European heritage and his love for Margot—so he must sing in his native major mode. Through adroit shifting between major and minor, we hear this single character express himself in his two personas, the major-mode Frenchman and the minor-mode Riff leader.

A similar harmonic technique exists in 'The Riff Song.' The verse of the heroic male choral number begins in D minor and centres on a sustained G sharp, a tritone away from the tonic, and a pitch that immediately establishes a sense of aural Otherness. The Riffs are not Europeans, and their tonal language immediately affirms this distinction. The refrain, which features their leader, the European-born Red Shadow, hovers between F major and D minor and thus confirms the dual identity (European and Riff leader) of Pierre/Red Shadow.

The 'Eastern and Western Love' sequence near the beginning of act 2 likewise employs musical means to distinguish between the two approaches to gender relations, Eastern polygamy and Western monogamy. Two Moroccans, Ali Ben Ali and Sid El Kar, explain their views of love in their respective songs 'Let Love Go' and 'One Flower Grows Alone in Your Garden,' both of which are in F minor. As non-Westerners, they perform in the minor mode. The vocal ranges of both men also prove to be exotic (for Broadway audiences), for Ali Ben Ali is a low bass and Sid El Kar is a high tenor. After they have expressed their views, Pierre enters with 'One Alone,' his ode to monogamy as clearly reflected in the title, in A-flat major. He expresses his European view in the major mode. Furthermore, he is a baritone, a mid-range, familiar voice, as opposed to the extreme ranges heard immediately before. The Christian world of monogamy, by appearing last in the sequence, dominates the Eastern, Islamic world of polygamy, indicating, though an Orientalist gaze, the latter to be inferior to the former.[16]

A related sort of treatment is evident in the music of the female characters. Margot is the soprano heroine who dreams of romance with one man in the effusive 'Romance,' with its resolutely major mode. Her foils are Clementina and Azuri, both personifications of an exotic Other. Clementina is one of the

Spanish dancing girls at the beginning of act 2 who performs her 'Song of the Brass Key' in a sultry mezzo voice; she is the progeny of Carmen from Georges Bizet's 1875 opera. The music begins in the minor mode but turns to major for the refrain. The liminal place of Spain in the musical and dramatic discourse is summoned here—Spain is exotic on one hand, akin to North Africa with its Moorish influence; and European on the other, for it too had acted as a European colonizing force in Morocco. Furthermore, as a mezzo, Clementina is as much a musical foil for Margot, a soprano, as a dramatic one. Azuri, likewise, is a Moroccan dancer who seeks revenge on men who have wronged her, including Paul Fontaine. She does not sing but appears over a slithering chromatic monophonic line in the orchestra filled with half steps and augmented seconds; her music—and life—lie far away from Margot's effusive major-mode world.

1929: A FAITHFUL RENDITION IN A NEW MEDIUM

Warner Bros. purchased exclusive motion picture rights to *The Desert Song* on 4 March 1928,[17] and the studio released two versions of its film the following year, a dialogue version and a nondialogue version, the latter of which included cue cards.[18] We focus here on the dialogue version, since it holds the distinction of being the first full-length screen adaptation of a Broadway musical with all-synchronized sound. Its conception and realization remain extremely close to the stage original in terms of plot, music, and general atmosphere. The creators' purpose was to recreate the theatrical original in a nascent medium.

The film starred musical actor and former baseball player John Boles (1895–1969) in the dual role of Pierre/Red Shadow opposite radio singer Carlotta King (1898–2000) as Margot, with Myrna Loy (1905–1993), already famous for her vamp roles, as Azuri. Harvey Gates fashioned the screenplay after the original stage script, and Roy Del Ruth directed the 123-minute feature. Louis Silvers served as music director and led the Vitaphone Orchestra, whose more than hundred members sat just off-camera.[19] *The Desert Song* was released on 8 April 1929.

But just how close to the original was this 1929 adaptation? The courts actually answered this question. Lillian Macloon, who held stage rights for the show west of and including Denver and Winnipeg, filed a suit against Warner Bros. She claimed that the film caused unfair competition for her stage productions.[20] Macloon lost the case as well as her appeal.[21] A similar instance occurred in the United Kingdom. The studio paid Lee Ephraim, who held the stage rights to the show, £1,000 to release *The Desert Song* film in London, noting that the trouble apparently was that the 'DESERT SONG' after a long run at the Drury Lane Theatre, was then being shown in the provinces, and Lee Ephraim, who held the rights, naturally had to be squared before he would submit to the competition of the film.[22]

While the romantic tale was maintained, even down to a great deal of specific dialogue, the comedic elements were severely curtailed. Benny and Susan are no longer a comic couple, and indeed, Benny (played by Johnny Arthur) is coded as homosexual.[23] After he falls off his horse and is brought to a Riff camp, suspected of being a spy, he slyly tells one of his captors, 'How's it goin', Big Boy?' Susan seems basically content with their asexual relationship, and after they spend a night together in the desert, she disappointingly confesses that nothing happened, for 'he was such a gentleman.' Whenever Benny and Susan appear, 'It'—their song in the original stage version concerning sex appeal—is heard in the underscoring, though the song itself is never featured.

As a pioneering work in the history of Hollywood film, this *Desert Song* also takes on a salient feature of 'silent-era' films, the omnipresence of musical underscoring. Rex Dunn created a tapestry based on Romberg's themes. Dunn's underscoring is rooted in standard Hollywood practice, where specific musical signifiers are associated with specific characters or screen events. This became known as a 'classical film score' and is a descendant of the Leitmotif system. For example, whenever the Riffs are conferring, 'The Riff Song' is heard, while 'French Military Marching Song' accompanies the French army.

The screenplay's adherence to the stage libretto includes its Orientalist aspects. Notably, the 'Eastern and Western Love' sequence appears intact, as do the culture-defining modal cues of the stage version. The vast desert terrain and its promise as a land of adventure and mystery, a central tenet of Orientalism, squares front and centre in this version. Several of the spectacular scenes appeared in Technicolor to enhance their allure.[24]

Critics lauded the effort though they qualified their praise. Harry Evans, writing in *Life* magazine, admired the film's sweeping desert vistas, which cinema could give its audiences in a way that live theatre could not. The incongruence between this level of realism and the sentimental romance of an operetta, though, posed a critical disruption:

> However, the effectiveness of these shots is one of the disturbing elements of the picture, because the realism created is in direct conflict with the theatrical atmosphere of the singing scenes. For instance, one moment you see a gang of Arabs riding over the sands hell bent on death and destruction, and the next they are shown in a typical stage interior humming tenor accompaniments while the lovers sing ditties at each other.[25]

Veracity and fantasy came head to head, and some sort of accord between the two narrative styles remained unresolved in the film. The reviewer for *Variety* offered a possible solution to the film's incongruity: 'It is not what might have been accomplished had picture license been taken, to which it would lend itself easily.'[26] Perhaps reworking the storyline and adjusting the placement of musical numbers would help alleviate the disparity between cinematic realism and operetta-like escapism.

This approach began to be considered in the late 1930s, when Warner Bros. was thinking about a new film of *The Desert Song*, one with a significantly altered plot. MGM did this with its 1930 treatment of *The New Moon*, Romberg and Hammerstein's operetta from 1928, where the setting was changed from eighteenth-century Louisiana to nineteenth-century Russia.[27] But before another full-length treatment arrived, the studio released a highly condensed version of the operetta to showcase its most famous songs.

1932: A VITAFONE SHORT

Called *The Red Shadow*, the nineteen-minute short directed by Ray Mack showcased the talents of Alexander Gray as Pierre/ The Red Shadow and Bernice Claire as Margot. The stars had appeared together on stage in *The Desert Song* many times and recreated their beloved theatrical performances for the camera.

As in the 1929 version, all the dialogue is underscored, this time by David Mendoza, a staff composer at Warner Bros. Mendoza also created a shortened paraphrase of 'Azuri's Dance' for the film.

The basic romantic plot of Pierre/The Red Shadow and Margot is all that remains of the multilayered storyline. As would be expected, the film includes shortened versions (usually refrains) of the operetta's most endearing music. It begins with two refrains of the evocative title song followed immediately by the rousing 'Riff Song.' The leads offer a duet rendition of 'One Alone.' The exotically tinged 'One Flower Grows Alone in a Garden'[28] (from the 'Eastern and Western Love' sequence) appears in its entirety, and the film concludes with stirring choral reprises of 'Riff Song' and the title song.

The practice of adding new songs to film versions of *The Desert Song* begins here. (This was becoming standard practice in film adaptations of Broadway musicals.) Cliff Hess created a new song, 'Morocco Bound,' that was supposed to create a sense of exotic Otherness early in the film. In the final cut, only an instrumental version appears as brief underscoring. 'Romance,' Margot's effusive ode in the original, likewise appears only as instrumental background music.

The Red Shadow distilled *The Desert Song* to its most basic escapist romantic elements and offered its audiences abridged performances of its most popular musical numbers. This was a strong reminder that the music of *The Desert Song* is its most enduring quality.

UNREALIZED TREATMENTS, 1936–1942

Since Warner Bros. held the exclusive rights to film adaptations of *The Desert Song*, in the 1930s, it began developing new storylines to surround the songs in a way that was less stilted and more plausible than in the 1929 adaptation. As the studio executives learned, audiences were much more willing to suspend belief in a live theatrical performance than they were in the cinema when it came to a musical treatment of a contemporary subject. In 1935, MGM's film adaptation of Victor Herbert's *Naughty Marietta* placed the singing team of Jeannette MacDonald and Nelson Eddy firmly in the public consciousness in a vehicle that prided itself on its historical escapism. Since *The Desert Song* was set in the recent past, this type of historical distancing was simply not possible. Therefore, creative restructurings of the narrative were necessary, ones that would keep a disguised male lead firmly in place while altering other aspects of the story. These treatments ranged from the nearly comical, where the whole idea of the Red Shadow is a publicity stunt, to the politically realistic, complete with Nazis. Elements of several of these unrealized efforts would eventually appear in subsequent film versions.

Several versions of the tale appeared during the 1930s and early 1940s. In Robert Lord's treatment from December 1934, Paul Fontaine is engaged to marry Margot Lambert, but when he shows up late at a Parisian restaurant, the rake Pierre dances with her. This infuriates Pierre's uncle, the General, who orders Pierre to resign from the army. Pierre and his friend Benny, a journalist, go to Algiers, where the Caliph Ali Ben Ali hires Pierre to command his army and Benny to be his publicity person. Since Ali wants publicity, Pierre and Benny concoct the story of the Red Shadow and print stories about how Ali Ben Ali plans to kill the menace. Meanwhile, Margot arrives in Algiers, confessing love for Pierre. The Riffs attack the French, and the Red Shadow kidnaps Margot. He removes his mask, and Margot 'laughs and kisses him.' At the end, Margot and Pierre are aboard a ship bound for Paris. At a costume party, Margot is wearing a native Moorish costume and Pierre is dressed as the Red Shadow. In this fanciful treatment, Margot learns of her lover's dual identity early on, and Morocco is literally shown to be a source for make-believe costumes. Fantasy trumps any sense of reality.

On 25 March 1936, Warner Bros. and Technicolor Motion Picture Corporation agreed to make a full-length film version of *The Desert Song*.[29] Seton I. Miller prepared a preliminary scenario, dated 17 April 1936, and a version marked 'Miller's Script with [Robert] Lord's changes' from 7 July 1936 includes the directive to 'eliminate as much operetta mood as possible.'[30] It is in this version that the Red Shadow is renamed El Khobar, as happens in the subsequent films. (Because of fears surrounding communism, calling a hero 'The Red Shadow' had become untenable. So he becomes El Khobar, which is actually the name of a city in Saudi Arabia.)

Pierre becomes Paul Bernard, and Margot is now Liane. In the new plot, the Riffs kidnap Fontaine, who plans to marry Liane, and El Khobar rescues him. El Khobar then carries Liane, who knows he really is Paul, off to the desert. El Khobar is arrested, sentenced to die, and Bennie and Opal (the Susan character) slip El Khobar a gun so that he can escape. El Khobar and Liane ride off together as the film ends.

Central to this discussion is the agreement that Romberg and Hammerstein signed to write a new song for the film, due no later than 1 November 1936. The agreement stipulated that the song could not be used in any other film until it had appeared in the new version of *The Desert Song* and that Romberg could use the song on any radio program on which he appeared, as long as he would not use it without the consent of Warner Bros. prior to the picture's opening.[31] The new song, 'As Lovely as You Seem,' is a wistful romance for Paul to sing to Liane.[32]

On 16 April 1937, the proposed film was cancelled.[33] The previous August, R. J. Obringer noted that casting and 'other production problems' were delaying the project.[34] Warner Bros. returned to the property in the summer of 1938, with a new screenplay by Michael Fessier and Warren Duff.[35] Pierre becomes Paul Bonnard, Margot is now light opera star Liane Dupre, and David Lansing is an Englishman who assumes Bennie's character role. Making Margot a singer would allow for diegetic—that is, more cinematically realistic—performances of Romberg's music. As with previous efforts in the 1930s, this version was also shelved.

In August 1941, Robert Buckner and Charles Grayson proposed yet another new treatment for the operetta, which they described as 'a valuable piece of studio property, a million-dollar title and one of the greatest musical scores of our times.'[36] They found the story outdated and wanted to infuse it with 'modern feeling' and 'real human beings instead of "Chocolate Soldiers," '[37] a reference to the overt artifice of operettas such as Oscar Straus's *The Chocolate Soldier*. Their version would be set in current times, with Nazi-occupied Vichy France ruling Morocco, and would feature two brothers with differing political views—one a supporter of the Vichy state and the other a supporter of Free France under Charles De Gaulle—who are in love with the same woman. Buckner and Grayson described the set-up: 'The three of them together typify vividly the France of today, brother against brother, each believing his to be the right side; and the girl whose emotions are torn by loyalties.'[38]

In the proposed scenario, the Nazis are using slave labour to build a railroad across the Sahara to Dakar. The sole hope for the unwilling labourers lies in the Red Shadow. As in the original, the heroic Red Shadow has a mild-mannered alter ego, now called Paul Bonnard. The authors envisioned this as a role for Errol Flynn, claiming that it was 'difficult to think of anyone else with the same color and dash that he could give the famous role.'[39] Although Errol Flynn would be a massive audience draw, this was a musical and Flynn was not known as a singer. To address this, the creators envisioned a new character, Raoul Bonnard, Paul's brother, to be played by Dennis Morgan. Raoul, who was a singer in Paris before the war, supports the Vichy government. The proposed scenario would thus provide two male leads—a swashbuckling hero (Flynn) and a singing sibling rival (Morgan). Furthermore, they introduced Denise Bonet as a singer from Paris who comes to Morocco to be near Raoul and becomes smitten with Paul. Raoul learns of his brother's dual identity, and after a skirmish at the German governor's palace, Raoul and Denise watch Paul ride off into the desert to continue his fight for freedom.

A version dated 18 April 1942 outlines a revised approach to the basic story. The Errol Flynn-inspired Paul is jettisoned, as is the part of Raoul. Paul, whose dual identity again provides a fundamental plot point, is to have 'a natural voice.'[40] His alter ego, now called El Khobar, is seen 'not as a crack-pot renegade' but as someone who supports 'the poor and the weak—the little guys of the earth.'[41] Denise is still a singer, now the star 'of one of those bush-league light opera troupes.'[42] Benoit, the troupe's manager, hears Paul sing and wants to make him a star. The notion of diegetic and dramatically believable reasons for songs to be sung is central to this vision of the storyline.

1942: HOME-FRONT PROPAGANDA

On 17 December 1943, nearly fifteen months after its completion, Warner Brothers finally released its second full-length cinematic version of *The Desert Song*. Since many Hollywood studios were producing home-front propaganda musicals at the time, Robert Buckner's adaptation of *The Desert Song* followed suit.[43] The disguised hero (Dennis Morgan) in the ninety-six-minute film's story of Nazi machinations in North Africa in 1937 is no longer a former French soldier but rather Paul Hudson, an American pianist who rides off to continue his fight for justice rather than remain with his beloved French chanteuse, Margot (Irene Manning).[44] The addition of North African–sounding music and the diegetic presentation of much of the score provide a sense of documentary realism that helps shift the Orientalist markers from 1920s' exotic resonances to 1940s' real-world monikers.

The Technicolor production offered plenty of spectacular desert scenery. The location filming took place at the Canyon de Chelly National Monument in Arizona and near Gallup, New Mexico.

The delay in the film's release was largely due to its depiction of the French in North Africa. In December 1942, the Office of War Information's Bureau of Motion Pictures decreed that the film presented an unsympathetic image of the French and recommended either a wholesale revision or not screening the film until the war was over. Indeed, for much of the film, the Vichy government is depicted as the true France. Fontaine, the military commander in Morocco, works in collusion with a dishonest Caid who himself is conspiring with the Nazis. The situation changes, though not soon enough.

Even after the film was released, concerns remained about how the French appeared in the film. In an inter-office memo from Robert Schless to J. L. Warner dated 7 February 1944, Schless mentioned some cuts requested by the French, including the elimination of certain lines of Paul's dialogue such as 'Why doesn't France export some of its love of freedom?' and his self-reply to the question, 'And what did they get out of our civilization?,' 'Only a kick in the face.'[45] (Both comments remain in the DVD of the film released in 2014.)

Nazis in the Desert: The Musical

In this adaptation, Nazi campaigns in North Africa form the basic premise, overshadowing the romance. The film opens in Geneva in the summer of 1939, where the Germans scheme to build a railroad across the Sahara. Slave labour is being used to build the railroad, including captured Riffs and various opponents of the Vichy French. This scenario echoed a real situation in North Africa, for in the early 1940s, the Vichy government was constructing a railroad through French North Africa. Caid Yousseff, the film's fictional villain (in a menacing portrayal by Victor Francen), is a local leader who colludes with the Nazis to enslave his countrymen.

The scene shifts to Morocco, where Johnny Walsh, an American journalist working for the American Press Bureau (and drolly played by Lynne Overman), shares living accommodation with another American, Paul Bonnard (Dennis Morgan), a mild-mannered pianist and café orchestra leader. We first meet Paul while he is sitting in the bathtub intoning plenty of Riff motifs (the opening four notes of 'The Riff Song') and a version of 'One Flower Grows Alone in Your Garden' in a style imitating Islamic chant. We also learn that El Khobar has succeeded Abd-El-Krim, one of the real-life inspirations for the original 1926 *The Desert Song*, as the Riff leader, thus tying the cinematic remake to the stage original.

Paul signals his fellow Riffs by playing the Riff motif on the piano, which becomes a full-fledged instrumental rendition of 'The Riff Song' featuring the café orchestra. The Riffs hear the motif and pass it along, until a posse assembles near the Ben Nour Prison Camp, where the railroad is being built, and attacks it. The Riffs take Tarbouch, one of Youssef's deputies, as prisoner.

Margot, a singer recently arrived from Paris, makes her debut at the Benoit Concert Palace with a song expressly written for the film, 'Gay Parisienne,' an effervescent waltz with a sprightly coloratura obbligato. She follows this with the refrain of 'Romance.' Caid Youssef enters during the next song on the program, 'Fifi's Song.' He updates the suave French commander, Colonel Fontaine (played by Bruce Cabot) on the railroad's progress; they are both concerned that Tarbouch will tell El Khobar what he knows about the real reason for the railroad—a quicker pathway between Nazi Germany and South America. Johnny overhears and quickly goes to phone his paper, only to be stopped by François, the French censor, who pushes down the button on the phone and abruptly ends the call.

Fontaine wants to show Margot a local café and takes her to Au Chien Fidele (At Faithful Dog), owned by the comically eccentric Pere FanFan (played by Gene Lockhart), who constantly cools himself with an electric fan. Fontaine suspects some café owners of being Riff informants, including FanFan, and really wants to go check up on him. He tells Margot that FanFan had been a Legionnaire but 'went native' and befriended the Moroccans who come to his establishment. His café, unlike the Benoit Concert Palace, is filled with smoke (from hookahs) and features sensual dancing women. It is the physical embodiment of the Oriental Other, a stark contrast to the Eurocentricism of the Benoit Concert Palace.

Paul just happens to be playing piano at FanFan's café, and when Margot and Fontaine sit near him, he begins playing 'One Alone.' He asks Margot if she knows the song—she replies that she does, but that she has not heard it in a long time. This is another reference to the legacy of *The Desert Song*—it had been sixteen years, after all, since the show had opened on Broadway.

Paul's infuses the Riff motif into his rendition of the song, and Margot, remembering the melody of 'One Alone,' joins in. The aural and visual worlds collide here, for North African instruments appear on screen (as opposed to the Western instruments of the Benoit Concert Hall) but produce Western sounds. The Riff motif, which Paul uses to warn the Riffs of Fontaine's presence, causes the café to empty, leaving only him, Margot, and Fontaine.

Paul, disguised as El Khobar, takes Margot secretly to his Riff camp, where he reveals his dual identity to her, with 'One Alone' as underscoring. Paul sings 'The Desert Song' to his new-found love, and she joins him for the second refrain. He returns to FanFan's café, where he sings 'Long Live the Night' while accompanying himself on the piano. Johnny finds Margot at FanFan's, and Margot tells him that Paul and El Khobar are the same person.

The reporter goes to warn Paul of an impending French ambush on the Riff camp. When he finds him, he gives him his horse and surrenders to the French, carrying El Khobar's costume.

Fontaine comes to Margot's room and tells her that they've captured El Khobar and that he (Fontaine) may be transferred and promoted. He of course wants her to join him. The underscoring is telling here—a languid version of 'Romance' lets us know she is dreaming of Paul, and when Fontaine proposes marriage, she declines. The music shifts to 'One Alone' when she mentions Paul and unwittingly tells Fontaine that Paul is El Khobar.

Back at the Benoit Concert Hall, dancing girls provide a cabaret-style 'French Marching Song' featuring a solo turn for Margot. Paul talks to Fontaine about releasing Johnny, who the French still think is El Khobar. Fontaine tells Paul he knows that he is El Khobar, and Paul responds by telling Fontaine that the source of the railroad money is Berlin and the Nazis. Fontaine is genuinely surprised, and the two of them team up to expose Yousseff. They find Yousseff conferring with Germans, even speaking in German, and a fight erupts. Fontaine, realizing the Nazi machinations, becomes in effect a De Gaullist and promises to restore 'all rights and liberties to the Riff tribes.' Yousseff is killed, and in a final celebratory scene, El Khobar leads the entire cast in a refrain of the 'Riff Song.' Paul leads the horseback chorus as they leave to fight for justice, and Margot proudly waves him off.

American Propaganda

With Paul, the American, as the hero, the film definitely implies American strength and the power of just one American to effect change. Additionally, Paul and Margot emblematize a wartime couple: Paul fights for democracy and freedom while Margot loves and supports him. Through the efforts of individual Americans like Paul, the United States is shown to be assuming a vital role in curtailing the spread of the Nazi regime. In publicity materials and on the sheet music cover issued in association with the film, Morgan wears munitions sashes, an obvious military reference, while smiling broadly, proud of his wartime participation.

In order to make the film about American heroism in World War II, the romance between the principals had to be simplified. The original idea of a hero in disguise and a desert rescue fantasy were no longer appropriate. Margot learns Paul's identity relatively quickly and supports him in his efforts, including when he rides off at the end of the film and leaves her behind. The storyline shifts to a tale of defeating Nazis and away from one that kept audiences wondering when Margot will finally realize that the mild-mannered Paul (or Pierre) and El Khobar (or the Red Shadow) are one and the same person.

Cultural and Gender Constructions

El Khobar embodies Orientalism's tenet that the West constructs the Orient as needing the West to save it from itself. The Moroccans cannot deal with Yousseff themselves; they require Western intervention in the person of Paul/El Khobar. It is a Westerner, precisely an American, who leads the attack on Yousseff's palace, killing the Caid, along with several Nazis.

Furthermore, the film presents a stereotype of Arab leaders as villainous and Arabs in general as inferior to the French. The fundamentally benign Morocco of the original has become vilified. A single enemy is created in Yousseff, whereas no single villain exists in the 1926 original; tyranny and oppression are the enemies. Yousseff exploits his own people and is a Nazi sympathizer.

Knowing the film was set in the immediate past, Warner Bros. was concerned about making the film as authentic as possible. Jamiel Hassan was hired to perform Arabic chants,[46] and a research record in the WBA lists purchases that include maps, pictures, guides to pronunciation, the February 1942 issue of *Free World* with an article on Morocco, and various props, including a Moroccan four-wheeled cart.[47]

Along with a near-documentary desire for authenticity, the Colonial Gaze of the original is magnified. El Khobar, champion of the Riffs, calls his followers 'savages about their freedom.'[48] A French bartender despairingly remarks, in another scene, 'It's a shame these Muhammadans don't drink.'[49] The desire for realism makes these remarks especially striking.

Not incidentally, this film version of *The Desert Song*, which was completed in 1942, was not granted a general export licence until 1944. Even then it carried a provision not allowing sale in countries with significant Arab or Muslim populations, according to studio records because it could be interpreted as glorifying a revolt.[50] Its reductionist depictions of Moroccans as either evil or weak and in desperate need of external aid could have been another factor.

European cultural attitudes also appear in how the characters describe the music they are experiencing. Margot describes the title song as 'weird music,' reflecting her Eurocentric worldview. Paul chants the pentatonic opening of the verse ('My desert is waiting'), and Margot comments that it is a 'strange chant,' to which Paul replies that it is an 'old Toric love song.' When he reaches the tonal refrain ('Blue heaven'), aural tension is released with the arrival of the major mode. Margot takes over the second refrain, something she is capable of doing since the refrain is tonal, European-style music.

In addition to cultural difference, sexualized Otherness also appears in this version of *The Desert Song*. Sylvia Opert, who played Azuri, performed what one reviewer called 'a hedonistic native dance'[51]; another critic noted that 'a sleekly provocative dancer, Sylvia Opert, puts on quite a one-girl show.'[52]

The sensual lure of the desert is foregrounded in Opert's performances.

Whereas Bennie was coded as gay in the 1929 version, here it is the French censor, François (played by the German actor Curt Bois), whose performance engenders an effete quality. He tells Johnny, the American reporter and really the only person in the film with whom he interacts, that he feels unloved, and also informs him about an impending attack in order to gain his friendship. He is a definite outsider and his dress, mannerisms, and speech place him squarely against the macho heroics of the other male characters, including Johnny. He is the only French character who actually speaks with a non-American accent in the film, something that emphasizes his Otherness. During the scenes featuring Johnnie and François, 'It' plays in the underscoring, just as it did for those with Bennie in the 1929 film. Bennie's gay coding in 1929 connected to François's in the 1943 adaptation through this common musical number.

Music of the Cabaret and the Desert

The 1943 release of *The Desert Song* includes music from the original stage work as well as new songs in a Broadway style and diegetic music that evokes a sense of Moroccan Other. Since the film was envisioned as wartime propaganda, dramatic realism was of greater importance than in a fundamentally escapist work. Hence, a diegetic use of music, when music is performed or heard on screen, becomes paramount in creating a sense of narrative believability.

Six songs from the original stage version appear in the film: 'The Riff Song,'[53] 'One Flower Grows Alone in Your Garden,' 'Romance,' 'One Alone,' 'The Desert Song,' and the 'French Military Marching Song.' The film's producer, Robert Buckner, wanted to use what he considered the musical's three principal songs—'The Riff Song,' 'The Desert Song,' and 'One Alone'—and condense others.[54]

Three new numbers were created for the film, all of which are performed in diegetic contexts: 'Gay Parisienne' (music by Serge Walter, lyrics by Jack Scholl), 'Fifi's Song' (music by Romberg, lyrics by Jack Scholl), and 'Long Live the Night' (music by Romberg, lyrics by Mario Silva and Jack Scholl). 'Gay Parisienne' introduces the film's audience to the singing voice of Irene Manning, and Buckner wanted a new song for this moment.[55] 'Fifi's Song,' a feature for a male vocalist that also appears in the first Benoit Concert Hall cabaret sequence, has its musical source in 'Then You Will Know,' a duet for Margot and Pierre from the original stage operetta. In the film, with new lyrics about what a man will do if woman after woman refuses him, it becomes a Maurice Chevalier-style feature for a male singer. Leo F. Forbstein, the film's music director, wanted to use a Chevalier-style song at this point in the film, but they were all under copyright.[56] So, he returned to the 1926 *Desert Song* and chose a song that was not going to appear in the film. 'Long Live the Night' is a 1940s croon-style ballad that Paul sings at FanFan's café. The musical source for the refrain comes from the verse of 'The Desert Song' ('Why waste your time in vain romancing'). Mario Silva composed a new verse for the fetching song.

In addition to the songs and the essential choral renditions of 'The Riff Song,' other music appeared as underscoring, mostly in medleys alongside snippets of Romberg's music. Songs in the public domain such as the 'Marseillaise' and 'Die Wacht am Rhein' (The Watchman on the Rhein), a German patriotic song, provided nation-specific references (the 'Marseillaise' representing the Free French and 'Die Wacht' signifying the Nazis). Film composer Heinz Roemheld (who won an academy award for *Yankee Doodle Dandy*) provided atmospheric music for various scenes in the film, for which Ray Heindorf crafted arrangements.[57]

In addition to these European soundscapes, Warner Bros. staff composer Dave Bonnesar created numbers that provide diegetic aural stimuli to evoke the Moroccan setting: 'Mal El Sham' (Heights of Damascus), 'Asmar El Loon' (You're dark complected [sic]), and 'Howid Men Hina (Stop here),' and 'Rhana Meshwar' (We took a trip).[58] These feature largely in outdoor scenes, where they are played by street musicians on Arab-sounding instruments and are in stark contrast to the European musical atmospheres created by Romberg and Roemheld.

By including these allusions to actual non-Western music, Romberg's musical handling of cultural difference in songs such as 'One Flower Grows Alone in Your Garden,' as sung by Paul in his bathtub, demonstrates a musical hybridity. Instead of using major and minor to differentiate between European and non-European attitudes, melodic practices such as gapped scales and vocal timbre now come into play. Paul, in *how* he sings at the beginning of the film, demonstrates not just his awareness of various musical cultures (he is a musician, after all) but also his ability to navigate between cultures through musical means.

In order to allow for the diegetic performances, the romantic leads have both become musicians. Margot is a singer and Paul is a pianist and orchestra leader. Margot performs at Benoit's Concert Palace, a cabaret for the French in Morocco. Paul not only works as an orchestra leader and pianist at Benoit's but also plays piano at FanFan's Café.

'The Desert Song' occupies a liminal place in this diegetic/ nondiegetic realm. Paul and Margot sing the duet in the Riff camp, far from a concert hall or café. No orchestra is seen or heard on screen. The characters, though, describe the music, so they must be hearing it. (Margot calls it 'weird music' and Paul informs her that it is 'an old Toric love song.')

Music also functions as a dramatic device in this *Desert Song*. The Riff motif becomes a secret code for the Riff bands; its local origins are never explicitly stated but strongly implied. Its distinctive character of Otherness (set in a minor key, the Riff motif is a descending third, an ascending third, and a minor second) is familiar enough to audiences familiar with 'The Riff Song' to recognize it and associate it with the non-European Riffs. El Khobar and others sound the signal early in the film to rally the Riffs, and Paul infuses it into his rendition of 'One Alone' as a warning to the Riffs at FanFan's Café.

Reality versus Romance?

The World War II version of *The Desert Song* offers some breathtaking visual scenes and some fine musical performances. However, the attempts at dramatic realism put the film's story increasingly at odds with the escapist sentimentality of the musical numbers. While this dichotomy poses a challenge for any rendering of *The Desert Song*, as noted in the critical response to the 1929 version, it is especially evident in this adaptation. The film's attempts at authenticity through diegetic musical performance and the inclusion of non-European sounds in some ways only accentuate the inherent artifice of the musical theatre medium.

Critical response was mixed, but perhaps the most intense disfavour for the film came from fans. When Warner Bros. announced in the early 1950s that it was planning to remake *The Desert Song*, fans wrote directly to the studio to express their disdain at the previous version and their hopes for the new one. One wrote, 'What a mess the Dennis Morgan film a few years ago <u>was</u>—it should have been called "The Nazis in North Africa"—it was terrible to a lover of the superb "Desert

Song," its story & its music.'[59] Another expressed a similar sentiment: 'The one with Dennis Morgan—that should be forgotten—Irene Manning was awful—and the story was too terrible for words.'[60] For the third Warner Bros. adaptation, even less of the score would make it to the screen, and the plot would again be changed.

1953: A TECHNICOLOR FANTASY

The third full-length film adaptation of *The Desert Song*, starring Gordon MacRae and Kathryn Grayson, melds elements of the stage original with remnants of the 1943 release. Bruce Humberstone directed the adaptation, with Rudi Fehr as producer and Ray Heindorf as music director.[61] The setting is again 1920s French Morocco, and Margot does not realize the dual identity of her lover until the final scene. Yousseff is again the antagonist, though now he is a sheik. A gentler, kinder El Khobar is now a Robin Hood figure, for he and his Riff followers take only what Yousseff and his crew have stolen from them. Inter-Arab conflict thus becomes central to the plot of this *Desert Song*. Yousseff is a duplicitous villain, for he is behind a master plan to simultaneously starve villagers, garner further French support, and subsequently overthrow French rule.

Viva la France!

In this Cold War version of the tale, the French are portrayed as trustworthy while the Moroccans, especially the followers of Sheik Yousseff, ignite suspicion. Indeed, El Khobar and the Riffs never fight the French in this version; their sole adversary is the corrupt Sheik. The French want to secure peace with all peoples in Morocco. This radical transformation comes, according to cultural historian John Maier, because the United States wanted to slow down Moroccan independence movements since they could jeopardize US interests in the Mediterranean world, not only because of the potential loss of North Atlantic Treaty Organization (NATO) bases in Morocco but also because of the threat of a communist takeover.[62] The United States was on solid diplomatic terms with France, and this film reflects the close relationship between the two countries.

Charles Grayson crafted the revised plot from which Roland Kibbee developed the screenplay. The romantic leads are now Paul Bonnard (MacRae), an anthropology professor at the University of Paris, and Margot Birabeau (Grayson), the daughter of the French governing general. (Margot's surname in the film is that of Pierre in the stage original.) Margot, a coy student, is supposed to study with Professor Bonnard, but she shows absolutely no interest in doing so, for she would much rather flirt with Captain Claude Fontaine (Steve Cochran) and fantasize about the mysterious El Khobar. Bonnard is dedicated to the Riffs, knows the Qur'an, plays and sings traditional chants, and even provides them with Western medicines. The character of Benjamin Kidd (Dick Wesson) returns as the American newspaperman sent to cover the story of El Khobar. As in the 1943 version, his roommate is the mild-mannered Paul.

Fontaine informs General Birabeau (Ray Collins) that he wants to arm Yousseff (Raymond Massey) to help him get rid of the Riffs. Paul hears this and protests, remarking that the Riffs take only what has been taken from them. When Mindar, a traitorous Riff, wants to steal weapons and later strike Yousseff's palace, El Khobar dissuades him. Mindar eventually attacks El Khobar and is defeated. According to Riff law, Mindar must be bound and banished to the desert to die. El Khobar goes to the desert and rescues Mindar, shows him mercy, gives him passage to Tunis, and tells him to 'leave his hatred behind.'

Azuri (Allyn McLerie), a Riff dancer who is in love with El Khobar, watches this act of clemency.

Meanwhile, Yousseff has invited General Birabeau, Margot, and Claude to his palace, which provides a plot point for plenty of Orientalist dancing, including a solo number for Azuri. Yousseff plans to convince the French to give him weapons by having his own men dress as Riffs and attack the palace. Paul arrives and hears Margot humming 'One Flower Grows Alone in Your Garden' in a flower garden, to which he responds, as El Khobar, with 'One Alone.' El Khobar tells Margot he has come to prove that Yousseff is the enemy. She immediately tells Claude that El Khobar is in the garden, and when she returns, El Khobar whisks her off to the desert, where he shows her a village that Yousseff has burned to the ground. In a Riff compound, a group of musicians begins to play music, setting up the title song. Paul returns to Yousseff's palace to tell the General that Margot is unharmed and that the Riffs want to discuss peace. Benji, meanwhile, tries to convince the French that he saw a stockpile of weapons in the palace and follows Paul and the General to the Riff village.

When they arrive, the village is deserted. Hassan, a Riff left to die, tells Paul that Yousseff's men took 'the girl,' meaning Margot. Paul dons El Khobar's clothing, which Benji sees and thus learns of his secret identity. As El Khobar leaves the village, the French pursue him. El Khobar falls off his horse, and when the French unmask the mysterious man, they find Benji, who feigns the opening of 'The Riff Song.'

Benji leads the Riffs into Yousseff's palace through a secret entrance as Margot sings 'Long Live the Night,' which she calls her favourite song, to Yousseff. She keeps telling him that there's more to the song in order to buy time for the Riff invaders.[63] A note in the typescript musical synopsis suggests that Margot should act like Scheherezade in 1,001 Nights in the continual prolongation of her performance.[64]

After Yousseff is impaled, the truth about his stolen guns and devious plans are revealed. Paul enters with El Khobar's costume and tells the assembled group that the desert hero has died, to which the General replies that they owe El Khobar thanks and an apology. Margot is sad at the news and confesses, 'I loved him.' As in the original, Paul begins singing 'One Alone' and Margot recognizes his voice as that of El Khobar. A final reprise of 'The Riff Song' accompanies Paul, Margot, and the Riffs as they ride across the desert.

Orientalist Fantasies

As in the 1943 release, the Moroccans are portrayed here as inept and in need of European (e.g., French) rescue from themselves. Here, though, no outside threat from either the French or the Nazis exists—Yousseff injures his own people for his own gain. The French want to facilitate peace, despite Yousseff.

Attitudes towards non-European music are softened when compared with the 1943 version. Dave Bonnesar's ethnic-evoking musical sequences are backgrounded as underscoring, and Paul describes the pentatonic section of the verse of 'The Desert Song' ('My desert is waiting') as a 'Moorish folk chant.' Margot calls it 'beautiful,' and Paul elaborates, 'primitive and beautiful.' It is no longer 'weird,' as Margot described it in the 1943 version, but now 'primitive.' Its timelessness, like that of the desert, is still implied as part of the region's underdevelopment, according to an Orientalist gaze.

Authenticity

The creators of this adaptation did extensive research to evoke a sense of visual and, to a degree, aural authenticity. They requested a list of French marching commands, order arms, and other military calls, and Max Steiner, who was preparing musical underscoring, requested a book that included authentic French bugle calls.[65] The studio also sought images of Foreign Legion uniforms, information on the Riffs in the 1920s, and examples of Moroccan pottery, musical instruments, and rugs. Not knowing where to locate Arab instruments that would appear on-screen, the studio issued a request via a press release:

> Anybody got a gunibry? Or a zummarah? Or even a kuitra or an arghool?

Warner Bros.' music department is on the prowl for these Arabian musical instruments for scenes in 'The Desert Song,' and so far all they've been able to come up with is a pair of darboukas, and one old tamboura.

The gunibry is a kind of Moroccan drum, crudely constructed of a half a pumpkin covered with a sheepskin and strung with cat gut and twanged with a split quill. A kuitra comes from Tunisia and it's made with a tortoise shell, cat gut and played with a small plectrum. The tamboura is like a tambourine, only it's played with a vulture's feather. The others are reed instruments.[66]

The studio succeeded in its search, for several of these instruments appear in the film.[67]

Songs in the Desert

Only five songs from the original stage version appear in this version (one less than in 1942): 'The Riff Song,'[68] 'Romance,' 'The Desert Song,' 'One Flower Grows Alone in Your Garden,' and 'One Alone.' Two songs from the 1943 film were reprised: 'Gay Parisienne' and 'Long Live the Night.' Furthermore, the Riff motif serves the same function as an aural identifier as it did in the previous adaptation, though its inclusion was a point of contention during the film's development.[69]

The overtly diegetic treatment of most of the songs in the 1942 adaptation gives way here to nondiegetic appearances. The club and café atmospheres as venues for musical performance are no longer present. For example, Margot now sings 'Gay Parisienne' as she enters the French compound. No orchestra is in sight, though the soldiers accompany her as a male chorus.

The 'Eastern and Western Love' sequence from the original is reworked to offer a gendered approach to romance. Margot sings 'One Flower Grows Alone in Your Garden' as she wanders in a flower garden, interpreting the lyric as wanting to collect as many men as possible and not limiting herself to just one. El Khobar responds with 'One Alone'—he is the one and only man who can satisfy her.

Max Steiner created the cues that appear as underscoring. These are very short, ranging anywhere from five to fifty-five seconds. Steiner also arranged the 'Kooch Dance' for Azuri's (Allyn McLerie) performance at Yousseff's palace. His highly evocative orchestration calls for three balalaikas, two guitars, harp, piano, mandola (mandolin piano), celesta, and harp. Percussion instruments include finger cymbals, tam tam, small gong, timpani, and vibraphone.[70] This was a lavish production, and the conjuring of Orientalism in this scene returns to the nineteenth-century idea of splendid exoticism and a celebration of the female body.

El Khobar = Kal-El?

When this version of *The Desert Song* appeared, Superman was part of mainstream popular culture. With the shared story of a mild-mannered man's secret identity and the woman who loves him not realizing that the hero after whom she lusts and the man who pines for her are the same person, it's no surprise that some references to the tale exist in the film.

Coincidentally, Superman's Krypton name, Kal-El, is a shortened inversion of El Khobar. Almost not coincidentally, though, is the fact that Professor Paul Bonnard wears black-framed glasses, just like Clark Kent in Superman. When the film appeared, *Adventures of Superman* (1952–58) was showing on television. In one scene early in the film, Gordon MacRae looks like a bespectacled George Reeves as Clark Kent, and Kathryn Grayson's hair is styled in the same way as Noel Neill's as Lois Lane.[71] Paul even removes his glasses to see if Margot recognizes him as El Khobar; she does not. El Khobar, like Kal-El, is a man of peace who wants to help those who in need. Both oppose tyranny and genuinely care about the people they serve.

THE 1955 TELEVISION VERSION

On 7 May 1955 NBC broadcast a live eighty-eight-minute adaptation of the operetta with Nelson Eddy and Gale Sherwood as the romantic leads. The noted Hollywood baritone was thus given a chance to perform Romberg's famed score in a staged context. Metropolitan opera bass Salvatore Baccalone played Ali Ben Ali, offering a highly spiritual rendition of 'Let Love Go' in the 'Eastern and Western Love' sequence. William Friedberg, Neil Simon, and Will Glickman prepared the teleplay, which Max Liebman produced and directed. Charles Sanford and His Orchestra provided the orchestral underpinning. The plot is necessarily trimmed, though Romberg's music generally appears in its original contexts. The romantic tale is kept, while the comic subplot with Benny and Susan is completely excised—their characters do not even appear. We no longer have specific villains, tyranny and oppression are the forces to be defeated, as in the original.

Some plot elements were modified for the television version. For example, although set in 1925, the French want to establish a colony in Morocco, which historically they already had. Pierre likes to drink cognac, as opposed to picking wildflowers.

Several musical changes are also evident. Act 1 concludes with a new dream ballet that recalls the dream ballet that ends act 1 of *Oklahoma!* After Margot fantasizes about the Red Shadow (whose name returns to the original in this version) and sings a reprise of 'Romance,' the masked hero appears and intones a refrain of 'The Desert Song.' Dancers then take over from the singing stars. Rod Alexander's choreography is reminiscent of Agnes de Mille's in *Oklahoma!*, with parallel graceful moves and multiple lifts. At the end, the Red Shadow carries Margot off to the desert, and she doesn't resist.

In 'The Sabre Song,' Margot's solo expression of her love for the Red Shadow, the song begins in her mind, with extra reverb added to the sound. She doesn't move her lips until late in the song, when she expresses what she had previously only been thinking. This is something that could be accomplished on television through close-up shots and proved to be effective for the soliloquy.

Perhaps most striking, though, is the final duet, where Pierre and Margot sing 'The Desert Song' and not 'One Alone.' The production ends with the dreamy title song. During the end titles, though, the chorus provides a reprise of the refrain of 'One Alone.'

SHIFTING SAND

Orientalism as a cultural construct shifts over time, like sand in the desert. When it comes to *The Desert Song,* various factors affect these changes, ranging from real-world politics to film aesthetics. In the 1926 stage version and the 1929 film, the Moroccans are relatively benign, and the desert background is the canvas for a rescue fantasy with a disguised hero akin to *The Sheik*. In the 1942 and 1953 adaptations, though, the Moroccans are vilified and either collude with the Nazis or mistreat each other. The main Moroccan leader in both versions, Yousseff, is dishonest and oppresses his own people. The television version of 1955 returns largely to the original concept, coming full circle back to a tale of romance.

These adaptations also interrogate the conflation of operetta, a genre steeped in escapism and nostalgia, with contemporary real-world issues. The two perspectives seem to run counter to each other, even with cinematic practical solutions that include diegetic musical performances and having the characters themselves comment on the music they experience. Plots may change, contexts may shift, but what remains at the heart of any adaptation of *The Desert Song* are Romberg and Hammerstein's evocative and truly memorable songs. They are the sole reason, after all, that any of the adaptations were made.

NOTES

1. John Maier, *Desert Songs: Western Images of Morocco and Moroccan Images of the West* (Albany: State University of New York Press, 1996), 2.
2. For more on *The Desert Song*, see the author's 'Romance and Exoticism in North Africa: *The Desert Song*,' chap. 6, in *Sigmund Romberg* (New Haven, CT: Yale University Press, 2007), 155–180.
3. Robert Halliday (1891–1975) and Vivienne Segal (1897–1992) led the original cast. Halliday was a noted operetta baritone who also created the role of Robert Misson in Romberg and Hammerstein's *The New Moon* (1928). Segal was regarded as among the finest musical theatre singers of her generation. She made her Broadway debut in 1915 in Romberg's *The Blue Paradise* and later achieved fame as Vera Simpson in Rodgers and Hart's *Pal Joey* (1940) and as Morgan le Fay in the 1943 revival of the same team's *A Connecticut*

Yankee, where she introduced the morbidly delicious ballad 'To Keep My Love Alive.'

4. Harbach, Hammerstein, and Mandel, *The Desert Song* (London: Chappell, 1927), 23.

5. Edward W. Said, *Orientalism* (New York: Random House, 1978).

6. Alan Jenkins, *The Twenties* (New York: Universe Books, 1974), 205.

7. *The Desert Song*, 37.

8. *The Desert Song*, 48.

9. 'More Operetta: American Style, African Setting,' *Boston Transcript*, 9 November 1926.

10. Lord Chamberlain's Plays Correspondence Files, *The Desert Song*, Manuscripts Department, British Library, LC Plays 1927/4.

11. Other notable films in the genre include *Sahara Love* (1926), *The Son of the Sheik* (1926), *One Stolen Night* (1929), *Desert Nights* (1929), and *Morocco* (1930).

12. Valentino died of complications following surgery for a perforated ulcer. His particular type of ulcer became known as 'Valentino's syndrome.'

13. Bell's books included *The Desert and the Sown* (1907) and *Amurath to Amurath* (1911).

14. Jack G. Shaheen, *Reel Bad Arabs: How Hollywood Vilifies a People* (Brooklyn, NY: Olive Branch Press, 2001), 168.

15. Sigmund Romberg, 'A Peep into the Workshop of a Composer,' *Theatre Magazine* 48, no. 6 (December 1928): 27.

16. Ella Shohat, 'Gender and Culture of Empire: Toward a Feminist Ethnography of the Cinema,' in *Visions of the East: Orientalism in Film* (New Brunswick, NJ: Rutgers University Press, 1997), 39.

17. Memo from Philip B. Wattenberg to Harold Brekowitz, 22 March 1956, *The Desert Song* (1929), Warner Bros. Archive (hereafter WBA).

18. The music for the nondialogue version was recorded at the Vitaphone Studios in Brooklyn in early November 1929, well after the release of the dialogue version. It included not only Romberg's music but also excerpts of atmospheric works from other composers, such as John Ansell's 'The Grand Visier' and H. E. Haines's 'An Eastern Romance.'

19. Richard Barrios, *A Song in the Dark: The Birth of the Musical Film*, 2nd ed. (New York: Oxford University Press, 2010), 78. The

music was recorded at Warner Bros. in Hollywood on 13, 14, 20, and 21 March 1929. ('Notification of Intention to Use Musical Material,' *The Desert Song* [1929], WBA.)

20. Uncited document, *The Desert Song* (1929), WBA.
21. Barrios, *A Song in the Dark*, 78.
22. Typed letter, S. M. Green, London, to E. H. Murphy, Hollywood, 13 October 1931, *The Desert Song* (1929), WBA.
23. My thanks to Alastair Wright for pointing out this characterization.
24. Barrios, *A Song in the Dark*, 87.
25. Harry Evans, New York Life: Movies, 'The Desert Song,' *Life*, 24 May 1929, 23.
26. 'The Desert Song (Musical-Dialog),' *Variety*, 10 April 1929.
27. For more on film versions of *The New Moon*, see William Everett, 'Film Versions of Romberg's *The New Moon*: From New Orleans to Russia and Back Again,' in *Music, American Made: Essays in Honor of John Graziano*, ed. John Koegel (Sterling Heights, MI: Harmonie Park Press, 2011), 479–496.
28. The song is titled 'One Flower in Your Garden' on the music lists for *The Red Shadow* in the WBA.
29. Technicolor agreement, 25 March 1936, *The Desert Song*, WBA.
30. 'Miller's Script with Lord's Changes,' 7 July 1936, *The Desert Song*, WBA.
31. Romberg was a prominent radio personality in the 1930s, either hosting his own programs or appearing as a guest on others.
32. The lyrics for song are published in Amy Asch, ed., *The Complete Lyrics of Oscar Hammerstein II* (New York: Knopf, 2008), 402.
33. Note dated 16 April 1937, *The Desert Song*, WBA.
34. Inter-office communication from R. J. Obringer, 24 August 1936, *The Desert Song*, WBA.
35. *The Desert Song* screenplay, 20 July 1938, WBA.
36. Robert Buckner and Charles Grayson, 'A New Cure for "The Desert Song"'/'THE DESERT SONG: Presentation of a New Approach' (both titles appear on the document, the first on the title page and the second on first page of prose), 26 August 1941, 1, WBA.
37. Buckner and Grayson, 'A New Cure,' 1.
38. Buckner and Grayson, 'A New Cure,' 5.
39. Buckner and Grayson, 'A New Cure,' 4.

40. '"The Desert Song," Suggestion for a New Treatment,' folder 1846B, WBA, 2–3.
41. '"The Desert Song," Suggestion for a New Treatment,' 2–3.
42. '"The Desert Song," Suggestion for a New Treatment,' 2–3.
43. For more on World War II–era home front Hollywood musicals, see Jennifer R. Jenkins, '"Say It with Firecrackers": Defining the "War Musical" of the 1940s,' *American Music* 19, no. 3 (2001): 315–339.
44. This version of *The Desert Song* was not the only instance of a preexisting musical work being revised to reflect contemporary wartime America. *Carmen Jones*, Oscar Hammerstein II's revision of Georges Bizet's *Carmen*, opened on 2 December 1943 at the Broadway Theatre. A film version appeared in 1954.
45. Inter-office memo from Robert Schless to J. L. Warner, 7 February 1944, *The Desert Song* (1943), WBA.
46. Receipts for $25 on 23 May 1942 and $25 on 5 June 1942 are in the materials for *The Desert Song* (1942), WBA.
47. Research record, *The Desert Song* (1942), WBA.
48. Shaheen, *Reel Bad Arabs*, 168.
49. Shaheen, *Reel Bad Arabs*, 168.
50. Letter from Watterson R. Rothacker, Chairman, Office of Censorship, Los Angeles Board of Review, to Steve Trilling, 12 August 1944, *The Desert Song* (1942), WBA.
51. L.E.R., '"Desert Song" Colorful Melodrama,' *Hollywood Citizen-News*, 24 January 1944.
52. Bosley Crowther, 'The Screen: "The Desert Song," Modernized Version of the Old Operetta, with Dennis Morgan, Irene Manning, Opens at Hollywood,' *New York Times*, 18 December 1923.
53. Jack Scholl revised the lyrics to refer to El Khobar and not the Red Shadow.
54. Letter from R. J. Obringer to Morris Ebenstein, 7 May 1942, *The Desert Song* (1942), correspondence file, WBA.
55. Letter from R. J. Obringer to Morris Ebenstein, 16 May 1942, *The Desert Song* (1942), correspondence file, WBA.
56. Letter from Victor Blau to Leo Forbstein, 20 May 1942, *The Desert Song* (1942), WBA.
57. 'Music for Underscoring,' box 253, Musical scores, *The Desert Song* (1942), WBA.

58. The translations appear on the music parts in the WBA.

59. Wesley Chase, letter to Warner Bros., 6 August 1951, *The Desert Song* (1953), WBA.

60. Mrs Laban T. Johnston, letter to Warner Bros., 8 August 1951, *The Desert Song* (1953), WBA.

61. Heindorf provided the song arrangements for the numbers featuring Kathryn Grayson and Gordon MacRae, while Norman Luboff prepared the vocal arrangements. Murray Cutter was the credited orchestrator. Original orchestral scores and parts are extant at the WBA.

62. Maier, *Desert Songs*, 25.

63. Because of the increased length of the song due to its dramatic purpose, Sammy Cahn wrote lyrics for an additional refrain of 'Long Live the Night' (Contract, 9 August 1952, *The Desert Song* [1953], WBA).

64. Musical breakdown, 3 April 1952, based on script of 23 February 1952, *The Desert Song* (1953), WBA.

65. Research request list, *The Desert Song* (1953), WBA.

66. Carl Combs, Press release HO-91251, *The Desert Song* (1953), WBA.

67. Production notes for press releases, *The Desert Song* (1953), WBA.

68. The revised lyrics for the 1942 version that refer to El Khobar were reused here.

69. Rudi Fehr felt its use was inconsistent, first to have the Riffs hide and later to call El Khobar. (Rudi Fehr, memo to Steve Trilling, 29 February 1952, *The Desert Song* [1953], WBA.) Roland Kibbee, though, thought it was necessary to introduce the motif before it is used to summon El Khobar. (Roland Kibbee, memo to Rudi Fehr and Bruce Humberstone, 21 February 1952, *The Desert Song* [1953], WBA.)

70. Scores and sketches, music materials, reel 9, part 2, *The Desert Song* (1953), WBA.

71. Neill joined the cast in the second season, taking over the role of Lois Lane from Phyllis Coates.

7

'You Will Know That She is Our Annie'

Comparing Three Adaptations of a Broadway Classic

IAN SAPIRO

■ □ ■

Please take good care of our little darling. Her name is Annie. She was born on October 28th. We will be back to get her soon. We have left half of a silver locket around her neck and kept the other half so that when we come back for her you will know that she's our baby.[1]

THUS READS ANNIE'S NOTE, LEFT with her on the steps of New York's Municipal Orphanage by her parents in the stage musical *Annie*. The show, which opened on Broadway in April 1977 and transferred to London's West End around a year later, was written by Thomas Meehan with music by Charles Strouse and lyrics by Martin Charnin. Columbia Pictures produced a film version in 1982 featuring additional songs by Strouse and Charnin, and their music is also used exclusively in Disney's 1999 television movie adaptation. By contrast, while Will Gluck's 2014 film of *Annie* includes modifications of several of Strouse and Charnin's numbers, this is the only one of the adaptations that includes songs not written by the show's original composer and lyricist.[2]

This chapter focuses primarily on the relationships between the stage musical and these three adaptations but also considers intertextual connections between the different screen versions of *Annie*. The first part of the chapter considers some of the issues that arise with the creation of multiple remakes, a phenomenon particularly prevalent with films, though more rarely with screen musicals. The critical perspectives that frame the analysis of these adaptations are outlined, followed by a broad overview of each movie and consideration of their approaches to the show's underlying narrative. The final and most substantial part of the chapter is devoted to the musical aspects of the films, and explores in detail matters relating to the pictures' musical profiles and the various scores' narrative agency, coherence, and sound. Importantly, although the chapter includes criticism of each screen version there is no intention to demonstrate that any adaptation is 'better' or 'worse' than any other; rather, the aim is to offer thoughts on how each picture might be better understood and interpreted, and how 'our Annie' might therefore be identified within the stage show's three screen 'children.'[3]

FRAMING THE ADAPTATIONS

Stage musicals have been adapted for the screen since the earliest years of sound film, but in the vast majority of cases when a musical has made this transition it has done so only once. Indeed, there very few shows for which two screen-musical adaptations exist—*Anything Goes*; *Bye Bye Birdie*; *Girl Crazy*; *Gypsy*; *The King and I*; *The Music Man*; *No, No, Nanette*; *Showboat*; and *South Pacific*—and *Annie* is particularly rare in being transferred three times.[4] This status as a thrice-adapted musical raises questions as to precisely what has driven producers and directors to return to this show. As Linda Hutcheon notes, stage-to-screen adaptation has 'an obvious financial appeal,' especially given that 'a successful Broadway play will be seen by 1 to 8 million people; but a movie or television adaptation will find an audience of many millions more.'[5] However, while commercial gain is doubtless almost always a significant factor in the decision to produce a film version of a musical, as Miguel Mera observes, 'The most prevalent error is that many studies simply view the reinvented text as parasitical—cashing-in on the success of the source—as if this is the only reason that re-invention occurs. By taking this stance the re-invented text can only ever be found wanting.'[6] Indeed, the contrasts between the three screen *Annies*—which include aspects of narrative structure, music, characters and characterization, casting, setting, politics, and technology—indicate that each set of filmmakers considered their product to have a different relationship with its source(s).

Robert Stam applies Gérard Genette's concept of hypertextuality to film adaptation, arguing that 'filmic adaptations are hypertexts derived from pre-existing hypotexts,'[7] while Thomas Leitch suggests that filmic remakes of other films establish a 'triangular relationship among themselves, the original film they remake, and the property on which both films are based.'[8] Not only does the presence of the third screen *Annie* render Leitch's two-dimensional triangle into a three-dimensional tetrahedron in which direct relationships exist between four versions of the show, but both the original musical and the first film draw on the cartoon strip *Little Orphan Annie*. The resulting relational diagram shown in Figure 7.1 therefore also features a spur connecting these two versions to the original source. Indeed, as Stam notes, 'The diverse prior adaptations of a [text] can come to form a larger, cumulative

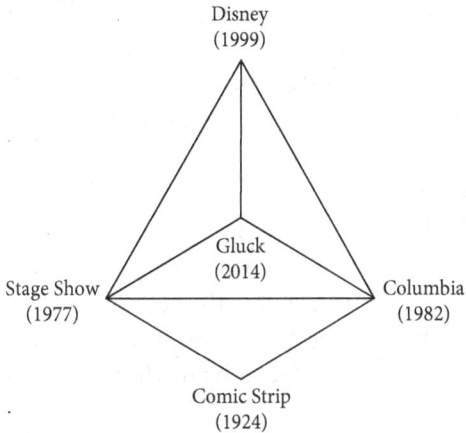

FIGURE 7.1 Tetrahedral relationship between the stage show and its three filmic adaptations, with an additional spur to the Little Orphan Annie comic strip

hypotext available to the filmmaker,'[9] a perspective with which Christine Geraghty concurs, observing that in addition to links with its primary source, 'an adaptation might also draw on memories, understandings, and associations with other versions of the original.'[10] As these views indicate, it is important to consider the possible and potential influence of the Columbia film on the Disney remake, and of both these iterations on the 2014 film within this investigation.[11]

In his consideration of remade films, 'Invention/Re-invention,' Miguel Mera acknowledges the idea of hypertextuality, but opts instead 'to use the term re-invention because it suggests a continuing sense of exploration and discovery.'[12] A further advantage of this solution to the terminological quagmire inherent in discussions of adaptations is that reinvention does not have its origins in literary theory, as is the case for many alternative terms.[13] Additionally, while there is an implication that an 'adaptation' is based heavily on and therefore might be constrained by one or more source texts, the same is not necessarily true of a 'reinvention,' this latter term suggesting an increased level of creativity in the making of the new work that is particularly useful when considering films based on other sources. Indeed, although a significant amount of criticism received by adaptations (and filmic adaptations in particular) stems from the idea of fidelity to the original text, Cartmell and Whelehan suggest that 'film reviewers today are often unconcerned as to whether a film adaptation is "faithful" [since] it is the additions, not the deletions to the source that are largely responsible for an adaptation's box-office and critical success,'[14] lending further support to the idea of reinvention.

Changes to the plot are common when stories are adapted from one medium to another, not least because the nature of, for instance, the screen, is quite different to that of the stage, and there are some things that can be achieved or will work more successfully in one format than another. In the case of *these* films, it should also be considered that the Disney version is a made-for-*television* movie, whereas the other two are cinematic productions. Narrative changes resulting from a stage-to-screen transfer will often lead to alterations to the music, causing yet more divergence from the source, but this does not necessarily mean that the changes are inappropriate or do not work, nor that the adapted version is in any way a lesser work than the original. Importantly, therefore, while this investigation considers the ways in which each screen iteration has changed (literally reinvented) the stage show of *Annie*, the critical evaluations must not be reduced to a simple question of 'fidelity.' In keeping with this perspective, and as outlined at the start of this chapter, the intention is to 'explore' (to use Mera's term) the reinventions of *Annie* rather than to pass judgement on their respective levels of commercial, cultural, or musical merit.

ANNIE, BORN 1977, 1982, 1999, AND 2014

Acclaimed by Gerald Bordman as the 'the season's biggest hit' and awarded the somewhat dubious distinction by Thomas Hischak of being 'the most successful musical ever made from a comic strip,' the stage show of *Annie* collected the 1977 Tony Award for Best Musical and ran for 2,377 performances in its initial Broadway run.[15] The show transferred to London in 1978 where its run, while not as extensive, lasted three and a half years, and although it closed before its Broadway counterpart, Columbia's film of the show was already in production by that time. Writing in 1985, just three years after the release of this first filmic reinvention, Thomas G. Aylesworth comments that while the stage musical 'was a warm, intimate, pleasant show, with songs to match,' Columbia's film 'missed the point of intimacy and was turned into an overblown production by director John Huston, who was filming his first musical.'[16] Aylesworth suggests the film had a budget in excess of $40 million, Hischak putting the figure at $52 million, and labelling the production 'one of the most expensive flops in the history of Columbia Pictures.'[17]

The film retains most of the main elements of the stage show's plot, but Carol Sobieski's screenplay introduces two characters from the comic strip that are not in the musical—Warbucks's bodyguard, Punjab, and chauffeur, the Asp—though neither contributes musically or narratively in a significant way until Punjab's involvement in the closing sequence. Sobieski also radically altered the climax of the story so that rather than Annie's kidnappers being arrested at Warbucks's mansion they are captured only after chasing her to the top of the B&O Bridge on the Baltimore and Ohio Railroad and trying to kill her. The chase sequence is an excellent example of Aylesworth's criticism of the picture, since it replaces a much more intimate scene from the stage musical in which Annie finally finds out that her parents are dead and her emotional relationship with Warbucks is strengthened. Indeed, the show's creators were highly critical of Houston and producer Ray Stark's film, calling it 'preposterous,' 'terrible,' and 'cock-eyed.'[18] and voicing particular displeasure at Stark's decision to reset the story around American Independence Day rather than Christmas because the film was shot in summer and he felt it was too expensive to make fake snow.[19]

The Disney reinvention returns the setting to winter and draws much more heavily on the specifics of the musical's plot than the Columbia picture. Indeed, this second screen *Annie* can be seen as what Leitch defines as a 'readaptation,' since it 'ignores or treats as inconsequential' the earlier Columbia film, instead prioritizing fidelity to the original text, translated to the filmic medium.[20] The screenplay by Irene Mecchi, whose credits prior to *Annie* include the animated Disney films *The Lion King*, *The Hunchback of Notre Dame*, and *Hercules*, introduces very little that cannot be readily traced back to the stage show, and as will be discussed in greater detail later in this chapter, some of the musical decisions taken in the first film are reversed in this reinvention. This version being made for television rather than cinema is clearly a factor here, with the intended presentation on a small screen—and doubtless being made on a much smaller budget—resulting in a more constrained development of the show's underlying narrative.[21] Jessica Sternfeld commends director Rob Marshall, who 'infused the potentially sticky-sweet show with unflagging wit and even bite' without needing to rely on extravagances such as helicopters and high-speed pursuits.[22]

The 2014 film is a contemporary reimagining of the *Annie* story and is far more akin to the Columbia movie than the Disney in terms of scale and spectacle. Rather than being an orphan, Annie is in foster care with Miss Hannigan and accidentally meets the Warbucks figure—renamed as Benjamin Stacks—when he pulls her out of the way of a truck as she runs into the road. She moves in with him as part of a plan to get him elected as the mayor of New York City, and she is reunited with her parents, who of course turn out to be fakes, by Stacks's campaign manager, Guy, who realizes that the publicity and popularity boost will win Stacks the election. Given the size of the hypotext that precedes it, it is perhaps unsurprising that the picture seems to straddle three of Leitch's categories of filmic remake: it can be read as an 'update' of the stage show, which it both reveres and revises while trying to bring the story up to date; it is, as shown below, arguably a 'homage' to the Columbia film; and it is also a re-adaptation of *Annie* inasmuch as it overlooks the presence of the Disney film, much as that production disregarded the Columbia movie.

These assertions are reinforced by Will Gluck's director commentary on the DVD release,[23] in which he suggests that this *Annie* has been made with a lot of reverence for the original stage show and the Columbia picture but fails to make any mention of the 1999 television movie. The first of several tributes occurs at the very outset of the film, with shots of a girl called Annie with masses of curly red hair delivering a presentation. This is a misdirection, however: the teacher calls up another girl, also called Annie, and it is she who is the star of this story. Her presentation is on President Roosevelt—another nod to the original show—and she takes the class through an admittedly superficial account of the New Deal that the stage Annie apparently helped inspire. While these connections might be readily apparent to any viewer with a working knowledge of a previous *Annie*, there are also more subtle references. In the same scene, written on the chalkboard is a list of American presidents, but the names of the musical's creators, Martin Charnin, Charles Strouse, and Thomas Meehan, are interpolated into the list in tribute.

The influence of the Columbia film is particularly apparent in some of the choreographic and narrative decisions. Several of the dance sections of 'It's the Hard-Knock Life,' such as the plate-throwing sequence in the kitchen, resonate strongly with similar moves in Arlene Phillips's choreography, and while in the stage show and the Disney reinvention Annie does not actually leave Warbucks's mansion with her 'parents,' Gluck's film features a car chase through New York involving the police on the ground and members of the Stacks household pursuing from the air in a helicopter, closely mirroring the climactic sequence from Huston's picture. However, whereas in Sobieski's screenplay Annie is found thanks to the rather unlikely circumstance of Punjab identifying the kidnappers' car in the dark from a monocopter, the 2014 chase is brought right up to date, with Stacks and the others able to track Annie via posts on social media that tag her location as the car in which she is travelling moves through the city.

Leitch observes that filmic remakes might include what he terms 'special rewards for viewers who remember the original' that are in no way important to the overarching narrative but 'provide an optional bonus of pleasure to those in the know.'[24] As has been discussed, this is very much the case with the 2014 *Annie*, though there are times when these in-jokes can be interpreted in ways that conflict with the film's underlying premise or coherence. In his recent chapter on the *Annie* films, Olaf Jubin criticizes the 2014 picture for presenting viewers with several messages that appear to be incongruent with contemporary society, including asking 'why would Stacks be afraid to expose his baldness in a society where shaving your head is a popular fashion choice for men?'[25] While much of Jubin's criticism is very well made, this immaterial sequence is clearly not intended to be of any narrative consequence, and is simply

a visual 'one-liner' connecting Stacks to the traditional representation of Warbucks as bald, harking back to the overlooked
Victor Garber in 1999, to Albert Finney in 1982, and further to
the original 1977 stage Warbucks, Reid Shelton.[26]

MUSICAL PROFILES

The official trailers for both the Columbia and Disney movies
reference the stage musical, identifying it directly as the source
text for the screen reinvention, and while the same is not true
for the most recent screen *Annie*, the fact that the trailer is
saturated with the most recognizable songs from the show (albeit remixed) implies strongly that the film is based on the
show. Indeed, although in an interview for *Playbill* Charles
Strouse comments that Jay-Z was 'contracted to only use six of
the songs' from the show,[27] the film includes eight sung numbers from the musical with another two used as underscoring.
Table 7.1 shows the musical structure of the stage show and
each of the films, and reveals the structural importance of the
main numbers, the majority of which appear across all four
versions.

Leaving aside the opening credit sequence, once the
narrative begins there is considerable similarity across all
iterations, with 'Maybe' and 'It's the Hard-Knock Life' the
first two numbers presented. However, from here they break
down with varying levels of consistency of musical structuring
across the different productions. As noted, several key songs
are retained across the three screen reinventions. Besides
'Maybe' and 'It's the Hard-Knock Life,' the songs, 'Tomorrow,'
'Little Girls,' 'I Think I'm Gonna Like It Here,' 'Easy Street,'
'You're Never Fully Dressed without a Smile,' and 'I Don't
Need Anything but You' appear in the stage show and all of the
films, though in several cases their position and function in

the story differ from the original. Of course, some changes are made within musical numbers—some cosmetic, others more surgical—but these eight songs form the spine of each reinvention and maintain their strong connections to the stage show.

What Table 7.1 additionally shows clearly is how the filmic *Annies* relate musically not only to the stage show but also to each other. The parallels between the musical and the Disney film are quite apparent, with the omission of three chorus numbers ('We'd Like to Thank You,' 'You Won't Be an Orphan for Long,' and 'Annie') the only notable points of departure prior to final scenes. A small narrative shift supports an extra reprise of 'Little Girls' in the closing sequence, and the removal of politics from the story necessitates a repurposing and repositioning of the 'Tomorrow' reprise and the omission of 'New Deal for Christmas.' The latter is replaced consistently across all of the reinventions with 'I Don't Need Anything but You,' which is a reprise in the Disney version, having been sung originally at the same narrative point as the stage musical. Perhaps unexpectedly, the Columbia and Gluck *Annies* also bear similarities in terms of musical structuring, with several of the adjustments made to the order of songs in the first film replicated in the most recent iteration. Notably, both pictures switch 'I Think I'm Gonna Like It Here' and 'Little Girls,' place 'Easy Street' at the point at which the reprise of the number is heard in the stage show (omitting the reprise), and, as just noted, use 'I Don't Need Anything but You' as the pre-credit finale, though in the Columbia film this is the start of a medley. Notwithstanding this, the 2014 film's use of songs from the musical for instrumental underscoring means that it mimics the show's overall musical structure much more closely than its 1982 counterpart.

The stage show of *Annie* features the children's chorus in three numbers—'It's the Hard-Knock Life' and its reprise, and the reprise of 'You're Never Fully Dressed without a Smile'—and the adult chorus in a further six songs—'We'd

Table 7.1

LIST OF SONGS IN EACH VERSION OF ANNIE

Stage Musical (1977)	Columbia (1982)	Disney (1999)	Gluck (2014)
Overture (various)	Tomorrow (credits)	Overture (various)	Overture (various)
Maybe	Maybe	Maybe	Maybe
It's the Hard-Knock Life	It's the Hard-Knock Life	It's the Hard-Knock Life	It's the Hard-Knock Life
It's the Hard-Knock Life (R)		It's the Hard-Knock Life (R)	
Tomorrow	Dumb Dog	Tomorrow	Tomorrow
We'd Like to Thank You	Sandy		Hard-Knock Life (R, U)
Little Girls	I'm Gonna Like It Here	Little Girls	I'm Gonna Like It Here
Little Girls (R)		Little Girls (R)	Maybe (U)
	Little Girls		Never Fully Dressed
	Maybe (R)		Little Girls
I'm Gonna Like It Here	Let's Go to the Movies	I'm Gonna Like It Here	
			NYC (U)
NYC	We Got Annie	NYC	
Easy Street	Sign	Easy Street	Maybe (U)
You Won't Be an Orphan			The City's Yours
Maybe (R)	Never Fully Dressed	Maybe (R)	
Never Fully Dressed	Never Fully Dressed (R)	Never Fully Dressed	Opportunity
Never Fully Dressed (R)	Tomorrow (R)	Never Fully Dressed (R)	

(continued)

Table 7.1

CONTINUED

Stage Musical (1977)	Columbia (1982)	Disney (1999)	Gluck (2014)
Easy Street (R)	Easy Street	Easy Street (R)	Easy Street
Tomorrow (R)			Tomorrow (R, U)
Something Was Missing		Something Was Missing	Something was Missing (U)
I Don't Need Anything		I Don't Need Anything	
Annie			
Maybe (R)	Maybe (R)	Maybe (R)	Who am I?
		Tomorrow (R)	
		Little Girls (Reprise)	
New Deal for Christmas	Finale (medley): I Don't Need Anything, We Got Annie (R), Tomorrow (R)	I Don't Need Anything (R)	Chase Sequence (various, U)
			I Don't Need Anything
Tomorrow (R, bows)	Tomorrow (R, credits)		Tomorrow (R, credits)
			Moonquake Lake (credits)
		End Credits	

Note: R indicates that the number is a reprise; U stands for instrumental underscoring rather than sung material.

Like to Thank You,' 'I Think I'm Gonna Like It Here,' 'NYC,' 'You Won't Be an Orphan for Long,' 'I Don't Need Anything but You,' and 'Annie'—as well as 'New Deal for Christmas' and the bows version of 'Tomorrow' for the full company. The Columbia film retains two of the three songs for children's chorus—'It's the Hard-Knock Life' and 'You're Never Fully Dressed without a Smile'—though the latter features only the principal orphans rather than the whole group, and the adult chorus performs in 'I Think I'm Gonna Like It Here,' 'Let's Go to the Movies' (which replaces the chorus number 'NYC'), and a new part-choral version of 'Tomorrow' over the opening credits. However, 'I Don't Need Anything but You' is stripped back to just the principals, most of the chorus is removed from 'We Got Annie' (itself a rewritten version of the chorus number 'Annie' from the stage show), and the rest of the original chorus numbers are removed from the film completely. In total, the film omits one third of the show's musical numbers, something that is perhaps particularly surprising given that it was released while *Annie* was still running on Broadway.

As indicated in Table 7.1, under half of the fourteen remaining songs in the Columbia movie are retained in their original positions, and four new songs are inserted into the picture: 'Dumb Dog,' 'Sandy,' 'Let's Go to the Movies,' and 'Sign.' The first two of these songs show Annie's love for Sandy, the stray dog she rescues from the pound, but they displace her first rendition of 'Tomorrow,' which, as discussed later, affects the underlying narrative of the story somewhat. 'Let's Go to the Movies' was originally designed to show off the singing and dancing talents of Ann Reinking, playing Grace, and although broadly speaking it serves a similar function to that of 'NYC'—introducing Annie to the City and its culture—it does not afford Warbucks the same opportunity for relaxation and nostalgia that starts his transformation from cold-hearted businessman to loving father figure. 'Sign,' the last new insertion, is a duet for Warbucks and Hannigan that neither seems to enjoy very much, in which she tries to seduce him while he repeatedly pesters her to authorize his adoption of Annie. Although written by Strouse and Charnin, none of the new songs enhance the musical palette of the film particularly, and their inclusion arguably weakens some aspects of the story.

While the structure and songs of the Disney film are much closer to that of the original show, it is the adult chorus that is the main casualty of this small-screen reinvention. It is notable that the songs omitted from the television version are 'We'd Like to Thank You,' 'You Won't Be an Orphan for Long,' 'Annie' and 'New Deal for Christmas,' all of which feature the chorus prominently in the stage show, with 'NYC' (reintroduced in place of 'Let's Go to the Movies') and 'I Don't Need Anything but You' rewritten to remove the chorus parts. Although it does not feature the chorus, 'You're Never Fully Dressed without a Smile' is also heavily abridged, with just a snippet of the main song featuring on the radio before the children perform their reprise of the number. However, prior to the final scene these are the only significant musical deviations from the stage show (accepting that there is also a significant amount of reorchestration, some rearranging in dance numbers, and the underscoring, where it exists, is generally new). The only new material in the film comes right at the end, with a second airing of the 'Little Girls Reprise,' a short reprise of 'I Don't Need Anything but You' to act as a finale, and instrumental end credits based around 'Maybe' rather than 'Tomorrow.'

In his discussion of film and theatre, Neil Sinyard notes that 'because a film has to reach a wider audience than a play, the play is sometimes in danger of either being simplified or diluted in order to make it more acceptable and accessible to the mass public.'[28] Such a statement applies just as aptly to musicals as plays, with perhaps the principal method of dilution coming from the removal of chorus songs when a show becomes a film.

While such changes to the role of the chorus do not impact greatly on the story in either the 1982 or 1999 reinventions of *Annie*—indeed, the removal of 'You Won't Be an Orphan for Long,' which is a weak song, arguably strengthens the narrative—such simplification can adversely affect the picture. The opening of Tim Burton's 2007 film of Stephen Sondheim's *Sweeney Todd* is a case in point. The chorus is largely excised (butchered, even) from the picture, with the result that 'The Ballad of Sweeney Todd' not only fails to present the audience with the background to the story through Sondheim's lyrics but also lacks the most haunting and chilling elements of the song: the dramatic and chromatic vocal harmonies. Cost is surely not an issue—Columbia clearly had the budget to retain more of the chorus singing in *Annie*, for example—indicating that it may simply be an aesthetic choice. Perhaps the tendency to value the visual over the aural in films leads to a perception that a large cast gives a picture grandeur whereas a singing chorus brings unnecessary complexity. Whatever the reason, it might be hoped that this trend will be at least slowed by the inclusion of a large chorus in the groundbreaking 2012 screen version of *Les Misérables*, particularly given the many ways in which the picture has revolutionized film musicals.[29] With this in mind, the music in Will Gluck's 2014 *Annie* is considered in detail later in this chapter, alongside consideration of that reinvention as a contemporary screen musical.

Constructing a framework for each film with reference to the placement of named songs offers an overview of the way in which apparently recognizable music supports each adaptation of *Annie*, but a comparison such as that presented in Table 7.1 does not provide any detail regarding the function, agency, or even sound of these musical numbers. Evaluation of these aspects of the music requires close consideration of selected songs from each reinvention, starting with the most famous of the show's numbers, 'Tomorrow.'

TOMORROW: NARRATIVE AGENCY
THROUGH SONG

According to Bordman, '"Tomorrow," Annie's paean of hope for the future, became the last Broadway show song for many seasons to enjoy widespread appeal.'[30] Indeed, while narratively the song features no more often in the stage show than 'Maybe,' 'It's the Hard-Knock Life,' 'Little Girls,' 'You're Never Fully Dressed without a Smile,' and 'Easy Street,' each of which is reprised, 'Tomorrow' also opens and closes the show overture and is the music for the final company bows. This bookending of the show promotes 'Tomorrow' disproportionately in the memory of the audience, who are likely to recall it more clearly than other songs owing to the serial position effect.[31] Similarly, the opening credits of the Columbia film showcase 'Tomorrow,' but this new version combines Annie singing solo and a choral rendition rather than being a purely instrumental overture, thrusting the song's story into the foreground far sooner than in the musical. This artificially increases even further the apparent importance of 'Tomorrow' to the story, not least because the stage overture features several other of the main melodies whereas the filmic version is musically single-minded. This being the case, it is particularly surprising to find that the first proper musical divergence within the actual film arrives at the point when Annie should sing her solo version of 'Tomorrow,' as noted earlier, a change that results in the song's not acquiring the same sort of personal connection with Annie that it has in the stage show. Indeed, although film critic Pauline Kael observes that Annie 'bawls out "Tomorrow" regularly, on schedule,'[32] the song actually features only once within the filmic narrative, when Annie and Warbucks visit President Roosevelt in Washington, DC, at the point when the reprise is heard in the original. In the musical, the cabinet members observe the worsening state of the economy, unemployment, and

the potential of war in Europe—the setting is the mid-1930s—
and out of their despair Annie raises their spirits with a reprise
of 'Tomorrow' that drives Roosevelt and his ministers to set the
country on the road to recovery through the New Deal. After
Annie and Warbucks leave, the president leads his cabinet in
another chorus.

Perhaps ironically, this is an occasion where fidelity to the
source generates a musical problem in the adapted film. In the
scene in the stage musical, Annie begins to speak the words
of 'Tomorrow' only to be shouted down by the cabinet before
she can complete the verse, and when Roosevelt encourages her
to sing, she continues from where she stopped. As shown in
Table 7.2, the impact of this is that the first A section of the
song's structure is omitted from this reprise, since the music
leads on naturally from the preceding dialogue—the text of the
(almost) complete first A section—as can be heard in ▶ audio
example 7.1. Columbia's Annie sings exactly the same material
as her stage forebear, but the dialogue that leads to this moment
is significantly different, as ▶ video example 21.1 demonstrates,
meaning that the song is incomplete; in this context there is no
logical musical reason for the omission of the first A section,
unbalancing the song. When 'Tomorrow' is repeated by Annie,
Warbucks, and the Roosevelts immediately afterwards it starts
with the previously omitted phrase, which was also present at
the very opening of the film as the song played through the
credits. Indeed, it seems therefore that the reason the start is
removed in the Washington, DC scene is simply because that is
what is sung—though not all that is heard—in the stage show.

There is also a small change in the song lyric that marks
a notable difference in Columbia's reinvention. Onstage when
Roosevelt and his cabinet repeat the song, the president seals
the creation of the New Deal through a subtle lyric change in
the song's C section, so that rather than 'always,' tomorrow
is 'only' a day away. However, in Columbia's version of the

story Roosevelt asks Annie and Warbucks for help delivering the New Deal, and it is Annie rather than the president who proclaims tomorrow is 'only' a day away (indicated in italics in Table 7.2). Indeed, this is the only version of the lyric used in the film, with Annie also singing 'only' in the opening credit track. The shift from 'always' to 'only' is quite noticeable in the musical, and it supports the idea that, as president, Roosevelt actually holds the power to improve people's quality of life (to bring the sun out) as the country recovers from the Depression. Removing this subtle change means that one of the key musico-narrative aspects of the original score is lost, and having Annie sing 'only' surely ascribes too much influence and responsibility to a young girl.[33]

Paradoxically, 'Tomorrow' leads to similar though opposite problems in Gluck's *Annie*. The song is restored to its position in the first part of the narrative, in alignment with the original show, and it expresses Annie's longing to find her parents, thus enabling the audience to empathize with her and her situation. Indeed, the main 'Tomorrow' sequence contains some of the most inspired cinematography in the 2014 film, as can be seen in ⊙ video example 21.2. Annie walks back to Hannigan's after a secret trip to the public records office to try to gather information on her parents, and as she passes through the city she sees reflections of parents with their children wherever she looks. In reality, however, none of these children exist, and when the actual people are revealed they are usually carrying out mundane activities such as pulling a mail cart, throwing a bucket on a building site, and carrying a sofa. Sadly, while this imagination in the visual imagery gives the song additional depth, the film has no sung reprise of 'Tomorrow' until the end credits. It therefore appears only once in this reinvention, and as a result it is arguably no more important a song for the protagonist than any other that she sings. Indeed, when it does return at the end of the film, complete with marching band, parade,

Table 7.2

LYRICAL STRUCTURE OF ANNIE'S SOLO FROM THE 'TOMORROW REPRISE' FROM THE STAGE SHOW AND THE ONLY NARRATIVE RENDITION OF 'TOMORROW' FROM THE COLUMBIA FILM (AUTHOR'S EMPHASIS)

Version A—4 bars [SPOKEN]	A—4 bars	B—5 bars	A'—4 bars	C—4 bars
Stage The sun'll come out tomorrow/ bet your bottom dollar that tomorrow/ there'll be . . .	Just thinking about tomorrow/ clears away the cobwebs and the sorrow/ til there's none.	When I'm stuck with a day that's grey and lonely/ I just stick out my chin, and grin, and say/oh.	The sun'll come out tomorrow/ so you gotta hang on til tomorrow/come what may.	Tomorrow, tomorrow, I love you, tomorrow/ you're *always* a day away.
Columbia (Different dialogue				Tomorrow, tomorrow, I love you, tomorrow/ you're *only* a day away.
Film ˈleading into song)				

Source: Thomas Meehan, Charles Strouse, and Martin Charnin, *Annie. Libretto Vocal Book*, 99–100; *Annie*, directed by John Huston (Columbia Tristar Home Entertainment, [1982] 2004) [DVD], 1:25:25–1:26:14.

balloons, and full choreography, tomorrow is still 'always' a day away, despite Annie's adoption by Stacks, which rather misses the whole point of the song.

While the omission of politics means that the placement of the 'Tomorrow' reprise in the Disney film also differs from the stage show, the narrative function of the song is retained much more closely in this reinvention. The agency lost from 'Tomorrow' in the Columbia picture is restored, with the song taking pride of place in the first act of the picture as it does in the 2014 movie. However, even though there is no trip to Washington, DC, in this version, the reprise of 'Tomorrow' still plays a key role in the narrative, coupled in this adaptation with a reprise of Annie's other personal song, 'Maybe.' Surprisingly, however, these numbers are sung to Annie by Grace after Mr and Mrs Mudge are apparently shown to be Annie's parents and she realizes she will have to leave Warbucks. While the removal of the political aspects of the show does have an impact on the structure of the narrative, it is the reassignment of the reprises of both 'Maybe' and 'Tomorrow' to Grace, rather than Annie herself, that most affects the interpretation of the story. Giving Grace, who up to that point has been a relatively peripheral character, the two songs that encapsulate Annie's character, enhances her standing and importance to the story, and to Annie. She is portrayed as a staunch supporter of Annie in all of the films, but only in this reinvention does she get to prove her love for the orphan by singing to her using Annie's own musical material. Her key position in the narrative is confirmed by enabling her to change 'always' to 'only' in the closing line of 'Tomorrow,' signalling her guiding hand in Annie's future. Director Rob Marshall's clear understanding of the two songs' agency is further demonstrated by the use of 'Maybe' rather than 'Tomorrow' for the closing credit sequence. After all, it is this song that Annie returns to at key points in her personal story—the very start, after Warbucks says he will look for her parents, and on the morning she is set to leave Warbucks with her 'parents'—indicating that 'Maybe' is actually the show's most important number.

(UN-)'EASY STREET'

'Easy Street' is another number that is treated quite differently in all three reinventions. The placement of the song in each film has already been noted, but the impact of such a repositioning requires closer attention. In the stage show and the Disney picture the song is a light-hearted number about the life the Hannigans always wanted, and while the lyrics include a vague notion of using Annie to get to Warbucks and his money, the number serves mainly to emphasize that these characters are the villains of the piece. It is only in the second act dialogue scene that culminates with the 'Easy Street' reprise that Rooster and Lily outline to Hannigan their plan to pose as Annie's parents in order to claim the reward money, and they appeal to her for information that will help them convince Warbucks that they really are Annie's mum and dad. There is nothing further actually shown in the stage musical, but it is clear that Hannigan furnishes them with the information found in Annie's note and, importantly, tells them of the existence of the silver locket left with Annie by her parents. It is this detail that appears to confirm that Annie is indeed their little girl, though the libretto includes a performance direction that Rooster's comparison of his and Annie's half lockets is done 'very quickly, too quickly,'[34] indicating that he does not have the real locket section.

There is no false locket in Disney's reinvention, with Rooster and Lily's knowledge of the necklace enough to convince Warbucks and the others that they are Annie's parents; and while this makes a little more sense than for the Hannigans to rely on a fake locket, in many ways it is equally problematic in the context of the story. Given the lengths to which Warbucks has gone to locate Annie's parents, it seems astounding that he does not insist on seeing both parts of the locket for himself to be sure the claim is genuine, especially as by this time he wants to adopt Annie himself and would therefore be particularly keen to be able to dismiss any claim to her as false.

In the Columbia film, 'Easy Street' is heard after Warbucks offers a large financial reward to any responders who can prove they are Annie's parents, and the whole number is therefore entwined with the idea of obtaining this money and then disposing of the child. During the song, Hannigan reveals that Annie's parents were killed several years earlier in a vehicle accident, and that the police sent their possessions to her to be looked after. As a result, she is able to provide the locket half for Rooster and Lily, resolving the issue from the stage show (and the Disney film) discussed earlier. The dancing in the bulk of the song retains an air of slapstick comedy, especially in the way Hannigan is pushed around by the other two,[35] with the editors of the *Consumer Guide* going so far as to suggest that 'compared to everything else in the film it stands out like a gem.'[36] However, the change of narrative context means the start of the song is somewhat darker than in the original show, and there is also an uncomfortable sexuality to the opening of the number that feels quite out of place in a family film. This is particularly notable when Rooster opens the envelope that contains the locket and reveals it slowly to Hannigan and Lily. As emphasized in ▶ video example 21.3, his drawn-out and salacious 'E' at the start of the lyric 'Easy Street' seems to drive the two women into some sort of orgasmic frenzy, and Lily writhes around on the desk in apparent ecstasy as he lowers the locket seductively onto her face. While these actions may be designed to empha-size quite how evil Rooster is in this reinvention—he actually tries to kill Annie when she escapes and destroys Warbucks's cheque, an intention only ever hinted at in other versions of the story—they seem quite inappropriate given the film's target audience.[37]

There is a marked difference between the Columbia and Disney representations of the relationships between Rooster, Lily, and Hannigan, which results in contrasting interpretations of the way in which the trio operate. Whereas Lily is Rooster's first priority in the Columbia film, his prin-cipal loyalty is clearly to his sister, Hannigan, in the Disney version. Indeed, Disney's Lily matches the stage show's char-acter description—'a floozy and bimbo'—very closely, leading Hannigan to decide that she, rather than Lily, will accom-pany Rooster as Mrs Mudge, Annie's apparent mother. Lily is left in charge of the orphans and it is this that ultimately foils the criminals' scheme: the orphans trick Lily into re-vealing the plan by convincing her that Rooster has no in-tention of returning for her once he and Hannigan have the money, a circumstance in which Columbia's Lily would never have ended up.

Rooster and Lily are both absent from Will Gluck's rein-vention, with their role taken on by Stacks's campaign man-ager, Guy, who stands to receive a substantial pay packet if he can get his employer elected mayor of New York City. Guy sings 'Easy Street' to Hannigan in a bar as he explains his plan to find fake parents for Annie to increase Stacks's chance of winning the election, darkening the number in a similar manner to the Columbia version and again linking it with the notion of removing Annie for personal gain.[38] Additionally, while the chorus is retained, 'Easy Street' is effectively a new song that is based on and borrows from the original musical and lyrical material, and it is not the only number to receive this sort of treatment. Indeed, in addition to considering Gluck's *Annie* with regard to the stage show and the other filmic reinventions, attention must be paid to the quite radical changes to the sound of the music, and to the status of this reinvention as a contemporary film musical.

MUSIC IN WILL GLUCK'S *ANNIE*

Jay-Z, who co-produced the 2014 film, first engaged professionally with the music of *Annie* in his 1998 hit 'Hard-Knock Life (Ghetto Anthem),' but the film's musical soundscape eschews the hip-hop/rap stylings of this track in favour of a fairly generic pop sound. The soundtrack combines new arrangements of some of the existing songs, new songs based on the show's songs (as is the case with 'Easy Street'), and totally new songs, with significant variety in the level of success across the picture.

There is an effort to embed music into the fabric of the film practically from the outset as the camera follows Annie as she races away from school at the end of the day and heads off into New York City. Her journey is accompanied by an overture of sorts that not only presents several of the songs from the original show but also integrates many of them into the city: the sound effects of roadworks, truck doors, and car horns all synchronize with the music; a young woman listening to music on headphones sings a riff from 'Tomorrow'; 'It's the Hard-Knock Life' could be interpreted as being on the radio in a taxi and the melody is taken up by bicycle bells; and part of 'I Think I'm Gonna Like It Here' is performed by a band busking on the subway platform. Olaf Jubin notes that 'at first this conceit seems like a charming attempt to apprise audiences that the urban sounds of New York City form the soundtrack of our heroine's life'; however, as the film progresses, 'it gets more and more desperate and unconvincing,'[39] and indeed further use in 'It's the Hard-Knock Life' of what might roughly be termed as musical bricolage is more annoying and distracting than engaging and interesting. Perhaps the greatest success of the overture is the misdirection caused by the music (which is 'Tomorrow' at this point) ending as Annie arrives at Stacks's product launch. However, while most of the action does indeed revolve around the familial relationship that develops between Annie and Stacks, her mad dash from school is not so that she can get a new phone; Annie moves on after only a momentary pause to complete what is revealed to be a weekly pilgrimage to the Domani restaurant where she was abandoned by her parents.

Some of the reinvented songs work reasonably well— there is an interesting rearrangement of 'Maybe' that perhaps emphasizes the closeness of Annie's foster-child group, for instance—and the idea of paying tribute to the original stage show results in some songs that have been excised as vocal numbers used within the picture as instrumental underscoring. However, when the original song has served only as the basis for a number, the results are more mixed. 'I Think I'm Gonna Like It Here' retains the narrative idea of the show song but presents it in a more contemporary setting. Tennis courts and servants are replaced with notions of thought-controlled and voice-activated technologies, and there is enough of the main melody and chorus lyric in the remix to at least capture the essence of the Broadway number. The song also plays on some of the elements of the original number, continuing the idea of homage identified by Gluck in his director's commentary; for example, while the 1977 (and 1982) Annie is astonished that Warbuck's swimming pool is inside his house, for the twenty-first-century youngster the surprise is that Stacks's pool knows what temperature she would like it to be. By contrast, 'Little Girls' departs quite significantly from the source materials and suffers from a loss of identity as a result. Indeed, it is almost unrecognizable as a version of the same song since the two have so little in common aside from the title lyric. While the cinematography again nods towards elements of the Columbia film through the appearance of the foster children every-where Hannigan looks, the song is 'perfunctory and shallow rather than transcendent,'[40] and fails to reach the heights of the original.[41]

The four completely new songs—'The City's Yours,' 'Opportunity,' 'Who Am I?,' and 'Moonquake Lake,' by Greg Kurstin and Sia Furler—also fail to offer anything particu-larly inspiring or memorable to the film musically, lyrically, or narratively. Functionally, the first three replace 'You're Never Fully Dressed' (Annie becoming famous), the 'Tomorrow' reprise (Annie lifts the spirits with a song of hope for the fu-ture), and the reprise of 'Maybe' (Annie, and in this version of the story also Stacks and Hannigan, consider what the future will bring), but in all three cases the substitution weakens the musical profile of the picture, particularly through the loss of the reprises of Annie's main songs. The fourth, 'Moonquake Lake,' is the title song of a movie Annie and her friends are taken to by Stacks but is actually only heard over *Annie*'s closing credits.[42] Indeed, it seems likely that the intention in adding the new tracks was to garner an Oscar nomina-tion for Best Original Song—as is usually the case in screen adaptations of stage musicals—an endeavour in which the writers were unsuccessful. Annie's solo, 'Opportunity,' was nominated for a Golden Globe, but it lost out to 'Glory' from *Selma*, which also won the Academy Award.

However, for me at least, all thoughts on the quality of the music are tempered by two related factors that identify *Annie* as an outlier in terms of contemporary film musicals. Despite efforts made to modernize the narrative and musical content of the show for this reinvention, the filmmakers—all of whom were novices in the production of movie musicals—seem to have been unaware of the significant changes wrought in the industry by the film of *Les Misérables* two years earlier. In his director commentary Gluck informs viewers that the songs were prerecorded in the studio,[43] and although the cast were also recorded singing on set and the final soundtrack is a mix of these recordings, the use of prerecorded vocals is quite apparent across the picture, especially given some of the choreography carried out while singing.[44] The other issue is the fact that, as Lapin derisively remarks, the songs are 'overproduced with slimy AutoTune [*sic*],'[45] with Jason Clark even more disparaging in his review for *Entertainment Weekly*: 'Musically, *Annie* is a disaster. The melodious original score by Charles Strouse and Martin Charnin gets the full-on Autotune pap treatment, which takes to these songs about as well as a lute to death metal.'[46] While it might be argued that this has been done to align the picture with the post-X-Factor auto-tune aesthetic, it sounds more like a necessity than a stylistic preference, particularly in the case of Annie herself, Quvenzhané Wallis.[47] While Depression-era politics may root the original *Annie* story in the 1930s, the stage show and the first two films can at least offer an element of nostalgia to audiences; Gluck's film is entrenched in the early twenty-first century by the audible results of these technological decisions, which might mean bizarrely that it dates far faster than any of its predecessors.

CONCLUSION

Columbia's film from 1982 remains the most widely known screen version of *Annie*, and the visual and narrative references to this first picture in the 2014 reimagining only serve to reinforce this point. Indeed, despite Disney's offering being the closest to the stage musical in both narrative and musical terms, and the programme doing very well when it was broadcast on ABC in 1999, the lack of a cinematic release means that it has never received the level of exposure afforded to the other two movies. It also lacks some of the 'star power' found in the other films' casts, with Columbia's movie headlined by Albert Finney and Carol Burnett, and Gluck's by Jamie Foxx, Cameron Diaz, and Quvenzhané Wallis, the only one of the three Annies not making her screen debut in the role.[48] While the Disney cast includes Oscar winner Kathy Bates and a number of Tony-award winning Broadway performers including Audra MacDonald, Alan Cumming, and Kristen Chenoweth, they perhaps do not carry the same level of celebrity among the film-watching public.

It was noted at the start of this chapter that there was no intention to prove that any of these reinventions was 'better' or 'worse' than any of the others, and that remains the case. This exploration has considered not only the ways in which the films are similar to and different from the original stage show but also each other, and the impacts (whether intentional or unintentional) that some of the musical and narrative decisions taken in the creation of each reinvention have had on the ways in which the story, songs, and characters are presented and received. While there are undoubtedly contrasting areas of strength and weakness in each of the three screen versions of *Annie*, each one adapts the preceding hypotextual material in different ways and to different ends. Indeed, it seems that *Annie*'s identity remains as mysterious as that of the character's mother and father. In each film, imposters needed only a few key details to be accepted as Annie's parents, and so too each screen reinvention offers just enough of the original narrative and music for a new generation of viewers to recognize and accept it as 'their *Annie*.'

NOTES

1. Thomas Meehan, Charles Strouse, and Martin Charnin, *Annie. Libretto Vocal Book* (New York: Musical Theatre International, 1977), 3.
2. Columbia Pictures was actually involved in the production of all three films; the 1999 television movie was a coproduction with Disney, and Village Roadshow Pictures and Overbrook Entertainment produced the 2014 film for Columbia. However, for clarity, all references in this chapter to 'Columbia's *Annie*' relate to the 1982 film.
3. Olaf Jubin poses the question of why it has been difficult to transfer *Annie* onto the screen, exploring many of the production decisions behind each of these adaptations and considering their relative levels of commercial and artistic success. See Olaf Jubin, 'The Trouble with "Little Girls": *Annie* on the Big (and Small) Screen,' in *Twenty-First Century Musicals: From Stage to Screen*, ed. George Rodosthenous (New York: Routledge, 2017), 196–211.
4. *Annie Get Your Gun* and *The Desert Song*, the latter of which is discussed by William A. Everett in his chapter in this volume, have also been adapted for the screen on multiple occasions. *Once upon a Mattress* has been filmed three times, though both the 1965 and 1972 versions are effectively recordings of the stage show for the screen—there was a live audience at the filming and the production is theatrical rather than filmic in look—rather than screen musicals. Accordingly, it is more akin to *The Sound of Music*, which exists on screen as a film musical (1965) and as two live television musicals (NBC 2013, ITV 2015), than to *Annie*.
5. Linda Hutcheon, *A Theory of Adaptation* (New York: Routledge, 2006), 5.
6. Miguel Mera, 'Invention/Re-invention,' *Music Sound and the Moving Image* 3, no. 1 (Spring 2009): 1–20, 2.
7. Robert Stam, 'Introduction: The Theory and Practice of Adaptation,' in *Literature and Film: A Guide to the Theory and Practice of Film Adaptation*, ed. Robert Stam and Alessandra Raengo (Oxford: Blackwell, 2005), 1–52, 31.
8. Thomas Leitch, 'Twice-Told Tales: Disavowal and the Rhetoric of the Remake,' in *Dead Ringers: The Remake in Theory and Practice*,

ed. Jennifer Forrest and Leonard R. Koos (New York: State University of New York Press, 2002), 37–62, 40.

9. Stam, 'Introduction: The Theory and Practice of Adaptation,' 31.

10. Christine Geraghty, *Now a Major Motion Picture: Film Adaptations of Literature and Drama* (Lanham, MD: Rowman & Littlefield, 2008), 4.

11. The comic strip is acknowledged as the inspiration for the stage show and is arguably the fundamental hypotext for any consideration of *Annie*. However, the purpose of this chapter is not to critique the musical as an adaptation in itself but as a source for filmic adaptation, and since neither the 1999 nor the 2014 film draws on the cartoon (as indicated by the lack of connecting lines in Figure 7.1), the stage musical is taken as the point of origin unless otherwise noted.

12. Mera, 'Invention/Re-invention,' 2.

13. Mera, 'Invention/Re-invention,' 2.

14. Deborah Cartmell and Imelda Whelehan, *Screen Adaptation: Impure Cinema* (Basingstoke: Palgrave MacMillan, 2010), 73.

15. Gerald Bordman, *Musical Theatre: A Chronicle* (New York: Oxford University Press, 1986), 685; Thomas Hischak, *The Oxford Companion to the American Musical: Theatre, Film and Television* (New York: Oxford University Press, 2008), 23.

16. Thomas G. Aylesworth, *Broadway to Hollywood: Musicals from Stage to Screen* (Twickenham: Hamlyn, 1985), 251.

17. Aylesworth, *Broadway to Hollywood*, 251; Hischak, *The Oxford Companion to the American Musical*, 24.

18. Robert Simonson, 'Second Floor of Sardi's with Martin Charnin, Thomas Meehan and Charles Strouse: A Drink with the *Annie* Creators,' *Playbill*, 21 March 2013, http://www.playbill.com/arti cle/second-floor-of-sardis-with-martin-charnin-thomas-mee han-and-charles-strouse-a-drink-with-the-annie-creators-com-203656, accessed 18 July 2018.

19. Simonson, 'Second Floor of Sardi's,' accessed 30 June 2017.

20. Leitch, 'Twice-Told Tales,' 45.

21. Geoffrey Block considers all four of Disney's television musical adaptations in 'Disney as Broadway *Auteur*: The Disney Versions of Broadway Musicals for Television in the Late 1990s and Early 2000s,' in *The Disney Musical on Stage and*

Screen: Critical Approaches from 'Snow White' to 'Frozen,' ed. George Rodosthenous (London: Bloomsbury, 2017), 83–99.

22. Jessica Sternfeld, 'Revisiting Classic Musicals: Revivals, Films, Television and Recordings,' *The Cambridge Companion to the Musical*, 2nd ed., ed. William A. Everett and Paul R. Laird (Cambridge: Cambridge University Press, 2008), 325–339, 337.

23. Will Gluck, 'Director's Commentary,' *Annie* (Sony Pictures Home Entertainment, [2014] 2015) [DVD].

24. Leitch, 'Twice-Told Tales,' 42.

25. Jubin, 'The Trouble with "Little Girls," ' 204.

26. Indeed, though he describes the scene as 'controversial,' Will Gluck confirms it is another of the filmmakers' homages to earlier iterations of *Annie*. Gluck, 'Director's Commentary.'

27. Simonson, 'Second Floor of Sardi's,' accessed 30 June 2017.

28. Neil Sinyard, *Filming Literature: The Art of Screen Adaptation* (London: Croom Helm, 1986), 160.

29. See Ian Sapiro, 'Beyond the Barricade: Adapting *Les Misérables* for the Cinema,' in *Contemporary Musical Film*, ed. K. J. Donnelly and Elizabeth Carroll (Edinburgh: Edinburgh University Press, 2017), 123–139.

30. Bordman, *Musical Theatre*, 685.

31. The serial position effect is the psychological phenomenon whereby items heard at the start and end of a list are more readily recalled than those in the middle. See Angela K. Troyer, 'Serial Position Effect,' *Encyclopedia of Clinical Neuropsychology*, ed. Jeffrey S. Kreutzer, John DeLuca, and Bruce Caplan (New York: Springer, 2011), 2263–2264.

32. Pauline Kael, *Taking It All In: Film Writings 1980–1983* (London: Arena, 1987), 344.

33. The character description for Annie on the website of the performing rights holder, Music Theatre International, gives her age as ten to twelve years old. See Music Theatre International, '*Annie*: Full Cast Info,' *Music Theatre International*, 2018, http://www.mtishows.co.uk/full-cast-info/509, accessed 18 July 2018.

34. Meehan, Strouse and Charnin, *Annie. Libretto Vocal Book*, 122.

35. Huston and Stark originally conceived their version of 'Easy Street' as an extravagant showstopper number filmed on a $1million specially constructed street set. However, they were

forced to rethink the song when viewing it within the context of the whole film after principal photography had been completed, reshooting it in the orphanage. Perhaps ironically, Disney's song begins in the orphanage but moves outside to the street for a dance break and the final part of the song. See Kenneth Turan, 'Hollywood Puts Its Money on *Annie*,' *New York Times Magazine*, 2 May 1982, http://www.nytimes.com/1982/05/02/magazine/hollywood-puts-its-money-on-annie.html, accessed 18 July 2018.

36. Editors of the *Consumer Guide* with Phillip J. Kaplan, *The Best, Worst & Most Unusual: Hollywood Musicals* (New York: Beekman House, 1983), 148.

37. Olaf Jubin notes similarly that the scene on the B&O Bridge in which Rooster tries to kill Annie 'is both confusing and too suspenseful for little children,' again calling into question the suitability of parts of the film for its target audience. See Jubin, 'The Trouble with "Little Girls,"' 199.

38. Jubin dissects the narrative and cinematographic issues with the 'Easy Street' sequence in 'The Trouble with "Little Girls,"' 206–207.

39. Jubin, 'The Trouble with "Little Girls,"' 206.

40. Andrew Lapin, '21st-century Musicals Still Haven't Found a Way Out of the Woods,' *The Dissolve*, 12 January 2015, https://thedissolve.com/features/exposition/876-2014s-musicals-might-just-save-us-all/, accessed 18 July 2018.

41. The song's cause is not helped by the fact that Cameron Diaz is weaker vocally than the other Hannigans: Dorothy Loudon (Broadway), Carol Burnett (Columbia), and Kathy Bates (Disney).

42. Contemporary films often feature a pop song over the closing credits rather than repeating music from the main score, with some songs, such as Take That's 'Rule the World' from *Stardust* (2007), written specifically for this purpose to connect the track to the film's narrative. However, it is very unusual for a film *musical* to introduce new material at this point, placing *Annie* out of alignment not only with the other reinventions but with its genre more broadly.

43. Gluck, 'Director's Commentary.'

44. To date, *Annie* is the only film musical produced since *Les Misérables* (2012) that does not feature any 'pure' live on-set singing. See Sapiro, 'Beyond the Barricade,' 134.
45. Lapin, '21st-century Musicals Still Haven't Found a Way Out of the Woods,' accessed 30 June 2017.
46. Jason Clark, 'Annie,' *Entertainment Weekly*, 25 December 2014, http://ew.com/article/2014/12/25/annie-4/, accessed 18 July 2018.
47. Jamie Foxx suffers the most in this respect, since although he can sing, his vocal is as overproduced as everyone else's.
48. Wallis made her debut two years before *Annie* in *Beasts of the Southern Wild*, for which she was nominated for an Oscar for Best Performance by an Actress in a Leading Role. See IMDB, 'Quvenzhané Wallis,' *Internet Movie Database*, 2018, http://www.imdb.com/name/nm4832920/?ref_=nv_sr_2, accessed 18 July 2018.

8

The Many Faces of *Rio Rita*

JOHN GRAZIANO

■ □ ■

THE CRITICAL AND FINANCIAL SUCCESS of *Rio Rita* in February 1927 could not have come at a better time for Florenz Ziegfeld. The *Follies* were no longer guaranteed moneymakers, partially due to the restraints on drinking alcoholic beverages imposed by Prohibition, nor were Ziegfeld's standard book shows providing him with a substantial profit. He was being sued continually by people who worked for him[1]; he was constantly in debt, partly due to his high stakes gambling habit and his extravagant spending; and he had to fund the monthly expenses of $10,000 for his estate, Burkeley Crest, in New York State's posh village, Hastings-on-Hudson. In the midst of all his financial problems, Ziegfeld dreamed of building a new theatre that would be named after him. In partnership with William Randolph Hearst, he decided to locate the theatre far from Times Square, on West 54th Street, across from the Warwick Hotel, which was owned by Hearst. The theatre was designed by the well-known architect/illustrator/set designer Joseph Urban (1872–1933);[2] it cost $2.5 million and accommodated 1,666 ticket holders. The stage was huge (almost ninety-one feet across and forty feet deep); Urban's fanciful murals decorated the entire theatre.[3]

Ziegfeld had hoped that *Show Boat* would be the first show to play at his new theatre, but when the creative team said it was not ready, *Rio Rita* received that honor, premiering on 2 February 1927.[4] While the musical was in development, its place of honor in opening the Ziegfeld Theatre was not contemplated. As is clear from the earliest sheet music covers, copyrighted in 1926, the show was not yet associated with any theatre. When it became apparent that *Show Boat* would not open the house, the cover was changed to advertise Ziegfeld's new theatre (see Figure 8.1), and two numbers, 'Are You There?' and 'Sweetheart,' were added to *Rio Rita*.

During the tryouts in Boston and several other cities, major tinkering took place. At the Colonial Theatre in Boston, for example, an extant programme from 27 December 1926 shows that 'Sweetheart' (a thirty-two-bar song without a verse) was not yet a part of the first act, and that act 2, in three scenes, was still not in its final form. But by the time the production reached the Forrest Theatre in Philadelphia in mid-January, the *New York Times* reported that there was an 'endless' line for tickets; Ziegfeld said he would try to meet audience demand by extending the run.[5]

Once the New York premiere was set for opening night at his new theatre, Ziegfeld set the price for orchestra seats at $27.50. Thereafter, they were priced at $5.50.[6] Crowds thronged the streets outside the theatre for glimpses of the celebrities attending the premiere.[7]

Rio Rita has a book by Guy Bolton (1884–1979), already known for his scripts for the Princess shows with P. G. Wodehouse (1881–1975), and Fred Thompson (1884–1949), who previously worked with Bolton on the Gershwins' *Lady, Be Good!* The lyrics are by Joseph McCarthy (1885–1943), who was one of the stable of writers Zeigfeld hired for the various editions of his *Follies*; he contributed to the 1919, 1920, 1923, and 1924 editions, but was best known to the public for his 1918

FIGURE 8.1 2nd sheet music cover for Broadway production of Rio Rita.

hit song, 'I'm Always Chasing Rainbows,' for which he wrote both lyrics and music. Harry Tierney (1890–1965), another regular member of the Ziegfeld creative team, wrote the music for *Rio Rita*. He had contributed songs to a number of the *Follies*;

had written the music for *Irene* (1919), which introduced the extremely popular 'Alice Blue Gown'; and had provided Ziegfeld with the score for his last money-making book show, *Kid Boots* (1923), which starred Eddie Cantor.

Rio Rita was given a typical Ziegfeld spectacular production, with a chorus of twenty-seven male and eighty-six female singers/dancers. Urban designed five lavish sets and one of Ziegfeld's favourite collaborators, John Harkrider (1899–1982), designed the spectacular costumes. Sammy Lee (1890–1968), already known for his choreography of *Lady, Be Good!* and *No, No, Nanette*, choreographed most of the dances, but Albertina Rasch (1891–1967) provided the choreography for the six numbers in which her sixteen specialty dancers, the Albertina Rasch Girls, appeared. The show was orchestrated by Frank Barry (dates unknown); the Entr'acte was unusual—a two piano 'specialty'—played by Constance Mering and Muriel Pollock.

J. Brooks Atkinson's review in the *Times* is effusive, while noting that the show was not groundbreaking: ' "Rio Rita" breaks no fresh trend into the hinterland of musical comedy; . . . But for sheer extravagance of beauty, animated and rhythmic, "Rio Rita" has no rival among its contemporaries.' Although Atkinson doesn't say whether he liked the music other than referring to the 'Rangers' March' as a ' "Vagabond King" type of marching song,' he applauds the spectacle while noting that by 11:00 PM, when he left, the identity of the Kinkajou had not yet been established:

> But that had not prevented inordinate beautiful dancing girls, or gringo cabaret girls, or Albertina Rasch dancers, or South-American troubadours or, for that matter, the original Central American Marimba Band (Nicaraguan hostages, perhaps?) from spinning across the stage, stamping their chic feet in unison or singing in chorus on any number of hot-blooded themes. In the

most lustrous costumes—silver sombreros, blood-red shirts, fluffy ballet stuffs, embroidered velvet waistcoats—they whirl in squads, one on the heel of another, until the stage was as furious in its design as the wall decorations. . . . The hippodromic proportions of 'Rio Rita,' splashed with bold brushfuls of color, were a feast to the eye.[8]

Arthur Pollock, in the *Brooklyn Daily Eagle*, lauded the show and praised the theatre, noting that it was unusual for its elliptical shape, which 'does away with all angles, [and] adds to the acoustics.' His review of the show centred on the star-turn performance of Ada-May, who 'was lovely. . . . [S]he turns out to be a charming comedienne who can sing a song with the best of them, effortlessly, buoyantly, dance in a manner always original and surprising, and make herself in all necessary respects, delightful.' Of *Rio Rita* itself, he said: 'It has a gracious beauty and fine manner.'[9]

Frank Vreeland of the *Evening Telegram* called *Rio Rita* an 'orgy of beauty and bounty. . . . [The book is] brisk if slightly conventional. . . . This production . . . primarily glorifies the American eye for beauty. . . . A bewitching feature which stopped the show was the Albertina Rasch ballet, providing the daintiest musical comedy number imaginable as a swaying flight of moonbeams.'[10]

From the time of its premiere, there has been some confusion as to whether *Rio Rita* is a musical comedy or an operetta.[11] At its Broadway opening in 1927, it was labelled a 'musical comedy' in advertising and on sheet music and a 'Romantic musical comedy' (is there any other kind?) on the piano-vocal score. For its film release in 1929, it was advertised as a 'Radio Picture Screen Operetta' and 'Fabulous Operetta.'

Some of the confusion may be the result of a recording of excerpts by the Victor Light Opera Company just two weeks after the show's successful premiere. The excerpts heard, with one exception, are the operetta-style songs, with soaring melodies, avoidance of 1920s syncopation, no use of slang, and so on; they provided a basis for the opinions of the many critics who labelled the show an operetta. The singers are unidentified except for J. Harold Murray, who is the only member of the original cast to appear on the recording. Operetta selections dominate the sheet music as well, with only three of eight numbers offering the Broadway-style songs.

An examination of the entire score, however, shows that *Rio Rita* is a hybrid, combining two distinct genres, operetta and 1920s musical comedy. Harry Tierney's music is distinct for each group of characters. Rita and Jim, as befits their true love, sing operetta-style numbers. Lovett, Bean, and their flapper girlfriends/wives, on the other hand, represent the crass New York crowd that club-hop during the spirit-free Prohibition. Their love is fickle and, in Lovett's case, pecuniary. Lovett is a sleazy lawyer, always involved in shady deals, while Chick is a naïve dupe, who usually has difficulty figuring out his next move. The music written for them and their girlfriends is in typical 1920s musical comedy style. As the drama takes place in Mexico, Tierney provides local-colour 'exotic' dances, including the Fado, for the elaborately costumed chorus and dancers, 100 strong, to provide Ziegfeldian grandeur in the big ensembles.

The storylines are kept separate; the characters in the first group never interact with those in the second group, until the triple wedding at the very end of *Rio Rita*. There is, however, no sense of disjunction in the show. I have not been able to discover which of the creators—Bolton, Thompson, McCarthy, or Tierney—had the idea to set the two plots to different musical styles. I also have not been successful in finding other musicals written before 1927 that use this particular musical device to consistently delineate characters of different classes that might have been used as a model for the show.[12]

The complicated main plot of *Rio Rita*, which features a se-cret identity villain and the Texas Rangers, is somewhat rem-iniscent of other 1920s shows;[13] it is set on the Texas border and in Mexico on the Rio Grande river, where one Roberto Ferguson, Rita's brother, is accused, by General Enrique Joselito Esteban, of being an arch-criminal bank robber, the Kinkajou. A Texas Ranger, Jim, who has fallen in love with Rita, is trying to arrest Roberto, but after some doubts, he realizes finally that the General, not her brother, is the Kinkajou. By cutting the ropes of a barge on which the General is having a party—at which time he is attempting to force Rita to marry him—Jim allows it to drift into United States waters, so he can arrest the villain. This (almost) classic love triangle between two suitors—one of whom is the villain—is augmented by the inclusion of Rita's brother, Roberto, who is accused by Esteban of being the Kinkajou. The drama keeps the audience in the dark about the Kinkajou's identity until the penultimate scene of act 2.

In contrast with the operetta-like intrigue of the main story, the secondary musical comedy plot centres around two American Easterners, Ed Lovett and Chick Bean, and Bean's two wives. Lovett is a not-too-honest lawyer who has secured a Mexican divorce for Bean, who has hurriedly married a second time (to Dolly). Following his Mexican marriage, however, Bean is informed by Lovett that the divorce is not valid in Texas, and he will, therefore, be considered a bigamist in the United States. Chick has to avoid sharing a bedroom with Dolly until the divorce is final. They lament their separation in the duet, 'Are You There?' To complicate matters even further, Bean's first wife, Katie, appears at General Esteban's floating barge to announce unexpectedly that she has inherited $3 million. Her announcement catches Lovett's attention and he pursues her. In the final scene, the three couples—Jim and Rita, Chick and Dolly, and Ed and Katie—are married in a moonlight cer-emony, three weeks after the Kinkajou's capture.

Bolton and Thomson's script is a canny mixture of melodrama and comedy. The scenes between Rita, Esteban, and Jim are serious, while those with Chick and Ed are snappy, with jokes and risqué dialogue. The characters are all operetta/musical comedy stock figures. Rita is a simple but upright young woman who cannot be swayed from her quest to marry Jim, though for a short time (the end of act 1), she tells him to go away forever. Jim is a rather bland but serious character, given to platitudes; he is a symbol of the law and in this somewhat lawless state and foreign country, it is his job to pursue bank robbers. More interesting is Esteban, who rejoices in being the villain. He, too, is single-minded about his secret career as a criminal, but he can also be suave when courting Rita. The comic scenes hew more closely to what audiences would have expected from the creators of the Princess musicals, including *Very Good Eddie* (1915), *Oh, Boy!* (1917), and *Oh Lady! Lady!* (1918). Lovett and Bean partake in fast repartee that reflects the musicals of the 1920s.

Tierney's score is probably his masterpiece. The various numbers that comprise the score are inventive, with unusual forms and extended period phrases.[14] 'The Best Little Lover in Town,' which is heard following the opening chorus and dance, introduces Ed Lovett with a chorus of girls. His spoken cue to the song is 'Five minutes alone with me, and you're a girl with a past.' Joseph McCarthy's lyrics for Lovett's syncopated number starts the show with an up-to-date double-entendre number. A thirty-two-bar verse begins with a clever rhyme: [Lovett] 'I'm chivalrous, but frivolous/I'm vigorous, quite rigorous,/ Should you add fastidious, Tut, tut!/Loquacious, Sagacious,/ I might add vivacious./[Girls] 'We must say, My gracious, you're a nut.' The thirty-six-measure chorus, sung entirely by Lovett, continues: 'Who is the best little lover in Town?/Just look me up when there's no one around,/Here in a crowd I seem tragic;/ But, oh! you'll be proud of my parlour magic./I never rest, Oh!

I can't settle down,/ With all the affairs that I've found./For I'm busy all day/giving samples away./The best little lover in town.' It is followed by a sixteen-bar patter section that is sung by all. The chorus is heard once again, as both a vocal and a dance.

Tierney's next two numbers shift from musical comedy to operetta; they do not conform to the verse/chorus form that one would expect to hear. Rita muses about her love for Jim to a brief 'air,' 'Sweetheart,' which is immediately followed by 'River Song' (see ex. 8.1). This latter number is musically significant, since it is combined later in the act with the chorus of the title song, 'Rio Rita' and also closes act 1 (ex. 8.2).

The large-scale Finale to act 1 (249 measures), which brings the drama to its traditional crisis point, is unusual in structure and also quite effective, eschewing complete statements of reprises. It is episodic, combining sung fragments from several of the numbers heard earlier with new music and underscored spoken dialogue in a variety of tempos, and in a number of different keys, beginning in E minor and ending in E-flat major, with a large central section in F major. Tierney opens the finale (mm. 1–38) with a Sousa-like march rhythm in 6/8 for General Esteban, his soldiers, and Rita, in which Esteban convinces her that Jim is an American spy who really does not love her. The music changes tempo to accommodate Rita's questioning feelings. She replies 'I must believe you then' (ex. 8.3) to a new strain, but breaks off singing. The accompaniment continues with repetitions of her plaintive phrase while Esteban speaks, telling his men to kill Jim on sight.

After he leaves, Rita sings a dreamy waltz (mm. 53–80). Her plaint, 'A fool had a dream/By the river of dreams' is set to a new melody with large leaps that is reminiscent of 'River Song' (ex. 8.4).

The formal structure is again incomplete; after two eight-measure periods, the B section begins, but it breaks off after four measures. There is no return to the opening A material.

EXAMPLE 8.1 *Rio Rita*, 'River Song.' (mm. 1-8)

EXAMPLE 8.2 *Rio Rita*, 'River Song' and 'Rio Rita' combined. (mm. 41-48)

EXAMPLE 8.3 *Rio Rita*, act 1 finale, mm. 39-50.

EXAMPLE 8.4 *Rio Rita*, act 1 finale, 'A fool . . .' (mm. 53-60)

Instead, Jim enters, singing the opening strain of the chorus of 'Rio Rita.' His singing is interrupted by a reprise of the waltz, 'When You're in Love, You'll Waltz' heard under a conversation between Jim and Rita. Jim then reprises his strain from that song (ex. 8.5), but Rita does not join him at its close as she did in the original duet.

The waltz continues, though Jim's singing is interrupted by a servant, who delivers a letter from Esteban that has false information in an effort to trap him. To an abrupt change of tempo, Jim tells Rita he has to go but can't tell her why. She is angry and tells him to go forever: (Sung) 'You're not here for me. (spoken) But through me, the Kinkajou!' She asks him to leave and never return. The chorus has entered during their confrontation, and excitedly supports her (in F minor). After professing his love for her, Jim prepares to leave (mm. 186–199). As he turns to walk through the gate of her hacienda, which will result in his death from Esteban's men, a slow dirge-like passage is heard (ex. 8.6); Rita shouts 'Stop! Wait! Not through that gate.' Jim escapes.

Over a brief underscored passage, Esteban accuses Rita of loving Jim. She denies it. As he leaves, Rita reprises measures 17–24 of 'River Song,' with a slight, but significant change of text.

'River Song' text	Finale text
And there beneath the palms,	Twas there, beneath the palms
We met, and we knew	We met, and we knew
A dream, with all its charms, came true,	A dream with all its charms, came true,
All life began there.	And now, it's ended.

EXAMPLE 8.5 *Rio Rita*, act 1 finale, 'If you're in love' (mm. 100–120).

EXAMPLE 8.6 *Rio Rita*, act 1 finale, 'Dirge' (200-208)

RITA: Stop! Wait! Noth through that gate.

Her reverie is interrupted by Jim, who from afar (offstage) sings a variant of the first strain of the chorus to 'Rio Rita.' The act ends as Rita and the hacienda denizens sing the final four measures of 'River Song.'

Six new numbers are introduced in the second act, including three dance specialities. In addition to Dolly and Lovett's comic duet 'I Can Speak Espanol,' the most talked-about dance of the show, Albertina Rasch's 'Black and White Ballet' is seen (ex. 8.7).

The lyrics for 'Following the Sun Around,' offer another example of how the creators straddled the fence between operetta and musical comedy. When the chorus is first heard, sung by Jim, it is a serious love plaint. Set to a wide-ranging operetta-type melody (ex. 8.8), Jim's lyric suggests the hopelessness of his love affair: 'I'll spend my days/Chasing after sunshine,/ Some day one ray may steal through./Can't change my ways,/ Always hoping some time/Someone else may learn/To care as I do./There's only one beneath the sun/That I've ever found./ If she would smile on me a while,/'Twould change things all around;/Until then, I'll spend my days/Chasing after sunshine/ Following the sun around.'

Later in the act, a reprise of the song's chorus, now titled 'Moonshine' is sung by Chick Bean.[15] Now it is no longer a love plaint but a primer that comments on how one gets around the problems of prohibition. Chick sings: 'I'll spend my nights/ Chasing after moonshine,/How I love my mountain dew./Must have my rights,/Morning, night, or moontime,/I must have my little toddy or two./It's natural that the things we want are real hard to get./They made our country dry, but my! They made our cities twice as wet./I'll spend my nights/Chasing after moonshine,/Following the Vans around.'

Unlike the stellar cast he was to contract for *Show Boat*, the performers chosen for *Rio Rita* were Ziegfeld regulars, well known to the public but not of superstar quality. Ethelind

EXAMPLE 8.7 *Rio Rita*, act 2, 'The Black and White Ballet' (mm. 1–20)

EXAMPLE 8.8 *Rio Rita*, act 2, 'Following the sun around'.

Terry (1899–1984) was cast as Rio Rita. She had appeared in the Music Box Revue of 1922 and had a small part in Ziegfeld's *Kid Boots*.[16] J. Harold Murray (1891–1940) was cast as Captain Jim. Rita's brother, Roberto, and General Esteban were played by Walter Petrie (dates unknown) and Vincent Serrano (1866–1935), respectively. The two comic roles, Ed Lovett and Chick Bean, teamed Robert Woolsey (1888–1938) and Bert Wheeler (1895–1968) for the first time.[17] Their comic interactions clicked with both critics and audiences, and they were the only Broadway cast members who were signed to recreate their roles in the first film version.

When *Show Boat* was ready to open at the Ziegfeld Theatre in December 1927, *Rio Rita* was relocated to the Lyric Theatre, where it remained until Rudolf Friml's *The Three Musketeers* opened in March 1928. Ticket sales were still strong, so *Rita* ended the last few months of its Broadway run of 494 performances at the Majestic Theatre.[18] Shortly thereafter, Ziegfeld and Hearst were approached by the RKO studio, which purchased the screen rights to the show for $85,000.[19] With the advent of sound, films of Broadway musicals were a natural to attract audiences to the recently built movie palaces. In 1929, fifty-two musicals were released by the studios.[20] *Rio Rita*, which is the second Broadway musical to be released as a film, was a huge success; it was voted one of the ten best films of the year.[21]

THE 1929 FILM

Although *Rita* has been categorized as 'virtually a filmed transcription of the play,'[22] there are significant differences between it and its Broadway predecessor. While the plot was not changed substantially, it was 'adapted' by the director, Luther Reed (1888–1961). Some musical numbers were dropped, others were combined, and one new number, the duet/quartet/ chorus dance, 'Sweetheart, We Need Each Other,' was added as a replacement for 'Are You There?,' possibly because the studio may have felt the latter's lyrics were too risqué for movie audiences. 'You're Always in My Arms' was added, a result of its reinstatment as part of the film, but 'I'm Out on the Loose To-Night' was dropped, even though it is heard in the film.[23] Sheet music with pictures of the stars was published when the film opened in England.

Urban's sets were discarded, as were the dances choreographed by Lee and Rasch. Rita and Jim were sung by Bebe Daniels (1901–1971) and John Boles (1895–1969), and Esteban, now renamed General Ravinoff, a Russian exile living in Mexico, and Roberto were played by Georges Renavent (1894–1969) and Don Alvarado (1904–1967), respectively; Woolsey and Wheeler (Ed Lovett and Chick Bean) recreated their original vaudeville-*shtick* roles.[24] The new choreography was by Pearl Eaton (1898–1958).

As is the case with many early musicals, the 1932 rerelease that survives and is currently available is not complete; several writers have reported that the original version, in fifteen reels, was reduced to ten in the rerelease, cutting about forty minutes from the film.[25] Warner Bros. is said to have the complete 140 minute RCA Photophone recording, though this statement has not been confirmed.[26] Several 'lost' segments are available on YouTube; they include the Kinkajou scene from the beginning of the film, some of the deleted opening colour sequence dance that corresponds to the beginning of act 2, and the sound portion of John Boles singing 'Following the Sun Around,' number 24 in the piano-vocal score. RKO was able to film only the last forty minutes in the Technicolor process, due to the limited availability of their colour camera.[27]

Some of the script was rewritten by Russell Mack, though most of the Woolsey and Wheeler segments are from the original Broadway show. The ending was changed significantly; the triple wedding at Jim's house is now a single wedding taking place on the barge immediately after Ravinoff's arrest. Musically, the movie opens with 'The Kinkajou,' which in the Broadway version is heard in act 1, scene 3. Similar musical changes occur throughout the film. Somewhat surprisingly, 'You're Always in My Arms,' no. 13 in the vocal score, which was dropped from the show on Broadway, was restored to the movie version. The show's act 1 finale survives almost intact, with only a brief section omitted. Finally, the newly added 'Sweetheart, We Need Each Other' became a major number in the Technicolor portion of the film. It is in a traditional verse/chorus form, though with a little twist. A sixteen-measure verse is followed by the refrain, which has a 'B' section of only four measures (ex. 8.9). This gives the song a decidedly strange metric balance, the result of which can be seen in the somewhat awkward performance by Bert Wheeler and Dorothy Lee.

The choreography, while imitative of Ziegfeld's opulent production, is massive and clearly underrehearsed. Although RKO hoped to make a big splash with *Rio Rita*, it was shot on a tight budget in twenty-four days (26 June to 20 July), leaving little time to rehearse adequately the big chorus and dance numbers.[28] The public and the critics, however, overlooked these artistic issues, and clearly were entranced by this 'talkie' musical. Mordaunt Hall's review lauds the spectacle, while noting somewhat incorrectly that Luther Reed, 'has contented himself in making virtually an audible animated photographic conception of the successful Ziegfeld show.' The singing, dancing, and costumes were high points for him:

> Chorus girls appear as if by a magic wand ready to dispel the gloom of the lovers with their presence, their singing and dancing. . . . Rita has many gowns, each one more bewitching than the other. . . . [She] has a bridal dress . . . [which is] not

EXAMPLE 8.9 *Rio Rita*, 'Sweetheart, we need each other', chorus, mm. 17–20.

any more fascinating than the metallic cloth gown in which [she] appears at the ball. . . . [A]lthough some of the scenes [in the Technicolor process] are not quite in focus, the effect is invariably beautiful. . . . There are several impressive spectacular passages in this film, and those that are in prismatic hues are always interesting because of their loveliness. . . . It is an evening of good music, enjoyable fun and constant screen-fulls of striking scenes that cause one to wonder how much such a production cost.[29]

RKO grossed about $2,000,000 and netted a $935,000 profit.[30] *Rio Rita* was so popular that it was rereleased in 1932, even though by that time, many of the film's production values were decidedly primitive. During the 1930s and into the 1940s, *Rio Rita* also remained viable on the stage, performed by various road companies around the country. It also was seen by audiences in vaudeville houses in an abbreviated version that accompanied feature movies. It was still being performed as late as 1941; a production with Joe E. Brown, Peter Lind Hayes, and Mary Healy was seen in San Francisco in June of that year.[31]

THE 1942 FILM

MGM licenced the rights to *Rio Rita* sometime in 1940.[32] Louis B. Mayer (1884–1957) negotiated a deal with Universal Pictures, who held the contract for the comic team of Bud Abbott (1895–1974) and Lou Costello (1906–1959), to borrow them to make three pictures, one per year, at a salary of $150,000 per year.[33] Pandro S. Berman (1905–1996) served as producer and S. Sylvan Simon (1910–1951) directed, shooting the movie between 10 November 1941 and 14 January 1942.[34] In a clear effort to duplicate Woolsey and Wheeler's comic success in the original show, MGM reimagined the musical remake as a vehicle for the preeminent early-1940s comic team, Abbott and Costello, who combined burlesque show physical comedy with word play, but unlike Wheeler and Woolsey, did not sing or dance. Abbott's unchanging straight-man persona was the smooth-talking 'idea' man who comes up with dangerous and/or foolish schemes that his partner is asked to carry out. Costello epitomized the poor soul—the common blue-collar everyman, short in stature, fairly fat, with a distinct New York accent, most likely a resident of Brooklyn, and very literal-minded—who often was taken advantage of but usually came out triumphant by the end of each comic misunderstanding. By 1942, they were a big box office hit, having starred as a team in seven comic films. They filled a lacuna that resulted when Robert Woolsey died in 1938. Other comic teams might have been hired for the remake, though they were not as close to the Woolsey and Wheeler model as were Abbott and Costello. The Marx Brothers, with their well-defined personalities, were still active in the early 1940s, but they were not really a good fit for the script as it was conceived. The Ritz Brothers, who appeared in several films during the 1930s, were another possibility, but there were three of them and they did not have superstar status. The only other comic team active in the late-1930s who might have been appropriate for the comic roles were 'Ole' Olsen (1892–1963) and 'Chic' Johnson (1891–1962), who delighted audiences with their somewhat off-beat surrealistic routines on Broadway and in several films, but they, too, were not in the same box office league as Abbott and Costello.

Once the studio had settled on *Rio Rita*, they decided to scrap most of Tierney's music. Only two numbers survive: the title song, 'Rio Rita,' and the 'Rangers's Song,' which includes a newly composed verse as well as an interpolated and un-credited Mexican song, 'Caliente,' sung mostly in Spanish, which is intertwined with the original chorus.[35] Harold Arlen (1905–1986) and 'Yip' Harburg (1896?–1981) were hired to write four new songs, but only one, 'Long before You Came Along' is heard in the film.[36] For a Brazilian dance sequence with a solo by the Brazilian dancer Eros Volúsia (1914–2004) that takes place before the broadcast of the club show at Rita's hotel, Nilo Barnet's 'Brazilian Dance,' which includes the well-known 'Tico, Tico' by Zequinha de Abreu (1880–1935) and 'Ora O Conga' by Osvaldo Costa de Lacerdo (1927–2011), is performed.

In addition to Abbott and Costello, the MGM cast comprised one young performer on the verge of stardom, and actors who were usually seen in supporting roles. Rita is played by nineteen-year-old Kathryn Grayson (1922–2010) in her first starring role; following the dancers at the club show, she unexpectedly sings an extended excerpt of the 'Shadow Song' ('Ombra leggiera') from Meyerbeer's *Dinorah*.[37] Her diverse repertory in the film showcased her as a talented singer who was comfortable both with Broadway song and opera.[38] Rita's love interest, Ricardo Montero, is played by John Carroll (1906–1979), a Hollywood veteran who appeared in many movies of the 1930s in supporting roles. Tom Conway (1904–1967) plays the part of the villain, Maurice Craindall. Although he, too, was most often cast as a supporting player, he starred as the Falcon in ten films in the 1940s. Musically, all the music in this film is diegetic; it differs from the Broadway show and first film version, which combine both diegetic and nondiegetic numbers.

The 1942 version of *Rio Rita* is related only vaguely to the original Broadway show and the first film. A new script, offering an improbable and episodic story, was written by Richard Connell (1893–1949) and Gladys Lehman (1892–1993); John Grant (1891–1955) provided special material for Abbott and Costello. Rita's last name has been changed from Ferguson to Winslow; she is still the youthful owner of a ranch hotel, the Vista del Rio, near the Mexican border in Texas. The remaining characters are newly minted. Instead of the Ranger, Jim, the romantic lead is a well-known crooner, Ricardo Montero, who is returning to Texas after ten years to visit his childhood home and to sing at the first national broadcast of the Fiesta that is being run by Rita at her hotel; she has been in love with him since she was a teen-ager. General Esteban is replaced by another villain, Maurice Craindall, who is the manager of the hotel but also a fifth col-umnist foreign agent and Nazi collaborator. Instead of the comic team Ed Lovett and Chick Bean, Abbott and Costello play Doc and 'Wishy' Dean, out-of-work New Yorkers.

Abbott and Costello's comic routines occupy almost two-thirds of the film, leaving little time for the remainder of the plot and the music. The comic routines incorporate some of the burlesque show physical and verbal antics for which they were well known. For example, in the opening scene, they are working in a pet store, which allows them to engage in the kind of long punning rapid-fire repartee for which they were famous. As the scene progresses, Doc receives a call from a customer, Mrs Pike, who wants to have her dog, a Pekingese, picked up:

DOC: Wishy, go over and get a Peke at Mrs Pike's.

WISHY: Why can't I take a good look?

DOC: I want you to get me Pike's Peke!

WISHY: Pike's Peak? What do you think I am? A mountain climber?

DOC: Go over to Mrs Pike's house. You'll see a Peke around the yard.

WISHY: I'll see a peek around the yard? What do you want me to do? Play hide-and-seek with the girl? Look, the boss, I mean, after all, told me to get busy with that white dog. He wants me to wash—

DOC: What white dog?

WISHY: The white one—you know, what do you call it? The—

DOC: Spitz.

WISHY: No-o-o. But he drools a little.

After being fired from the pet shop, Doc and Wishy get into the trunk of a car with New York plates, thinking it will take them home. It is Montero's car, however, which is headed for the hotel. Montero follows Rita to the Texas desert, where she is singing to an instrumental phonograph recording (!); they sing 'Long before You Came Along' together, and then join the Rangers in the 'Rangers' Song.'[39]

As part of his broadcast scheme (see below), Craindall has ordered fake apples that have short wave radios in them that will allow other fifth columnists to receive insurrection instructions. Among Craindall's generally dim-witted helpers are Jake, who menaces Doc and Wishy several times, and Lucette, a femme fatale, who tries to ensnare Montero after he overhears the spies. When Rita meets Doc and Wishy, after they have been chased by Jake and Craindall's other goons, she offers them jobs as hotel detectives.

After many twists and turns, including a scene with a 'talking' dog, who has swallowed one of the fake apples and after being petted, gives the score of a Brooklyn Dodgers baseball game, Montero is given a Nazi 'code book' by Wishy, which the spies try to retrieve. At the nightclub, Montero warms up before the broadcast by singing 'Rio Rita,' which is followed by the Brazilian dance sequence and Meyerbeer.[40] When Wishy goes to Craindall's office to tell him that there are Nazis at the hotel, he is chased by the Nazi goons; ultimately, after Wishy winds up in a laundry room washing machine, he and Doc are captured and tied up with a time bomb, set to go off in thirty minutes, at 11:25 PM. As a donkey appears in a window and Hitler's voice is heard, Jake gives the Nazi salute. Wishy turns to the talking donkey (Hitler) and says: 'I've heard your voice, but this is the first time I've seen your face.'

As the broadcast begins, with the orchestra playing 'Rio Rita,' Montero punches Craindall in the face to stop him from sending the coded message over the airwaves. A general fight breaks out, but suddenly the Rangers's Song is heard in the distance and all the Nazis except Jake flee. The hotel guests are baffled since the Rangers do not seem to be there, but then Doc and Wishy, who have somehow escaped their bonds, come into the ballroom with a herd of donkeys who have swallowed the radios. Wishy, it seems, has requested the Ranger's song from an El Paso radio station, and it is being broadcast at the precise moment it was needed. Montero catches Jake, but Wishy lets him escape. Though the audience does not see the manoeuvre, Wishy has quietly put the time bomb in Jake's pocket. When Ricardo asks Wishy why he let Jake go, he winks broadly at the movie audience. An explosion follows, killing all of the Nazis.[41] Costello, now no longer in his Wishy character, says: '11.25. (He waves at the movie audience.) Good night, folks.'

Although the comic antics of Abbott and Costello were crucial to the hoped-for financial success of *Rita*, this 1942 film, one of the first musicals to include Nazi characters, was also intended to offer a not-too-subtle propaganda message. While the German sympathizers think they are smart, they are shown to be rather stupid and inept in their several attempts to implement their scheme and to capture Montero, Wishy, and Doc. Their fifth column activity revolves around an impossibly flawed plan, in which they will distribute fake apples that have radios installed in place of the cores, which are intended to alert German sympathizers in American factories of the time for an attack. Unfortunately for them, the apples stolen by Wishy and Doc are ingested by the donkeys and the dog, who, at various crucial moments in the action, 'magically' speak. The denouement combines the talking animals, a time bomb, and the Germans' mistake of believing that a recording of the 'Ranger's Song' playing on the radios is actually the lawmen riding to the ranch to capture them.

There are many gaps in the plot that the writers have cheer-fully ignored. In bringing the comedy to its conclusion, they have not addressed why the Nazis would think that the Rangers would be returning to the hotel. The national broadcast has nothing to do with border issues. Nor have they addressed a resolution to the love interest between Rita and her older friend, an exotic 'other,' Ricardo, who is clearly understood to be a Mexican who grew up and went to school in Texas. Unlike the previous versions of *Rio Rita*, this movie does not have a love story as its underlying raison d'être. Indeed, at the film's conclusion, we do not even know whether Rita and Ricardo will continue their relationship and eventually marry. Rather, this *Rio Rita* is about the adventures of two unemployed working-class New Yorkers in Texas. Wishy and Doc, two av-erage and not-too-bright Americans, have been able to outwit sophisticated foreign agents. To audiences, however, they were cardboard stand-ins for Abbott and Costello, the most famous and most celebrated American comedians after 1940. Costello acknowledges his identity and fame when he breaks the fourth wall at the end to wave at the audience and wish them a 'good night.' American audiences implicitly understood that Lou Costello, an American everyman, with New York street smarts, had defeated the German agents. If everyone was able to do what he did, then the Nazis and their fifth column accomplices didn't stand a chance of taking over America.

CONCLUSIONS

The changing theatrical values seen in the three versions of *Rio Rita* respond to the changing political conditions in America from the late 1920s to the early 1940s. Ziegfeld's vo-luptuous production of an old-fashioned, somewhat creaky

book musical, with a cast of more than 100, reflected his pen-
chant for extravaganzas that featured opulent scenery and
an excess of minimally clad chorus girls in a variety of eye-
catching costumes, as well as the needs and excesses of the
decade leading to the financial collapse of the country in 1929.
By that time, the 'talking' film of the show had been released;
while it was not a replica of the original or as lavishly produced,
it brought audiences around the country a taste of Ziegfeld's
Broadway. As one of the first 'talkies,' filmed partly in two-
colour process Technicolor, it offered a sense of the Broadway
musical to those who had never seen one live. Film studios saw
the sound musical as a strong audience draw and were quick
to option some of Broadway's mega-hits, which, in addition to
Rio Rita, included *So Long, Letty, The Desert Song, Little Johnny
Jones*, and *Sally*, all of which were released in 1929.

By 1942, America had changed dramatically. The excesses
of the 1920s were long past; the decade-long depression was
slowly dissipating, and the country was embroiled in a world
conflict. Hollywood studios were continuing to produce many
escapist films to entertain their audiences; they also were, finally, after a decade of mostly ignoring the Nazi threat, now
involved in the American propaganda machine as well. This
second *Rio Rita* movie, though not very similar to the original,
fit Hollywood's new direction of the early 1940s—a Broadway
and film mega-hit that 1940s audiences surely remembered;
two popular comedians; a rising young singer to provide a bit
of 'high class' culture through an operatic selection; and the
defeat of enemy agents in the country.

Popular entertainment has regularly followed social and
political trends. The Hollywood studios have always tried,
sometimes successfully and other times not, to mirror the
larger trends. Ziegfeld's Broadway show was, as most Broadway
shows are, a delineation of a love triangle, in this case between
a young woman, an officer of the law, and a corrupt military

man from Mexico. The two film versions of *Rio Rita* provide an exemplar of how popular entertainment genres can be fuelled by changing social and political issues. The first version details several relationships between Americans, Mexicans, and a corrupt Russian exile. The basic plot was not changed, though audiences could now vent their anger at a military man from a Bolshevik country. By 1942, the Mexican bandits led by General Ravinoff in the first version were no longer needed to serve as the evil exotic 'Others'; German sympathizers had replaced them. The love story of Rita and Ricardo (and briefly her competitor, Lucette) was secondary to the story of Nazi agents on American soil. On its own patriotic terms, the 1942 version served its purpose; audiences would be entertained by the antics of its stars but also be made aware of the secret foreign intruders who were threatening to overthrow the American way of life. Understanding the changing social values seen in the Broadway show and the two film versions of *Rio Rita* offers us a well-defined view of popular entertainment in the context of early twentieth-century history.

NOTES

1. For example, Edward Royce, his director for several shows, including *Kid Boots* and *Sally*, sued him for breach of contract, stating that he was to receive 1 percent of the gross receipts of *Rio Rita* for his work directing the show for two weeks before he was fired. His suit states that Ziegfeld was $200,000 in debt, having lost $100,000 gambling in Florida in 1926 (*Brooklyn Daily Eagle*, 27 May 1927, p. 1).

2. Joseph Urban was born in Vienna, where he studied architecture. He emigrated to the United States in 1911. From 1914 to his death, he was associated with Ziegfeld, Hearst, the Boston Opera, and the Metropolitan Opera (*New York Times*, 11 July 1933, p. 17). The Ziegfeld Theatre was demolished in 1966 over the objections of some architectural historians and historic preservationists.

3. For details on the lavish decorations in the theatre, see Richard Ziegfeld and Paulette Ziegfeld, *The Ziegfeld Touch: The Life and Times of Florenz Ziegfeld, Jr* (New York: Harry N. Abrams, 1993), 134–135.

4. Ziegfeld first announced that the New York City opening would take place on 24 January (*New York Times*, 10 January 1927, p. 18), but because he extended the show's run in Philadelphia, he pushed back the New York opening.

5. *New York Times*, 17 February 1927, p. 18.

6. 'Ziegfeld Opening Feb, 2,' *New York Times*, 19 January 1927, p. 21.

7. 'Dreams of Girl and Producer Come True,' [Albany, NY] *Times-Union*, 3 February 1927, p. 9.

8. J. Brooks Atkinson, 'The Play: "Rio Rita" Riot,' *New York Times*, 3 February 1927, p. 18.

9. Arthur Pollock, 'Plays and Things: Florenz Ziegfeld Opens His Own New and Beautiful Theater with a Charming Musical Comedy Called "Rio Rita,"' *Brooklyn Daily Eagle*, 3 February 1927, p. 10A.

10. Burns Mantle, 'Zeigfeld in Double Success,' *Buffalo Courier-Express*, 13 February 1927, Stage and Screen Section, p. 1. The quote is from a letter Mantle received from Frank Vreeland, the [New York] *Evening Telegram* critic, informing him of the musical's opening in the city. Mantle had come down with the flu and was not able to review new shows for more than a week.

11. Defining the show's genre is a continuing issue. Gerald Bordman, for example, in *American Musical Theatre: A Chronicle*, 3rd ed. (New York: Oxford University Press, 2000), 472, says 'Though it was branded a musical comedy . . . the show was in reality an operetta.' Similarly, Donald J. Stubblebine, in *Broadway Sheet Music: A Comprehensive Listing, 1918–1937*, labels *Rio Rita* 'an old fashioned operetta' (Jefferson, NC: McFarland, 1996), 238; and Thomas Hischak refers to the show as a 'large-scale operetta' in *Broadway Plays and Musicals: Descriptions and Essential Facts of More than 14,000 Shows through 2007* (Jefferson, NC: McFarland, 2009), 389.

12. One might cite Richard Strauss's *Ariadne auf Naxos* as a predecessor work that features two types of music to represent the different characters, though they do interact with one another,

but since the opera was not premiered in the United States until 1946, I doubt that Tierney knew it.

13. Sigmund Romberg's *The Desert Song*, for example, also revolves around a secret identity; it opened on 30 November 1926, just two months before *Rita Rio*.

14. The 1927 piano-vocal score differs in part from the programme of the show that opened on Broadway. No. 13, a song for Rita, 'You're Always in My Arms,' is not listed in the programme. Two numbers, 'The Jumping Bean' and 'Montezuma's Daughter,' have been added to the second act. Perhaps an examination of the original orchestral parts, if they are extant, might shed more light on the development of the play from its previews to the final version.

15. The piano-vocal score assigns the reprise to Katie Bean.

16. *Rio Rita* was the high point of Terry's career. She was not successful in her film appearances and played bit parts through the 1930s.

17. RKO's choice of Woolsey to recreate the role of Lovett is remarkable given that he did not play the entire run of the show; he left sometime after October 1927 and was replaced by Walter Catlett (1889–1960), a well-known comedian who had film experience. He reassumed the role on the post-Broadway road tour.

18. While the show was on tour in Chicago, Ziegfeld was negotiating with Sir George Butt to bring *Rio Rita* with its American cast to London (*Brooklyn Daily Eagle*, 3 November 1928, p. 17). It opened there in 1930.

19. Richard B. Jewell, *RKO Radio Pictures: A Titan Is Born* (Berkeley: University of California Press, 2012), 25. Ziegfeld bragged during a bankruptcy lawsuit that he expected to be offered $100,000 for the rights.

20. IMDb 'Rio Rita (1929)' accessed 12 June 2018. In Jack Burton, *The Blue Book of Hollywood Musicals* (Watkins Glen, NY: Century House, 1953), 12–18, the performance total is given as 447.

21. *Rio Rita* opened in New York City on 15 September 1929; it was preceded by *The Desert Song*, which opened on 8 April 1929. Stanley Green in *The World of Musical Comedy* (New York: Ziff-Davis, 1960), 76, writes of the former, 'The 1929 film version with Bebe Daniels and John Boles was the first successful screen

adaptation of a Broadway musical.' The important word in his statement is 'successful'; although *The Desert Song* opened earlier than *Rio Rita*, it was not included as one of the ten best pictures of 1929. A film version of *Show Boat* also preceded *Rio Rita*; it was released in April 1929, but it is not an adaptation of Ziegfeld's musical. Along with two original screen musicals, *The Broadway Melody* and *Gold Diggers of Broadway*, *Rio Rita* was named one of the ten best pictures of 1929 in a poll taken by the industry paper, *Film Daily* (7 February 1930, p. 8).

22. Ted Sennett, *Hollywood Musicals* (New York: Harry N. Abrams, 1981), 48.

23. Several sources, including IMDb list E. Y. Harburg and Harold Arlen's 'Long Before You Came Along' as an added number to the 1929 film version. It was, however, written for and heard in the 1942 version; Arlen and Harburg wrote three additional songs ('A Couple of Caballeros,' 'Poor Whippoorwill,' and 'Such Unusual Weather') for the 1942 film, which were not used.

24. Woolsey and Wheeler were so popular with audiences that during the 1930s, they costarred in more than twenty comedies. Wheeler usually played the mark while Woolsey was the sharp dealmaker, usually concocting schemes that were barely legal.

25. The length of the original film has been estimated at 137 minutes by some commentators, and at 125 minutes by others. The currently available version is approximately 103 minutes. In his 1929 review, Mordaunt Hall noted that 'the last half of this handsome vocalized motion picture is filmed by the Technicolor process.' This statement cannot be correct, since the Technicolor portion is no more than forty minutes and might be as little as thirty-eight minutes. Much of the cut material from this part of the movie is or has been available on YouTube; it comprises about seven additional minutes. If the complete film was 137 minutes, then the first part of the movie would be approximately 100 minutes long, which means the current version is 28 (or 23) minutes short. A three-minute excerpt of the deleted Kinkajou number has surfaced, but no other missing fragments have emerged, nor is it possible to determine where they might have been in the original unless one can examine the length of each reel.

26. The Museum of Modern Art is said to have had a copy of the complete film, but it has been either misplaced, lost, or stolen.
27. Sennett, *Hollywood Musicals*, 48. Richard Barrios, *A Song in the Dark: The Birth of the Musical Film* (New York: Oxford University Press, 1995), 227. The currently available print of the film of the Technicolor portion corresponds to the second act of the show. The most important missing segments of the act are parts of the opening dance sequence on the barge, the pirate dance that follows 'Sweetheart, We Need Each Other,' and 'Following the Sun Around,' some of which are available on YouTube.
28. Edwin M. Bradley, *The First Hollywood Musicals: A Critical Filmography of 171 Features, 1927 through 1932* (Jefferson, NC: McFarland, 1996), 176.
29. Mordaunt Hall, 'The Screen: "A Ziegfeld Show on the Screen," *New York Times*, 7 October 1929, p. 29.
30. Richard B. Jewell, 'RKO Grosses, 1929–1951: The C. J. Tevlin Ledger,' *Historic Journal of Film, Radio and Television* 14 (): 37–49.
31. Reported in the *Syracuse Herald-Journal*, 2 June 1941, p. 16.
32. I have not yet uncovered whether MGM licenced *Rio Rita* from the Ziegfeld estate or RKO. I believe the studio contracted with RKO, since one of the provisions of the contract was that the 1929 version could not be publicly shown.
33. Originally, the sum was split 50/50, but after 1942, Costello received 60 percent of the sum.
34. Scott Allen Nollen, *Abbott and Costello on the Home Front: A Critical Study of the Wartime Films* (Jefferson, NC: McFarland, 2009), 49.
35. It is not the 1935 song, 'In Caliente,' by Mort Dixon and Allie Wrubel, which was heard in a number of films during the 1930s and 1940s. It may be an uncredited original song by Herbert Stothart, who was music director for the film.
36. See note 21.
37. The choice of an aria by Meyerbeer can only be speculated on, though as a showcase vehicle for the young star, it can hardly be surpassed. Given that *Dinorah* was no longer part of the standard repertory, one can ask why Grayson didn't sing the 'Bell Song' from Delibes's *Lakme* or 'Una voce poco fa' from Rossini's *Il barbiere di Siviglia*. These virtuoso pieces were known by

the general public through the recordings and appearances of the French soprano, Lily Pons (1898–1976). My guess is that Meyerbeer's aria is in triple metre, which allows Grayson to 'waltz' around the set while she is singing.

38. Grayson was MGM's replacement for Deanna Durbin, who moved to Universal Studios.

39. This is a major change from the original show. The Rangers, in this film, appear only once. When their song is heard at the climax of the movie, it is in a broadcast recording.

40. Grayson sings an abbreviated version of this well-known aria. After the opening segment (mm. 1–79), she skips to the final reprise (m. 159). A new cadenza is heard at measure 218, in which Grayson sings a G-flat 6, before concluding on an F6.

41. Lucette, however, has not been seen in this final scene; perhaps she did not attempt to escape in the car with the other Nazis. Her fate at the film's end is undetermined.

SELECT BIBLIOGRAPHY

Acevedo-Muñoz, Ernesto R. West Side Story *as Cinema: The Making and Impact of an American Masterpiece.* Lawrence: University Press of Kansas, 2013.

Altman, Rick, ed. *Genre: The Musical.* London: Routledge and Kegan Paul, 1981.

Altman, Rick. *The Hollywood Musical,* 2nd ed. Bloomington: Indiana University Press, 1993.

Andrew, Dudley. *Concepts in Film Theory.* Oxford: Oxford University Press, 1984.

Ansen, David. 'Madonna Tangos with Evita.' Newsweek, 15 December 1996.

Astaire, Fred. *Steps in Time.* New York: Harper, 1959.

Aylesworth, Thomas G. *Broadway to Hollywood: Musicals from Stage to Screen.* Twickenham, UK: Hamlyn, 1985.

Banfield, Stephen. *Jerome Kern.* New Haven, CT: Yale University Press, 2006.

Barrios, Richard. *A Song in the Dark: The Birth of the Musical Film.* New York: Oxford University Press, 1995.

Birkett, Danielle, and Dominic McHugh. *Adapting The Wizard of Oz: Musical Versions from Baum to MGM and Beyond.* New York: Oxford University Press, 2018.

Block, Geoffrey. *Enchanted Evenings*, 2nd ed. New York: Oxford University Press, 2009.

Block, Geoffrey. *Richard Rodgers*. New Haven, CT: Yale University Press, 2002.

Bordwell, David. *The Way Hollywood Tells It: Story and Style in Modern Movies*. Berkeley: University of California Press, 2006.

Bordman, Gerald. *American Musical Theatre: A Chronicle*, 3rd ed. New York: Oxford University Press, 2000.

Bordman, Gerald. *Jerome Kern: His Life and Music*. New York: Oxford University Press, 1980.

Bradley, Edwin M. *The First Hollywood Musicals: A Critical Filmography of 171 Features, 1927 through 1932*. Jefferson, NC: McFarland, 1996.

Brantley, Ben. Broadway Musicals. New York: Abrams, 2012.

Brown, Peter H. 'Desperately Seeking Evita.' Washington Post, 5 March 1989.

Burton, Jack. *The Blue Book of Hollywood Musicals*. Watkins Glen, NY: Century House, 1953.

Cantu, Maya. *American Cinderellas on the Broadway Musical Stage: Imagining the Working Girl from* Irene *to* Gypsy. Basingstoke, UK: Palgrave Macmillan, 2015.

Cartmell, Deborah, and Imelda Whelehan. *Screen Adaptation: Impure Cinema*. Basingstoke, UK: Palgrave Macmillan, 2010.

Casper, Joseph Andrew. *Stanley Donen*. Metuchen, NJ: Scarecrow Press, 1983.

Ciccone, Madonna. 'The Madonna Diaries. Vanity Fair, November 1996.

Citron, Stephen. Sondheim and Lloyd-Webber: The New Musical. New York: Oxford University Press, 2001.

Cohan, George M. *Twenty Years on Broadway and the Years It Took to Get There: The True Story of a Trouper's Life from the Cradle to the 'Closed Shop.'* New York: Harper and Brothers, 1925.

Cohan, Steven, ed. *Hollywood Musicals: The Film Reader*. London: Routledge, 2002.

Cohan, Steven, ed. *The Sound of Musicals*. London: BFI, 2010.

Croce, Arlene *The Fred Astaire and Ginger Rogers Book*. New York: Vintage Books, 1972.

Davis, Lorrie, with Rachel Gallagher. *Letting Down My Hair; Two Years with the Love Rock Tribe—from Dawning to Downing of Aquarius*. New York: A. Fields Books, 1973.

Decker, Todd. *Music Makes Me: Fred Astaire and Jazz*. Berkeley: University of California Press, 2011.

de Giere, Carol. *Defying Gravity: The Creative Career of Stephen Schwartz from Godspell to Wicked*. New York: Applause and Cinema Books, 2008.

de Giere, Carol. *The Godspell Experience: Inside a Transformative Musical*. Bethel, CT: Scene 1 Publishing, 2014.

De Mille, Agnes. *Dance to the Piper*. Introduction by J. Acocella. New York: New York Review Books, 2015 [1952].

Delamater, Jerome. *Dance in the Hollywood Musical*. Ann Arbor: UMI Research Press, 1981.

Doherty, Thomas. *Hollywood's Censor: Joseph I. Breen and the Production Code Administration*. New York: Columbia University Press, 2007.

Donnelly, K. J., and Elizabeth Carroll, eds., *Contemporary Musical Film*. Edinburgh: Edinburgh University Press, 2017.

Dyer, Richard. *Only Entertainment*, 2nd ed. London: Routledge, 2002.

Easton, Carol. *No Intermissions: The Life of Agnes De Mille*. New York: Da Capo Press, 2000.

Eddie Mannix Ledger. Los Angeles, Margaret Herrick Library, Center for Motion Picture Study.

Editors of *Consumer Guide* with Phillip J. Kaplan. *The Best, Worst and Most Unusual: Hollywood Musicals*. New York: Beekman House, 1983.

Edwards, Paul. 'Adaptation: Two Theories.' *Text and Performance Quarterly* 27, no. 4 (2007): 369–377.

Eller, Claudia. 'Crying's Over, "Evita" Finds Backers.' Los Angeles Times, 11 December 1993.

Elliott, Kamilla. *Rethinking the Novel/Film Debate*. Cambridge: Cambridge University Press, 2003.

Evans, Peter William. *Top Hat*. London: Wiley, 2010.

Everett, William A., and Paul R. Laird, eds. *The Cambridge Companion to the Musical*, 3rd. ed. New York: Cambridge University Press, 2017.

Everett, William A. *Sigmund Romberg*. New Haven, CT: Yale University Press, 2007.

Fehr, Richard, and Frederick G. Vogel. *Lullabies of Hollywood: Movie Music and the Movie Musical, 1915–1992*. Jefferson, NC: McFarland, 1993.

Feuer, Jane. *The Hollywood Musical*, 2nd ed. Basingstoke: Macmillan, 1993.

Fisher, James. *Historical Dictionary of American Theater: Beginnings*. Lanham, MD: Rowman and Littlefield, 2015.

Fordin, Hugh. *M-G-M's Greatest Musicals: The Arthur Freed Unit*. New York: Da Capo Press, 1996 [1975].

Forman, Miloš, with Jan Novak. *Turnaround: A Memoir*. Villard/Random House, 1993.

Forrest, Jennifer, and Leonard R. Koos, eds. *Dead Ringers: The Remake in Theory and Practice*. New York: State University of New York Press, 2002.

Forte, Allen. *The American Popular Ballad of the Golden Era 1924–1950*. Princeton, NJ: Princeton University Press, 1995.

Franceschina, John. *Hermes Pan: The Man Who Danced with Fred Astaire*. New York: Oxford University Press, 2012.

Furia, Philip, and Laurie Patterson. *The Songs of Hollywood*. New York: Oxford University Press, 2010.

Gardner, Kara A. *Agnes De Mille: Telling Stories in Broadway Dance*. New York: Oxford University Press, 2016.

Ganz, Andrew. 'In Upcoming Revival of Evita, Che Will Be the "Everyman," Not Che Guevara.' February 2012. Playbill.com.

Gänzl, Kurt. *Ganzl's Book of the Broadway Musical*. New York: Schirmer Books, 1995.

Geraghty, Christine. *Now a Major Motion Picture: Film Adaptations of Literature and Drama*. Lanham, MD: Rowman and Littlefield, 2008.

Giddins, Gary. *Bing Crosby: A Pocketful of Dreams, the Early Years, 1903–1940*. Boston: Little, Brown, 2001.

Gilbert, James. *Men in the Middle: Searching for Masculinity in the 1950s*. Chicago: University of Chicago Press, 2005.

Gontier, David F. Jr, and Timothy L. O'Brien. '13. Evita, 1996.' In The Films of Alan Parker, 1976–2003. Jefferson, NC: McFarlandgringoinbuenosaires.com.

Gorbman, Claudia. *Unheard Melodies: Narrative Film Music.* Bloomington: Indiana University Press, 1987.

Goldmark, Daniel. 'Adapting *The Jazz Singer* from Short Story to Screen: A Musical Profile.' *Journal of the American Musicological Society* 70, no. 3 (Fall 2017): 767–817.

Grant, Mark N. *The Rise and Fall of the Broadway Musical.* Boston: Northeastern University Press, 2004.

Gray, Susan. *Writers on Directors.* New York: Watson-Guptil, 1999.

Green, Stanley. *The World of Musical Comedy.* New York: Ziff-Davis, 1960.

Grode, Eric. *Hair: The Story of the Show that Defined a Generation.* Foreword by James Rado. Philadelphia: Running Press, 2010.

Hall, Sheldon. 'Tall Revenue Features: The Genealogy of the Modern Blockbuster.' In *Genre and Contemporary Hollywood*, edited by Steve Neale, 11–26. London: BFI, 2002.

Harris, Mark. *Pictures at a Revolution: Five Movies and the Birth of New Hollywood.* New York: Penguin Press, 2008.

Harvey, Stephen. *Directed by Vincente Minnelli.* Foreword by L. Minnelli. New York: Museum of Modern Art/Harper and Row, 1989.

Hemming, Roy. *The Melody Lingers On: The Great Songwriters and Their Movie Musicals.* New York: Newmarket, 1986.

Hirschhorn, Clive. *Gene Kelly: A Biography.* London: W. H. Allen, 1974.

Hischak, Thomas. *Broadway Plays and Musicals: Descriptions and Essential Facts of More Than 14,000 Shows through 2007.* Jefferson, NC: McFarland, 2009.

Hischak, Thomas S. *The Oxford Companion to the American Musical: Theatre, Film, and Television.* Oxford: Oxford University Press, 2008.

Hischak, Thomas S. *Through the Screen Door: What Happened to the Broadway Musical When It Went to Hollywood.* Lanham, MD: Scarecrow Press, 2004.

Hirschhorn, Clive. *Gene Kelly: A Biography.* Foreword by F. Sinatra. London: W. H. Allen, 1974.

Horn, Barbara Lee. *The Age of Hair: Evolution and Impact of Broadway's First Rock Musical.* New York: Greenwood Press, 1991.

Hubbert, Julie. '"Whatever Happened to Great Movie Music?" Cinéma Vérité and Hollywood Film Music of the Early 1970s.' *American Music* 21, no. 2 (2003): 180–213.

Hubbert, Julie, ed. *Celluloid Symphonies: Texts and Contexts in Film Music History.* Berkeley: University of California Press, 2011.

Hutcheon, Linda. 'The Politics of Postmodernism: Parody and History.' *Cultural Critique* 5 (1986): 179–207.

Hutcheon, Linda. *A Theory of Adaptation*, 2nd ed. New York: Routledge, 2013.

Hutcheon, Linda, and Mario J. Valdés. 'Irony, Nostalgia, and the Postmodern: A Dialogue.' *Poligrafías. Revista de Teoría Literaria y Literatura comparada* 3 (1998–2000): 18–41.

Jewell, Richard B. 'RKO Grosses, 1929–1951: The C. J. Tevlin Ledger.' *Historic Journal of Film, Radio and Television* 14 (1994): 37–49.

Jones, John Bush. *Our Musicals, Ourselves: A Social History of the American Musical Theatre.* Lebanon, NH: Brandeis University Press, 2003.

Kantor, Michael, and Lawrence Maslon. Broadway: The American Musical. New York: Bulfinch Press, 2004.

Kennedy, Matthew. *Roadshow! The Fall of Film Musicals in the 1960s.* New York: Oxford University Press, 2014.

Kessler, Kelly. *Destabilizing the Hollywood Musical: Music, Masculinity and Mayhem.* New York: Palgrave Macmillan, 2010.

Kimball, Robert, ed. *The Complete Lyrics of Cole Porter.* New York: Vintage Books, 1984.

King, Geoff. *New Hollywood Cinema: An Introduction.* New York: Columbia University Press, 2002.

Kirle, Bruce. *Unfinished Show Business: Broadway Musicals as Works-in-Process.* Carbondale: Southern Illinois University Press, 2005.

Klein, Amanda Ann. *American Film Cycles: Reframing Genres, Screening Social Problems, and Defining Subcultures.* Austin: University of Texas Press, 2011.

Knapp, Raymond. *The American Musical and the Formation of National Identity.* Princeton, NJ: Princeton University Press, 2005.

Knapp, Raymond. *The American Musical and the Performance of Personal Identity.* Princeton, NJ: Princeton University Press, 2006.

Knapp, Raymond, Mitchell Morris, and Stacy Wolf, eds. *The Oxford Handbook of the American Musical.* New York: Oxford University Press, 2011.

Kogan, Rick. 'The Original "Grease" Was Born in Chicago.' Chicago Tribune, 29 January 2016.

Kracauer, Siegfried. *Theory of Film: The Redemption of Physical Reality.* New York: Oxford University Press, 1960.

Laird, Paul R. *The Musical Theater of Stephen Schwartz.* Lanham, MD: Rowman and Littlefield, 2014.

Lawson-Peebles, Robert, ed. *Approaches to the American Musical.* Exeter, UK: University of Exeter Press, 1996.

Leitch, Thomas. 'Twelve Fallacies in Contemporary Adaptation Theory,' *Criticism* 45, no. 2 (Spring 2003): 150–153.

Lerner, Alan J. *The Street Where I Live: The Story of My Fair Lady, Gigi and Camelot.* London: Hodder and Stoughton, 1978.

Leve, James. *American Musical Theater.* New York: Oxford University Press, 2016.

Levy, Emanuel. *Vincente Minnelli: Hollywood's Dark Dreamer.* New York: St Martin's Press, 2009.

Long, Robert E. *Broadway, The Golden Years: Jerome Robbins and the Great Choreographer-Directors, 1940 to the Present.* New York: Continuum, 2001.

Lovensheimer, Jim. *South Pacific: Paradise Rewritten.* New York: Oxford University Press, 2010.

Magee, Jeffrey. *Irving Berlin's American Musical Theatre.* New York: Oxford University Press, 2012.

Mast, Gerald. *Can't Help Singin': The American Musical on Stage and Screen.* Woodstock, NY: Overlook, 1987.

McArthur, Colin. *Brigadoon, Braveheart and the Scots: Distortions of Scotland in Hollywood.* New York: I. B. Tauris, 2003.

McClary, Susan. *Feminine Endings: Music, Gender, and Sexuality.* Minneapolis: University of Minnesota Press, 1991.

McElhaney, Joe. *The Death of Classical Cinema: Hitchcock, Lang, Minnelli.* Albany: State University of New York Press, 2006.

McElhaney, Joe, ed. *Vincente Minnelli: The Art of Entertainment.* Detroit, MI: Wayne State University Press, 2009.

McHugh, Dominic. *Loverly: The Life and Times of My Fair Lady.* New York: Oxford University Press, 2012.

McHugh, Dominic, ed. *Alan Jay Lerner: A Lyricist's Letters.* New York: Oxford University Press, 2014.

McLean, Adrienne. *Being Rita Hayworth: Labor, Identity, and Hollywood Stardom.* New Brunswick: Rutgers University Press, 2004.

McMillin, Scott. *The Musical as Drama.* Princeton, NJ: Princeton University Press, 2006.

McNally, Karen. *When Frankie Went to Hollywood: Frank Sinatra and American Male Identity.* Urbana: University of Illinois Press, 2008.

Mera, Miguel. 'Invention/Re-invention.' *Music Sound and the Moving Image* 3, no. 1 (Spring 2009): 1–20.

Miller, Scott. 'Inside Evita." 2010. New Line Theatre.org.

Miller, Scott. *Rebels with Applause: Broadway's Groundbreaking Musicals.* Portsmouth, NH: Heinemann, 2001.

Minnelli, Vincente, with H. Arce. Foreword by A. J. Lerner. *Vincente Minnelli: I Remember It Well.* Hollywood, CA: Samuel French, 1990 [1974].

Mordden, Ethan. *The Hollywood Musical.* New York: St Martin's Press, 1981.

Mordden, Ethan. *When Broadway Went to Hollywood.* New York: Oxford University Press, 2016.

Morris, Mitchell. '*Cabaret,* America's Weimar, and the Mythologies of the Gay Subject.' *American Music* 22 (2004): 145–157.

Most, Andrea. *Making Americans: Jews and the Broadway Musical.* Cambridge, MA: Harvard University Press, 2004.

Mueller, John. *Astaire Dancing: The Musical Films.* New York: Wings, 1985.

Mundy, John. *Popular Music on Screen: From Hollywood Musical to Music Video.* Manchester: Manchester University Press, 1999.

Naremore, James, ed. *Film Adaptation.* London: Athlone Press, 2000.

Neale, Steve. *Genre and Hollywood.* London: Routledge, 2000.

Nollen, Scott Allen. *Abbott and Costello on the Home Front: A Critical Study of the Wartime Films.* Jefferson, NC: McFarland, 2009.

Norton, Richard C. *A Chronology of American Musical Theater,* vol. 2. New York: Oxford University Press, 2002.

O'Brien, Daniel. *The Frank Sinatra Film Guide.* London: Batsford, 1998.

O'Brien, Lucy. *Madonna: Like an Icon.* New York: Bantam Press, 2008.

Oja, Carol J. *Bernstein Meets Broadway: Collaborative Art in a Time of War.* Oxford: Oxford University Press, 2014.

O'Leary, James. '*Oklahoma!*,' 'Lousy Publicity,' and the Politics of Formal Integration in the American Musical Theater.' *Journal of Musicology* 31, no. 1 (Winter 2014): 139–182.

Parker, Alan. 'EVITA – Alan Parker – Director, Writer, Producer Official Website.' Web.

Patinkin, Sheldon. *'No Legs, No Jokes, No Chance': A History of the American Musical Theater.* Evanston: Northeastern University Press, 2008.

Pomerance, Murray. *The Eyes Have It: Cinema and the Reality Effect.* New Brunswick, NJ: Rutgers University Press, 2013.

Richards, Stanley, ed. *Great Rock Musicals.* New York: Stein and Day, 1979.

Rodosthenous, George. *Twenty-First Century Musicals: From Stage to Screen.* New York: Routledge, 2017.

Rodgers, Richard. *Musical Stages: An Autobiography.* New York: Da Capo Press, 1995.

Rogers, Ginger. *Ginger: My Story.* New York: HarperCollins, 1991.

Sanders, Julie. *Adaptation and Appropriation.* New York: Routledge, 2006.

Schreger, Charles. 'The Second Coming of Sound,' *Film Comment* 14, no. 5 (September/October 1978): 34–37.

Sennett, Ted. *Hollywood Musicals.* New York: Harry N. Abrams, 1981.

Sheward, David. New York review: Evita. 5 April 2012. Backstage. com.

Shmoop Editorial Team. 'Culture in the Reagan Era.' Shmoop. Web.

Sinyard, Neil. *Filming Literature: The Art of Screen Adaptation.* London: Croom Helm, 1986.

Slater, Thomas J. *Milos Forman: A Bio-Bibliography.* New York: Greenwood Press, 1987.

Smith, Helen. *There's a Place for Us: The Musical Theatre Works of Leonard Bernstein.* Farnham, UK: Ashgate Press, 2011.

Smith, Jeff. *Sounds of Commerce: Marketing Popular Film Music.* New York: Columbia University Press, 1998.

Spring, Katherine. *Saying It with Songs: Popular Music and the Coming of Sound to Hollywood Cinema.* New York: Oxford University Press, 2013.

Stam, Robert. 'Beyond Fidelity: The Dialogics of Adaptation.' In *Film Adaptation*, edited by James Naremore, 54–76. London: Athlone Press, 2000.

Stam, Robert. *Literature through Film: Realism, Magic, and the Art of Adaptation*. Malden, MA: Blackwell, 2005.

Stam, Robert, and Alessandra Raengo, eds. *Literature and Film: A Guide to the Theory and Practice of Adaptation*. Malden, MA: Blackwell, 2003.

Starr, Larry. *Gershwin*. New Haven, CT: Yale University Press, 2010.

Stempel, Larry. *Showtime: A History of the Broadway Musical Theater*. New York: W.W. Norton, 2010.

Sternfeld, Jessica. *The Megamusical*. Bloomington: Indiana University Press, 2006.

Stubblebine, Donald J. *Broadway Sheet Music: A Comprehensive Listing, 1918–1937*. Jefferson, NC: McFarland, 1996.

Studlar, Gaylyn. *Precocious Charms: Stars Performing Girlhood in Classical Hollywood Cinema*. Berkeley: University of California Press, 2013.

Swain, Joseph. *The Broadway Musical: A Critical and Musical Survey*. Lanham, MD: Scarecrow Press, 2002.

Symonds, Dominic. *We'll Have Manhattan*. New York: Oxford University Press, 2015.

Symonds, Dominic, and Millie Taylor, eds. *Gestures of Musical Theater: The Performativity of Song and Dance*. New York: Oxford University Press, 2014.

Taraborelli, J. Rando. Madonna: An Intimate Biography. New York: Simon and Schuster, 2002.

Taylor, John R., and A. Jackson. *The Hollywood Musical*. London: Secker and Warburg, 1971.

Tharp, Twyla. *Push Comes to Shove*. New York: Bantam, 1992.

Thelen, Lawrence. *The Show Makers: Great Directors of the American Musical Theatre*. New York: Routledge, 2000.

Thomas, Bob. *Astaire: The Man, the Dancer*. New York: St Martin's, 1984.

Thomas, Tony. *The Films of Gene Kelly: Song and Dance Man*. Foreword by F. Astaire. New York: Carol, 1991.

Traubner, Richard. *Operetta: A Theatrical History*, rev. ed. New York: Routledge, 2003.

Turk, Edward Baron. *Hollywood Diva*. Berkeley: University of California Press, 1998.

Whitfield, Sarah, ed. *Rethinking Musical Theatre*. Palgrave, 2019.

Wilder, Alec. *American Popular Song: The Great Innovators, 1900–1950*. New York: Oxford University Press, 1972.

Wilk, Max. *They're Playing Our Song*. New York: Zoetrope, 1986.

Winer, Deborah Grace. *On the Sunny Side of the Street: The Life and Lyrics of Dorothy Fields*. New York: Schirmer, 1997.

Wolf, Stacy. *Changed for Good: A Feminist History of the Broadway Musical*. New York: Oxford University Press, 2011.

Wolf, Stacy. *A Problem Like Maria: Gender and Sexuality in the American Musical*. Ann Arbor: University of Michigan Press, 2002.

Woller, Megan. '"Happ'ly-Ever-Aftering": Changing Social and Industry Conventions in Hollywood Musical Adaptations, 1960–75.' PhD diss., University of Illinois Urbana-Champaign, 2014.

Woller, Megan. 'The Lusty Court of *Camelot* (1967): Exploring Sexuality in the Hollywood Adaptation.' *Music and the Moving Image* 8, no. 1 (Spring 2015): 3–18.

Wollman, Elizabeth L. *Hard Times: The Adult Musical in 1970s New York City*. New York: Oxford University Press, 2013.

Wollman, Elizabeth L. *The Theater Will Rock: A History of the Rock Musical, from Hair to Hedwig*. Ann Arbor: University of Michigan Press, 2006.

Wood, Michael. *America in the Movies: Or, 'Santa Maria, It Had Slipped My Mind.'* New York: Columbia University Press, 1989.

Wood, Robin. *Hollywood from Vietnam to Reagan . . . and Beyond*. New York: Columbia University Press, 2003.

Yudkoff, Alan. *Gene Kelly: A Life of Dance and Dreams*. New York: Back Stage Books, 1999.

Ziegfeld, Richard, and Paulette Ziegfeld. *The Ziegfeld Touch: The Life and Times of Florenz Ziegfeld, Jr.* New York: Harry N. Abrams, 1993.

Zadan, Craig. *Sondheim and Co.*, 2nd ed. New York: Harper and Row, 1986.

INDEX

For the benefit of digital users, indexed terms that span two pages (e.g., 52–53) may, on occasion, appear on only one of those pages.

Tables and figures are indicated by *t* and *f* following the page number